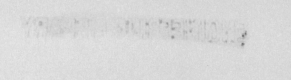

GREEN DESIGN FROM THEORY TO PRACTICE

EDITED BY
KEN YEANG AND ARTHUR SPECTOR

black dog
publishing

london uk

CONTENTS

FOREWORD
MADAME BEATRICE ROSENBERG DE ROTHSCHILD

The Jerusalem Seminar in Architecture series of events was founded in 1992 with the aim of examining and bringing important contemporary issues in architecture and urban planning to the attention of the professional community and the public. We have endeavoured to fulfil this commitment in the seven conferences held to date.

The most recent conference was in Jerusalem (25–27 January 2009) on the theme of "Green Design: from Theory to Practice". Its ambitious goal was to present an up-to-date account of the state of green architecture around the globe. With some 1,500 participants, the conference was effective in reaching professionals responsible for over 75 per cent of all local built activity (in the State of Israel). It was with a considerable sense of challenge and responsibility that we brought this community together for professional exchange.

We all share equal responsibility to improve the quality of our environment for future generations and to implement sustainable practices. It appears that today we have the technology to accomplish this task. Thus, the greatest challenge is to enlist our institutions—and indeed ourselves—to change the current mode of

thinking and habits. We hope the conference has been successful in advancing this objective.

Our Conference Chair, Ken Yeang and our Organising Committee put together a unique team of professionals and international experts who provided the audience with a comprehensive series of presentations. Dr Yeang was pivotal in making the conference successful and in demonstrating once again his leading position in this movement for over 35 years. Our special thanks are due to Arthur Spector for his dedication to the role of originating the event and as the Chair of the Organising Committee.

With appreciation for the breadth and quality of the presentations, and the feedback from participants, the Organising Committee moved forward in producing this collection of essays with an expanded list of contributors.

The Rothschild Foundation is pleased to have the opportunity to contribute its modest share to this vital effort towards our sustainable future. On behalf of the Chairman of the Foundation's Advisory Committee, Lord Rothschild, and the entire Committee, I hope that you enjoy and benefit from this publication.

INTRODUCTION
ARTHUR SPECTOR

Our intention in convening the Jerusalem Seminars in Architecture (first held in 1992) was to provide a forum to examine current important topics in architecture and urbanism. Our seventh seminar (2009) was dedicated to a critical examination of the state of green design. We invited some of the world's best professionals with expert knowledge in specific areas in this field to participate. Their presentations being comprehensive, instructive and informative, led to the obvious and compelling idea to publish the presentations for the benefit of a wider audience. Our aspiration in this volume is to contribute to enhancing all work that impacts on the environment.

At the outset, green architecture had suffered from a serious issue of imagery. The forms, materials and green technologies bolted onto the building form resulted in an additive architecture that was not integrated with the green design intentions and performance of the building. It appeared that the architecture had to put up with the green features and systems as a matter of necessity. In the case of healthcare projects, where the architect had made considerable efforts to resolve the programmatic needs in health planning with related infrastructure and non-compromising functions, there remained little opportunity afterwards to contend with the green functions of the building at such a late stage in the process.

Evident is the increasingly universal acceptance of the collective need to act for a common sustainable future. Sustainability has become an inherent part of global consciousness and is fast becoming a mandatory standard for all in the design profession. While many countries subscribe to and proclaim full support for sustainable principles, manifested predominantly by climate change, we have still to collectively and comprehensively set these principles in motion to impact all aspects of our urban environments. Our society and economies, including manufacturing and distributions systems, industrial agricultural systems, transportation systems and our rapidly growing cities, with their burgeoning utilities and unsustainable stock of buildings, require immediate rethinking

and prioritising. Achieving this successfully requires large-scale legislative changes at governmental level throughout the world. With the immense worldwide interest in sustainability, the ongoing devastation of our natural resources and the rapid diminishing of our energy resources, we need to jump-start and effect these changes globally, sooner rather than later.

We also need to encourage current and future generations of design professionals to be ecologically literate. While most of our planners are already aware of the need for such considerations in our urban environment, there remains a huge gap in knowing how to implement these intentions in our cities and built environment. As new green materials, clean technological systems and eco-products become exponentially available in the marketplace, it is just about impossible to keep track of them and more importantly, to fully understand and assess the real value of each new initiative or product without a very clear road map. We need to be aware of the superficiality of "greenwashing", which is evident in many of the professional journals.

While the ethical case for sustainability has been very eloquently made for several years, we have yet to take concerted action in implementation. The key intent of this book is to provide both the design professional and general public with the bases to act —to demystify key concepts and technologies and guide their inclusion in our work and our lives to optimise their values and benefits, besides clarifying their accompanying issues and costs.

This will lead to better management and coordination of all the emerging knowledge and systems. We need to qualify and quantify this information to enable us to use it effectively. To accomplish this, we need an easily understood and internationally recognised set of criteria to implement these new tools, systems and ideas successfully in our work.

A simple example is our inability to manage the most essential of our resources—water. The Meghalaya plateau in northeastern India is one of the wettest areas in the world. The area of Cherrapunji is well

The YMCA Complex in Jerusalem, Israel, Spector Amisar Ruskin Architects.

known as the city with the most rainfall in the world. Every year between 1,200 and 1,400 centimetres of rain fall on this region. Yet despite this, the area suffers from severe water shortage. The topsoil in Cherrapunji is eroded in the winter months primarily due to deforestation and mining. The terrain has lost its ability to absorb moisture and allow the growth of food in the region. Rainwater just drains off and ends up far below the plateau in the flats of Bangladesh. An essential resource is thus lost to the inhabitants of the area and its people have to buy potable water from an adjacent community. The technology to solve the problem is readily available, but the community has yet to organise itself to benefit from this natural resource, the simple and efficient management of which could change the community's quality of life.

While the focus of much of the world remains on the issue of non-renewable energy resources, there are now many alternative renewable energy systems with increased efficiency in performance and cost effectiveness. It is likely that within our lifetime we will see alternative energy sources that are clean, renewable and economically available to everyone. Energy, as with clean air, clean water and clean land, must be available to all.

A more difficult problem is the issue of waste emitted from the built environment. Our culture is essentially a throughput system that generates unmanageable quantities of waste, some contaminative. While there are solutions for energy production from waste, we are still a long way from any comprehensive global solution to handling waste and emissions.

Ultimately it is our lifestyles that must change. The management of this is primary if we are to inhabit a clean and healthy environment. There are many other pressing issues such as poverty, good housing and public health but all these become more difficult to solve if we do not have a clean environment. An overarching legislative infrastructure that manages, educates, defines qualities and measures performance in use is needed immediately. Most importantly, it must be readily accessible and easily understood by all.

These, then, are the most pressing challenges today. In an analogy of the architectural design process, we have now completed the "conceptual stage" in designing for our sustainable future, and next we have to delve deeply and quickly into the "design development stage" of green design and clean green technologies. A concurrent pressing necessity is the careful integration of all the different technologies to be efficiently and mutually supportive in our buildings.

Convincing the world that environmental issues are real is no longer the battlefront. We now have to focus on implementing green principles in our work in the most cost-effective way. This is our primary and immediate challenge. Three necessary ingredients are already here to make this happen. We already have many of the clean technologies. They are becoming affordable. Political motivation and support are emergent. Sustainability in architecture is no longer an option, or even an ethical consideration—it is the most crucial issue of our time if we are to leave the planet in a habitable state for future generations. The question is whether we can get it all done before the condition becomes irreversible.

This publication is dedicated to supporting this endeavour.

STRATEGIES FOR DESIGNING GREEN

KEN YEANG

INTRODUCTION

We are all aware of the numerous pressing global social issues to be addressed, such as abject poverty, providing clean water, adequate food and enclosures, proper sanitation and so forth. Ultimately, if we do not have a global environment with clean air, water and land, resolving the other pressing global social issues becomes even more difficult and expensive. Thus saving the environment is the most vital issue of the day.

For the designer, the compelling question is: how do we design for a sustainable future?

It would be a mistake to see green design as simply about eco-engineering. Engineering systems are indeed important (see the 'grey' infrastructure right) and technologies are rapidly developing and advancing towards a green architecture and built environment, but these are not the only considerations.

Neither is green design just about rating and accreditation systems (such as LEED or BREEAM), which are certainly useful references, but not comprehensive. They are useful as a partial checklist for some of the key considerations in green design and in proselytising to a wider audience. Yet, by not being comprehensive, many designers would ask, having achieved the highest level of rating (such as platinum), "where do we go from here?"

Clearly, green design has now entered the mainstream of architecture. Ask any architect about green design and you will get the same response—use of photovoltaics, wind generators, compliance with certification systems, planning as new urbanism, etc.. We need to question whether this is all there is to green design.

The contention is that achieving effective green design is much more than the above, and that green design is not as easy as had been imagined. It is complex. While still incomplete, there are a number of design strategies that can be adopted to get as close as we can to our goal of stasis with the natural environment in our built environment.

The first strategy is to view green design in terms of the weaving of four strands of infrastructure: the 'grey' (the engineering infrastructure, being eco-sustainable

THE FOUR STRANDS OF ECO-INFRASTRUCTURES

GREEN
Ecological Eco-Infrastructure: Nature's Utilities, Biodiversity Balancing, Ecological Connectivity, etc..

GREY
Engineering Eco-Infrastructure: Renewable Energy Systems, Eco-Technology, Carbon Neutral Systems, etc..

BLUE
Water Eco-Infrastructure: Sustainable Drainage, "Closing the Loop", Rainwater Harvesting, Water Efficient Fixtures, etc..

RED
Human Eco-Infrastructure: Enclosures, Hardscapes, Use of Materials, Products, Lifestyle and Regulatory Systems.

engineering systems and utilities), the 'blue' (water management and closing of the water cycle with sustainable drainage), the 'green' (the green eco-infrastructure, or nature's own utilities) and the 'red' (our built systems, spaces, hardscapes, society and regulatory systems). Green design is the blending of these four strands into a seamless system.

The Grey Infrastructure

The grey infrastructure is the usual urban engineering infrastructure of roads, drains, sewerage, water reticulation, telecommunications, energy and electric power distribution systems. These engineering systems should integrate with the green infrastructure rather than vice-versa, and should be designed to be sustainable.

The Blue Infrastructure

Parallel is the water infrastructure (the 'blue' infrastructure), where the water cycle should be managed to close the loop, although this is not always possible in areas of low rainfall. Rainwater needs to be harvested and recycled. Surface water needs to be retained within the site and returned to the land for the recharging of groundwater by means of filtration beds, pervious roadways and built surfaces, retention ponds and bio-swales. Water used in the built environment needs to be recovered and re-used wherever possible.

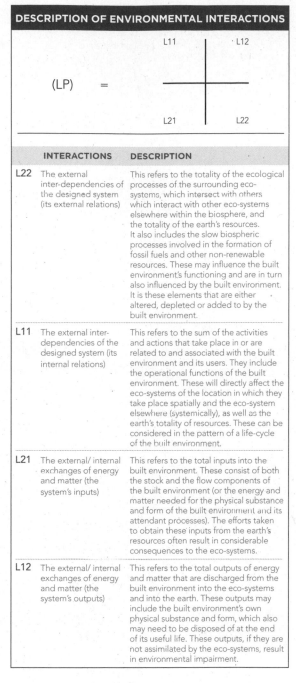

DESCRIPTION OF ENVIRONMENTAL INTERACTIONS

$$(LP) = \begin{array}{c|c} L11 & L12 \\ \hline L21 & L22 \end{array}$$

	INTERACTIONS	DESCRIPTION
L22	The external inter-dependencies of the designed system (its external relations)	This refers to the totality of the ecological processes of the surrounding eco-systems, which intersect with others which interact with other eco-systems elsewhere within the biosphere, and the totality of the earth's resources. It also includes the slow biospheric processes involved in the formation of fossil fuels and other non-renewable resources. These may influence the built environment's functioning and are in turn also influenced by the built environment. It is these elements that are either altered, depleted or added to by the built environment.
L11	The external inter-dependencies of the designed system (its internal relations)	This refers to the sum of the activities and actions that take place in or are related to and associated with the built environment and its users. They include the operational functions of the built environment. These will directly affect the eco-systems of the location in which they take place spatially and the eco-system elsewhere (systemically), as well as the earth's totality of resources. These can be considered in the pattern of a life-cycle of the built environment.
L21	The external/ internal exchanges of energy and matter (the system's inputs)	This refers to the total inputs into the built environment. These consist of both the stock and the flow components of the built environment (or the energy and matter needed for the physical substance and form of the built environment and its attendant processes). The efforts taken to obtain these inputs from the earth's resources often result in considerable consequences to the eco-systems.
L12	The external/ internal exchanges of energy and matter (the system's outputs)	This refers to the total outputs of energy and matter that are discharged from the built environment into the eco-systems and into the earth. These outputs may include the built environment's own physical substance and form, which also may need to be disposed of at the end of its useful life. These outputs, if they are not assimilated by the eco-systems, result in environmental impairment.

Site planning must consider a site's natural drainage patterns and provide surface-water management so that rainfall is not allowed to drain away. Combined with green eco-infrastructure, stormwater management enables the natural processes to infiltrate, evapo-transpire or capture and use stormwater on or near the site, potentially generating other environmental benefits.

Waterways should not be culverted but replaced by wetlands and buffer strips of ecologically functional meadow and woodland habitat. Sealed surfaces can reduce soil moisture and leave low-lying areas susceptible to flooding from excessive run-off. Wetland greenways need to be designed as sustainable drainage systems to provide ecological services. Buffers can be combined with linear green spaces to maximise their habitat improvement potential.

Eco-design must create sustainable urban drainage systems which can function as wetland habitats, not only to alleviate flooding but also to create buffer strips for habitats. While the width of the buffer may be constrained by existing land use, their integration through linear green spaces can deliver wider corridors. Surface-water management maximises habitat potential. Intermittent waterway tributaries can be linked using swales.

The Green Infrastructure

The green eco-infrastructure parallels the grey urban infrastructure of roads, drainage and utilities. This is an interconnected network of natural areas and open spaces that conserves natural eco-system values and functions and sustains clean air and water. It also enables the area to flourish as a natural habitat for a wide range of wildlife, delivering benefits to humans and the natural world alike. This eco-infrastructure is nature's infrastructure (parallel to our man-made infrastructures, designated as grey, blue and red infrastructures here), and in addition to providing cleaner water and enhancing water supplies, it can also result in cleaner air, a reduction in heat-island effect in urban areas, a moderation in the impact of climate change, increased energy efficiency and the protection of source water.

Having an eco-infrastructure in the masterplan is vital. Without it, no matter how advanced the eco-engineering, the masterplan remains simply engineering, and can in no way be called an ecological masterplan nor, in the case of larger developments, an eco-city.

Linear wildlife corridors connect existing green spaces with larger green areas, and can create new habitats in their own right. These may be in the form of newly linked woodland belts or wetlands, or existing landscape features such as overgrown railway lines, hedges and waterways. Any new green infrastructure must also enhance the natural functions of what is already there.

In the masterplanning process, the designer identifies existing green routes and areas, possible new routes and linkages for new connections in the landscape. At this point additional green landscape elements or zones can be integrated, such as linking with existing waterways that provide ecological services such as drainage to attenuate flooding.

This eco-infrastructure takes precedence over other engineering infrastructures in the masterplan. By creating, improving and rehabilitating the ecological connectivity of the immediate environment, the eco-infrastructure turns human intervention in the landscape from a negative into a positive. Its environmental benefits and values are a framework for natural systems that are fundamental to the viability of the area's plant and animal species and their habitat, such as healthy soil, water and air. It reverses the fragmentation of natural habitats and encourages biodiversity to restore eco-systems while providing the fabric for sustainable living, safeguarding and enhancing natural features.

The connectivity of the landscape with the built environment is both a horizontal and a vertical process. An obvious demonstration of horizontal connectivity is the provision of ecological corridors and links in regional and local planning which are crucial in making urban patterns more biologically viable. Connectivity over impervious surfaces can be achieved by using eco-bridges, undercrofts and ramps. Besides improved horizontal connectivity, vertical connectivity is also necessary, since most buildings are not single but multi-storey. Designers must extend eco-corridors upwards, with greenery spanning a building from its foundations to the rooftops.

The Red (or Human) Infrastructure

The human infrastructure is the human community, its built environment (buildings, houses, etc.), hardscapes and regulatory systems (laws, regulations, ethics, etc.). This is the social and human dimension that is often missing in the work of many green designers. It is clear that our lifestyles, our economies and industries, mobility, diet and food production all need to become sustainable.

SEAMLESS AND BENIGN BIO-INTEGRATION

The second design strategy is to regard green design as a seamless and benign environmental bio-integration of the artificial (the man-made) with the natural environment. It is failure to successfully integrate that is the cause of our environmental problems. If we are able to integrate our business processes, our designs and everything we do or make in the built environment (which by definition consists of our buildings, facilities, infrastructure, products, refrigerators, toys, etc.) with the natural environment in a seamless and benign way, there will be, in principle, no environmental problems whatsoever. Achieving this is, of course, easier said than done, but therein lies the challenge.

We can draw an analogy between eco-design and prosthetics in surgery. A medical prosthetic device has to integrate with its organic host—the human body. Failure to integrate results in dislocation. By analogy, this is what eco-design in our built environment and in our businesses should achieve: a physical, systemic and temporal integration of our man-made, built environment with our organic host in a benign and positive way. Eco-design essentially integrates our artificial systems, both mechanically and organically, with the host system.

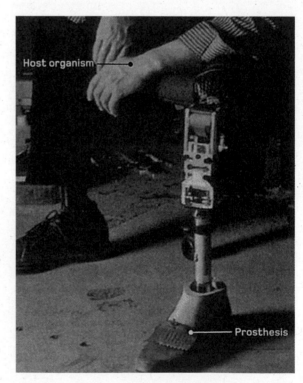

Host organism

Prosthesis

Eco-design as the vigilant monitoring and rectifying of environmental impairment.

Designing for bio-integration may be regarded as having three aspects: physical, systemic and temporal. Physical and systemic integration requires an understanding of the site's ecology. Any activity from our design or our business takes place with the intention to integrate benignly with the eco-system. We must understand an eco-system before imposing human activity upon it. Every site has an ecology with the capacity to withstand stresses imposed upon it. If it is stressed beyond this capacity, it becomes irrevocably damaged. Consequences range from minimal localised impact to the total devastation of the entire area (clearing of trees and vegetation, levelling of the topography, diversion of existing waterways, etc.).

We need first to ascertain an eco-system's structure and energy flow, its species diversity and other ecological properties and processes. Then we must identify which parts of the site (if any) can have different types of structures and activities, and which parts are particularly sensitive. Finally, we must consider the likely impact of the intended construction and use. This is, of course, a major undertaking. It needs to be done diurnally over the year, and in some instances longer. To reduce the timescale, landscape architects developed the sieve-mapping technique for landscaping mapping. This method generally treats the site's eco-system statically and may ignore dynamic forces within its layers, where there are complex interactions.

Another major issue is the systemic integration of our built forms, their operational systems and internal processes with the eco-systems in nature. This is crucial, because if our built systems and processes do not integrate with nature, they will remain disparate artificial items and potential pollutants. Their eventual integration after manufacture and use is only through biodegradation. Often, this requires a long-term natural process of decomposition.

Temporal integration involves the conservation of both renewable and non-renewable resources to ensure that they are sustainable for future generations. This includes designing low energy built systems that are independent of non-renewable energy resources.

ECOMIMESIS

A third strategy is to regard green design as 'ecomimesis', imitating eco-systems' processes, structure, features and functions. This is one of the cornerstones of eco-design. Our built environment must imitate eco-systems in all respects, e.g. recycling, using energy from the sun for photosynthesis, increasing energy efficiency, achieving an holistic balance of biotic and abiotic constituents in the eco-system.

Nature without humans exists in stasis. Can our businesses and our built environment imitate nature's processes, structure and functions, particularly its eco-systems? For instance, eco-systems have no waste. Everything is recycled within. By imitating this, our built environment will produce no waste. All emissions and products are continuously re-used, recycled and eventually re-integrated with the natural environment in tandem with efficient use of energy and material resources.

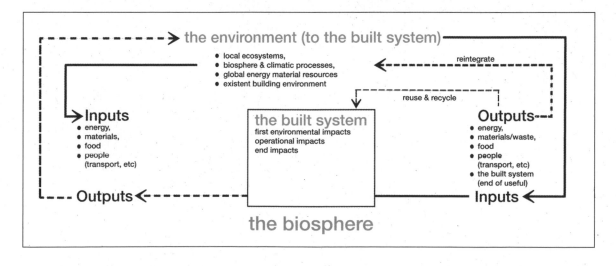

Eco-systems in a biosphere are definable units containing both biotic and abiotic constituents acting together as a whole. From this concept, our businesses and built environment should be designed analogously to the eco-system's physical content, composition and processes. We should regard architecture as artefacts which eventually need to be integrated with nature.

The material composition of our built environment is almost entirely inorganic, whereas eco-systems contain both biotic and abiotic constituents, or organic and inorganic components.

Our construction, manufacturing and other activities are, in effect, making the biosphere increasingly inorganic, artificial and biologically simplified. To continue without balancing the biotic content means simply adding to the biosphere's artificiality, thereby making it more and more inorganic. This results in the biological simplification of the biosphere and the reduction of its complexity and diversity. We must reverse this trend and balance our built environment with greater levels of biomass, ameliorating biodiversity and ecological connectivity.

Eco-design also requires the designer to use green materials and assemblies of materials, and components that facilitate re-use, recycling and re-integration for temporal integration with the eco-system. We need to be ecomimetic in our use of materials in the built environment. An eco-system generates no waste, one species' waste being another species' food—matter cycles continually through the web of life. It is this closing of the loop in re-use and recycling that our man-made environment must imitate.

RESTORING EXISTENT IMPAIRED

Fourthly, eco-design can be regarded as not only creating new artificial 'living' urban eco-systems or rehabilitating existing built environments and cities, but also restoring existent devastated eco-systems within the wider landscape of our designed system. We should, for instance, improve ecological linkages between our designed systems and business processes with the surrounding landscape, not only horizontally but vertically.

Achieving these linkages ensures a wider level of species connectivity, interaction, mobility and sharing of resources. Such real improvements in ecological nexus enhance biodiversity and further increase habitat resilience and species survival. Providing ecological corridors and linkages in regional planning is crucial in making urban patterns more biologically viable.

We must biologically integrate the inorganic aspects and processes of our built environment with the landscape so.that they become mutually eco-systemic. We must create 'man-made' eco-systems compatible with the eco-systems in nature. By doing so, we enhance man-made eco-systems' abilities to sustain life in the biosphere.

SELF-MONITORING SYSTEM

The fifth strategy for eco-design is to regard our designed system in the context of the biosphere globally as a series of interdependent interactions whose monitoring is necessary to ensure global environmental stasis and the repair of environmental devastation by humans, natural disasters and the impact of our human built environment, activities and industries. These environmental interactions need to be monitored for appropriate and immediate corrective action to be taken to maintain global ecological stability.

The above are strategies that can be used to approach green design and achieve a stable, sustainable environment. Green design has to go beyond conventional rating systems such as LEED or BREEAM, which are useful indices for comparing the green-ness of building designs. They are not, however, effective design tools. They are not comprehensive enough in addressing the issues of environmental design at local, regional and global levels.

Generally, ecological design is still very much in its infancy. The totally green building or green city does not yet exist. There is much more theoretical work, technical research and environmental studies that need to be done and tested before we can have a truly green built environment. We all need to continue this great pursuit.

UNDERSTANDING DRIVERS AND SETTING TARGETS FOR BIODIVERSITY IN URBAN GREEN DESIGN

MIKE WELLS, FLEUR TIMMER, ALISTAIR CARR

INTRODUCTION

Anthropogenic environmental changes are now threatening societal stability and the very fabric of civilisation around the world. They are also threatening the survival of possibly half of the species on earth and the lives of millions of people. With our increasing urbanisation as a species, it is essential that we directly address these threats through the application of effective green design within the urban realm. A key component of this is the creation of appropriate green infrastructure. But for green infrastructure not to be a 'greenwash', lacking significant functionality, all disciplines involved in urban design need a deeper understanding and recognition of the functional performance and values of green infrastructure and how to realise them in practice. This would help to make green design the mainstream approach in urbanism. Within this context, it is important to increase our awareness of the role of biodiversity in the functionality of green infrastructure in urban areas and the role of urban green infrastructure in preserving biodiversity.

Slow adoption of green infrastructure-led design in mainstream urban planning has been partly due to the difficulty of quantifying the very real benefits it brings. Various sustainability rating systems exist for urban design around the world, identifying some of the important measurements and targets. New systems are constantly emerging. However, even the very latest and best systems do not fully represent and give credit to all green infrastructure functionalities.

A key goal of 'eco-urbanism' is to achieve sustainable modern urban living despite burgeoning urban populations. Success will depend on ever-increasing sophistication of approaches to the design of green infrastructure and the development of quantitative, measurable targets for such design, linked to economic valuations. Central to this is the setting of quantitative or semi-quantitative targets for urban biodiversity within green infrastructure, relating not only to the preservation and enhancement of biodiversity itself, but specifically to the goods and services that biodiversity provides.

The combined pressures of global urban population growth, unsustainable use and degradation of natural resources and climate change are compelling mankind towards innovative green design in the places where most of us now live and work and recreate —our urban areas.[a]

POPULATION

Urban areas already contain more than 50 per cent of the global human population, and are anticipated to absorb all global population growth over the next four decades (an estimated 2.9 billion people[1]) whilst also accommodating further migrants from rural areas. The number of cities of over ten million inhabitants is expected to increase to account for over ten per cent of the world population by 2025.[2] Most of this growth will be in the less-developed countries. If the majority of growth were to occur in well-planned, high-density (not sprawling) cities, the associated increase in utilisation of energy and other resources and the associated increase in pollution might be greatly reduced.[3–6] In the developed world high-income city dwellers typically use less energy than equivalent suburban citizens, largely due to lower transport-related emissions.[7] Unfortunately, the majority of cities in developing countries are expanding by sprawl. However, even if this densification were to become the rule rather than the exception, urban life could well remain far from sustainable. Sustainability requires that the human environment be more than tolerable; it needs to be favourable, enabling people to thrive rather than merely exist, including the socially disadvantaged in society. [8–11, 12] These facts pose key challenges for green design.

NATURAL RESOURCES —PRODUCTIVE LAND

A key component of the ecological footprints[b] of cities is the production and transport of food. Carbon release from ploughing of soils in intensive arable farming and the general carbon footprint of modern 'industrial' agriculture are significant concerns, as are food imports.[13] For example, 81 per cent of the

For bibliographical references, see page 142.
[a] The distinction between urban and rural areas is complicated and multifaceted, and varies between and even within countries. The reader is referred to the latest guidance available from the United Nations Statistics Section on this matter.

[b] Ecological footprint of an urban area; the area of land needed to provide all the resources and services consumed and absorb all the waste produced.

food consumed in London originates from outside the UK with the associated carbon costs of transport, packaging and 'virtual water' (which has been described as 'exporting drought').[c, 14, 15]

Occasionally foreign imports can have lower carbon footprints than similar home-produced goods, but many of these cases relate to home-country production of crops out of season at high energy cost. Additionally, loss of productive land from growing city footprints is a concern at a time of such urban population growth.[16] Accordingly, many are now suggesting that we need to grow more of our food much closer to, and within, our urban areas on a sufficient scale to start creating real 'closed-loop' urban metabolisms.[17, 18] The emphasis here should ideally be on the use of large-scale permaculture techniques that conserve rather than release carbon from soils and make use of the vast quantities of organic waste produced in urban areas.

Examples such as Havana, Cuba where through necessity some 90 per cent of the city's fresh fruit and vegetables are grown in local farms and gardens have been recently much-vaunted.[19, 20]

There is still debate and uncertainty, however, as to what such enhanced urban and peri-urban food production could look like in decades to come and just how significantly it might contribute to the overall quantum of food consumed by urban citizens. Architectural magazines have recently been displaying many futuristic images of vertical and rooftop urban hydroponic farms, though it is not yet clear how such installations could ever be a viable alternative to traditional agriculture, even if the high carbon releases from the latter were factored in.[21, 22] In Canada at least one company, Omega Garden Int., is claiming commercially viable hydroponic food production with a carbon footprint lower per unit of productivity

[c] The ecological footprint of London, for example, a city which covers 0.6 per cent of UK land area but which is home to 12 per cent of the population is estimated to be an area equivalent to all of the productive land in the UK, though the footprint is globally dispersed.

than normal commercial rural agriculture. Additional advantages claimed are water economy and much reduced incidence of pests and disease. It still remains difficult, however, to see how any significant quantity of grains and pulses—staples of our diet for millennia—could ever be produced in, or even near, our cities and towns.

Nevertheless, even if a given urban food production technology or installation only makes a relatively small contribution to reducing the carbon footprint of our food, it may still be worth pursuing. This is not only to develop the technologies involved, but also as part of a multiple-strand approach to reducing the total carbon embodied in all the food consumed in urban areas, which should include reduction in demand. In the West, where problems of obesity are rife, a key strand needs to be education to reduce food intake and promote quality over quantity.

Moreover, whether or not a compelling direct economic/carbon case can be made for urban and peri-urban food production, there are other compelling arguments to pursue it in green design. These include the very great benefits in terms of social cohesion, individual health and reconnection with nature that such installations have been shown repeatedly to bring, with various associated economic benefits.[23, 24] We need more quantitative or semi-quantitative measurements of these benefits. We should also more frequently be asking "what can an approach that seeks to maximise native biodiversity bring to such food growing systems and their associated benefits?"

NATURAL RESOURCES —BIODIVERSITY

In the current "Anthropocene" period, man-induced losses, degradation, fragmentation, islandisation and pollution of habitats—contributing to and exacerbating climate change—are causing a mass extinction of species at a rate 1,000 to 10,000 times the estimated background rate. This is largely due to losses of rainforest and coral reef, but losses continue from all habitats.[d] Whilst some have suggested that

evidence for this loss threatening mankind's very existence is not strong, other evidence suggests that we may pay a high price given the inherently greater instability of degraded eco-systems.[25, 26] A well-publicised example is the loss of pollinators, especially bees, due largely to the loss of biodiverse habitats to make way for intensively farmed monocultures, where the cultivation techniques used are having adverse effects on habitats well beyond field boundaries.[27, 28] Apart from the enormous economic cost, this could in some cases trigger a cascade of local extinctions amongst associated species.[29–31, 32] According to one estimate, the eco-system goods and services of different natural or semi-natural habitats could have an economic value between 14 per cent and 75 per cent (depending on the habitat) greater than that of the simpler systems that have replaced them.[33] In light of the above, there has been a steady increase in policy aimed at reversing the trend of biodiversity loss since the Earth Summit in Rio de Janeiro in 1992, and the establishment of the Convention on Biological Diversity.[34] Green design and habitat creation in the urban realm have a significant role to play in this reversal.

CLIMATE CHANGE

Carbon footprint reductions from closed-loop metabolism in cities and high-density living will be focal to any serious efforts to minimise the effects of climate change. Green design can and must include effective measures that will help us adapt to the already inevitable changes. Examples of this include reducing urban heat island effects (and hence carbon costs of cooling) and reducing flood risk and damage to rivers in the context of more extreme and regular storm events.[35, 36] Once again, biodiversity has a significant enhancing role to play in this regard and also stands to benefit as climate change is itself threatening urban biodiversity through overheating and promotion of disease and invasive species.[37]

In summary, in addressing all the key pressing environmental issues of our time, green design in

---

d The result is predicted to be a 'mass extinction' comparable with the five other natural mass extinctions since the origins of life on earth some 3.5 billions years ago, and a loss of around half of global biodiversity. Recovery in species numbers from previous mass extinctions has taken hundreds of millions of years.

and around our urban areas has a focal role to play as a key component of 'Eco-urbanism'.[e, 38]

SUSTAINABLE URBAN LANDSCAPE DESIGN AND THE GREEN INFRASTRUCTURE CONCEPT

Until recently, proponents of urban densification have generally spoken little of the potential contributions to sustainability of green space or wildlife habitats in urban areas, and some still discount them. Reasons for this have included:

- Traditional conceptual schisms between what is 'town' and 'country' or indeed 'landscape' and 'urban realm'[39]
- The idea that towns were places where nature was controlled or suppressed[40]
- Lack of appreciation of the full potential value of green space in urban areas
- Commercial short-termism for capital gain
- High urban land values 'squeezing out' green spaces in our cities and towns.

Many landscape architects are only just realising the importance of ensuring sustainable design, and in the USA only in 2009 were assessment and benchmarking tools produced for sustainable urban landscape design to "enable built landscapes to support natural ecological functions by protecting existing eco-systems and regenerating ecological capacity where it has been lost".[41, 42]

In the late 1990s the Millennium Eco-system Assessment provided a classification which assigned the benefits that people derive from eco-systems into the following categories:[43]

- 'Supporting' (primary production and soils)
- 'Provision' (e.g. food, water, fibre, fuel, medicines)
- 'Regulating' (e.g. relating to climate, water, disease)
- 'Cultural' (e.g. spiritual, aesthetic, recreational and educational).

The value of these services to man was estimated at close to twice the Global Gross National Product.[44] Over the same period, the concept of 'green

infrastructure'—urban landscapes performing multiple functions for mankind—has rapidly attained a high profile.[45, 46] Green infrastructure has now been heralded, for example by the UK Town and Country Planning Association, as having an 'essential role' in the development of sustainable urban settlements.[47] Yeang has recently strengthened the status of green infrastructure by placing it in an equal categorisation of the following 'infrastructures': 'green' (vegetation/ natural and designed soft estate), 'blue' (surface water systems), 'red' (social—e.g. built forms, pedestrian networks) and 'grey' (hard engineering utilities).[48]

The multiple benefits of urban green infrastructure have been progressively characterised.[49–53] Perhaps one of the greatest benefits, and until recently least acknowledged, in terms of the sustainability of high-density urban populations, is the promotion of human health and psychological well-being with all associated economic benefits.[54–63]

'BIODIVERSITY PROVISION' VERSUS 'GREENING'

In practice, it is still often the case that green infrastructure is equated with general 'greening' with limited focus on biodiversity. The results of an increasing number of studies, however, are showing that (comparing between similar habitat types) biodiverse urban areas provide significantly enhanced eco-system services compared with comparable species-poor areas.

Of particular interest in this regard is a recent study that has shown clear links in a UK context between the biodiversity content of comparable urban landscapes and the well-being of the observer, even when the observer has little learned knowledge of, or particular interest in, biodiversity.[64] Attitudes towards 'wildscapes' in towns, already fairly positive in some northern mainland European countries like Germany (witness Emscher Park, Duisburg) may also be changing in countries such as the UK, where the traditional preference has been for highly manicured greenspace.[65, 66]

---

[e] 'The development of multi-dimensional sustainable communities within harmonious and balanced built environments', Ruano, M, *Ecourbanism*, 1999.

The history of living roofs, from eclectic roof gardens to biodiverse roofs based on construction rubble, is a fascinating journey through green design. Control over substrate composition and isolation from polluted surfaces and groundwater flows increase the chances of good natural/semi-natural habitat analogues being created on roofs, given time and patience. The authors are currently developing schemes for creating excellent heathland, neutral and calcareous grasslands on roofs for schemes throughout the UK. The conviction that these will succeed comes from examples such as the two illustrated here in Switzerland.

The first is on the Moos Lake water filtration plant in Wollishofen (Zurich, Switzerland). These living roofs were created in 1914 by transfer of displaced meadow soils onto some two hectares of concrete slab roofs, as it was thought that this would help stabilise temperatures in the stored water. The cross-sectional make-up is beautifully simple—some 15–20 centimetres of soil placed on a five centimetre sand and gravel drainage layer over a bitumen waterproofing—the whole roof draining naturally via a slight slope to an edging of 'Roman' tiles. The bitumen has only weathered close to the edges of the roofs, elsewhere being in perfect condition after 90 years. The vegetation, developed from the natural soil seedbank of the emplaced soils, is stunningly biodiverse (175 plant species including nine orchid species; there are over 6,000 Green-winged Orchids Orchis morio—illustrated). Moreover the roof habitats are an excellent analogue of the former ground-level meadow habitats, so good in fact that—as the original meadows of similar quality in the Canton have long been lost to agricultural 'improvement' —they are being considered for gazetting as a protected park.

Another example, on the Rossetti Building of the Cantonal Hospital in Basel next to the River Rhine, is an analogue of a river gravels habitat. This stony grassland with an undulating depth of local alluvial/gravel soils (mitigation for loss of these riverine habitats to industry) is again an excellent habitat for wildlife despite its limited size (1,500 square metres). It supports various uncommon invertebrates including several species of river edge habitats. It even partially floods in winter rains, further improving the niche diversity and similarities to flooded river edge gravels. As air conditioning is restricted in this part of Basel and the attractive architecture is achieved by glazing, the roof has a significant function in cooling the upper floor in summer.

A further example is of a rooftop meadow that has been monitored over a period in which its organic biomass has built up naturally and water features have been added until successful breeding by Lapwings Vanellus vanellus has occurred. The investigation forms part of a research project on roof-nesting by wading birds in Switzerland that is led by the leading Swiss living roof expert, Dr Stephan Brenneisen.

Nevertheless, attention must still be paid to the factors behind individual landscape preferences and dislikes so that design responses can 'broaden the constituency' for biodiversity.

Other examples are emerging. Better water-treatment performance may be achieved from more biodiverse wetlands compared with swards dominated by one or two tall emergent plant species.[67–69] Improved resilience in urban habitats to disease and environmental change and more sustainable productivity may result from greater complexity in comparable eco-systems.[70, 71] Livestock grazed on biodiverse grasslands may produce dairy and other products of a superior quality to those produced on agriculturally improved swards.[72]

Opinions differ as to whether urban green design can significantly assist in reversing some of the biodiversity losses described above. Earlier treatises on urban ecology stated that rarities did not tend to occur in urban areas.[73] More recent work has shown that urban biodiversity can indeed include a very valuable and often rare biota that to a large extent has been rendered extinct in the countryside by modern 'industrial' agriculture.[74, 75]

Even quite recently created living roofs can accommodate many rare species.[76–78] One might be tempted to dismiss living roof habitats as contrivances that are not 'fully functional eco-systems'. However, excellent analogues of valued natural habitats (or in the UK for example semi-natural habitats, virtually all truly wild habitat having been lost to man's activities) *can* be established in the heart of the urban realm on buildings given time.[79–82] These can be stable and support not only large populations of pollinators but also many other valued species (see examples from Switzerland on page 18).

In the UK, the change in awareness of the importance of biodiversity in green infrastructure is reflected in the recent guidance for net biodiversity gain (after full mitigation) in 'eco-towns', which provides biodiversity-led design principles for green infrastructure for the first time in the UK.[83]

ECLECTIC URBANSCAPES OR SEMI-NATURAL HABITAT ANALOGUES?

Having established that biodiversity in urban 'soft estate' is highly valuable; its incorporation can be approached in a number of ways. Typically the decision is an eclectic choice of species and substrates to create new urban 'ecologies'. Examples include the combination of new techniques for production of urban food with the sciences of permaculture and ecology to create new productive landscapes, the use of 'supernormal stimuli' to create particularly successful habitat features (such as certain artificial wildlife refuges) and the melding of habitat creation with artistry (such as on some living roofs).[f, 84] Using natural colonisation as a design tool often results in the commingling of native and non-native species as 'urban wildscapes' in what have been termed "recombinant" ecologies both of which have new 'culturo-biological' values.[85, 86] It is also true that urban habitats composed completely of alien species in urban areas can sometimes revive interest in the environment in social groups of foreign ethnic extraction, when the species have particular cultural resonance for the people involved.[87]

Native flora and fauna can and do thrive in a wide variety of such man-made habitats, occasionally preferring them to semi-natural habitats. However, analogues of fully functioning native semi-natural or wild eco-systems are likely, on the whole, to provide the best overall habitats for many native species simply because of the longer period of co-adaptation. Moreover, creating natural/semi-natural habitat analogues in cities can increase citizen awareness of bio-regional context, bringing sometimes significant benefits to people in terms of their performance at work, through their gaining a 'sense of place' or at least increased acceptance of wilder urban landscapes.[88, 89]

The idea, however, that we might be able to create functional copies of valued semi-natural habitats in urban areas has had generally less attention until relatively recently. The great number of non-native species present in urban areas together with the

---

f Supernormal stimuli are those which magnify the characteristics of a signal or releaser occurring in nature, such that a given animal responds to it in preference to the natural stimulus. One example is the preference shown by a Herring Gull chick to peck at a red football rather than the red spot at the base of its parent's beak when both are offered (pecking at the red spot in the natural situation elicits the regurgitation reflex of the parent, supplying food to the chick).

frequently challenging conditions of, for example, limited land availability, soil contamination, air pollution, water shortage, elevated temperatures, management difficulties and varied perceptions about what urban landscapes should look like, might suggest that efforts to create significant areas of good semi-natural/natural habitat analogues are unlikely to succeed.[90] Moreover, habitat creation in general, wherever it is undertaken, has been viewed with great caution by many nature conservationists who fear that an overstated ability to create valuable habitats could be used as an argument to destroy or move them for the purposes of development.[91, 92]

Nevertheless, certain semi-natural habitats such as wetlands *can* be created, with a very good approximation to many semi-natural eco-system functions, in relatively short timescales (less than a decade). An excellent example of this is the London Wetland Centre.[93]

Some grasslands of very high nature conservation value can be created in urban areas within several decades and do not necessarily support many non-native species.[94] The science of habitat creation has advanced steadily from the late 1980s, as the attached literature progression relating mainly to the UK attests [95–117], supplemented by a burgeoning global literature on restoration ecology. [118–122] In some countries, the database on the composition and autecology of plant communities is astonishingly detailed. Such references are not manuals for habitat design, but do give the green designer many cues as to how very good semi-natural habitat analogues might be created.[123] We predict that the functional differences between created and established semi-natural habitats in urban areas should continue to decrease as research progresses; and so the rationale for creating functional analogues in urban areas should strengthen over time.

PRESERVING THE BEST OF WHAT IS THERE NOW

It is now an established maxim that we must start our planning of green infrastructure by preserving, incorporating and buffering the best existing examples of habitats found in urban areas. This is not only because they can be surprisingly rich in species, but because they form clear source sites for colonisation of new green infrastructure. One of the best examples of this is the network of graded wildlife sites set up across the city by the London Ecology Unit.[124] This said, this piece is concerned more with the creation of new green infrastructure and habitats in urban areas.

SETTING SMART TARGETS FOR NEW GREEN INFRASTRUCTURE

Targets for design of new green infrastructure have been set in various ways over the years, with examples including the UK Accessible Natural Greenspace Targets (ANGST) system.[125] Another example is the UK Town and Country Planning Association's recommended ratio of green infrastructure to built form in eco-towns.[126] But to consider biodiversity targets in green design is to go to the next level of detail and involves comprehensive consideration of individual 'ecological features'.

The term "ecological feature" was coined by the UK Institute of Ecology and Environmental Management as a catch-all term for definable ecological units such as species, assemblages, habitats and whole eco-systems.[127] Each feature will have certain key requirements and as part of a wider matrix, be able to deliver a wide variety of eco-system services. The frequent absence of clear, specific and well-explained functional targets for all intended ecological features at the outset of projects often results in many eco-system services not being secured. Even in one of the more advanced fields of habitat creation and restoration—wetland creation and restoration—the setting of goals and metrics that define functional success and then monitoring them adequately have long been seen as major shortcomings in most design projects.[128, 129]

Using the language of business planning, biodiversity targets should be 'SMART'—Specific, Measurable, Achievable, Realistic and Time-scaled. Targets should specifically include the *absence*, or low occurrence, of undesired phenomena. Examples include the exclusion of invasive alien species, dangerous supernormal stimuli, mirror effects of glazing leading to death by collision, disruptions and entrapment by lighting, and adverse effects relating to roads.[130–133]

TARGETING RELEVANT ECOLOGICAL FEATURES—CONSIDERING ALL CURRENCIES OF VALUE

The obvious starting point for selecting biodiversity targets in green design is the Biodiversity Action Planning (BAP) system, where it exists.[135] Such plans list priority habitats and species which merit particular conservation effort. In the UK, for example, plans have or are being prepared for 65 habitats and 1,150 species.[136] Sometimes strategic BAP objectives are quantified, e.g. the restoration or creation of a certain number of hectares of habitat in a given area.

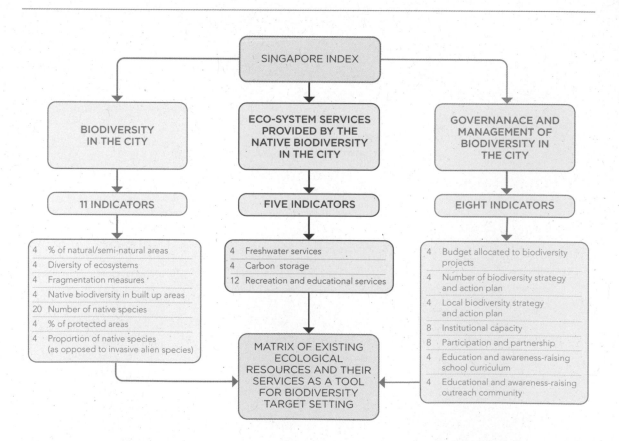

Other strategic objectives may relate to maintaining or restoring strategic connectivity and green networks in fragmented landscapes, which is often being defined by "biodiversity opportunity mapping".[137–138] Many such plans also consider ecological buffering values.[139] Where such plans do not exist, it can be time-consuming to list species and habitats relevant to the green design of a given urban area. It is essential, however, to make every effort to obtain the information, including by contextual field survey if necessary.

But biodiversity/genetic resource conservation value per se is not the only selection criterion in green design. Clear distinction should be made between intrinsic biodiversity value, social value and direct economic values of ecological features. Consideration should also be given to social equity in habitat provision as the quantum of urban biodiversity can be inversely proportional to the socioeconomic status of neighbourhoods.[140] In other words, poorer areas of town often have less soft estate, smaller gardens and generally less biodiversity than more affluent areas. This further widens social and health divides and disadvantages in society. Moreover, controlling for socioeconomic factors, crime rates have been shown to be higher in areas where there is less green infrastructure.[141]

Within each categorisation of value, as much sub-categorisation as possible should be attempted. In relation to species, for example, values may include the following:

Biodiversity 'Innate' and 'Ecosystem Support' Values

- 'Priority'—due to its innate biodiversity value which may be assessed, for example, on the basis of rarity or its value as a particularly high-quality example of its kind
- 'Flagship'—species that champion the biodiversity of the wider landscape in which they are found, often because of their conspicuousness, appealing appearance/behaviour or cultural iconography
- 'Keystone'—having a disproportionate effect in the functioning of the local environment
- 'Umbrella'—useful in making conservation-related decisions, typically because protecting these species indirectly protects a wide variety of other species and habitats.

Provision Values

- 'Edible' e.g. for a fish species that is part of an exploited fishery whether near to or far from the site (many of the most important cities in the world border the estuarine reaches of major rivers)
- 'Energy' e.g. a species that can also be used as a biomass fuel crop.

Regulating and Supporting Values

- 'Temperature regulating' and 'air quality improvement' effects of species which form significant parts of urban vegetation (all plant species contribute to this to some extent, but some species are better than others, and some are potentially harmful).[142]
- 'Water cleansing' species in wetlands, especially microbes and oxygenating plants
- Soil creation and stabilising species including a great diversity of invertebrates, fungi (such as mycorrhizae), microbes and other meio- and micro-fauna and flora of healthy soils.

Social/Amenity/Cultural/Educational Values

- 'Early warning'—species that may give an early warning of threats to our own health rather like a Canary in a coal mine. Classic examples include the Peregrine Falcon and DDT, lichen assemblages and sulphur dioxide and invertebrate populations in rivers and water pollution
- 'Healing/health-inducing'—for example, a species of bird with particularly melodious song or perhaps a plant with particularly appealing perfume; or species contributing to a valued whole eco-system aesthetic such as 'lushness' or 'multicoloured beauty' to which we respond positively.

Sources of potential strategic objectives for promotion of ecological features for social/amenity/cultural values may include some of the better Biodiversity Action Plans (such as that for London), but also other publications of government or charitable organisations. Objectives may include promoting species strongly associated with place and place names or with religious traditions.[143]

Recently, an international panel of biodiversity experts under the auspices of the Convention on Biological Diversity has devised the Singapore Index on Cities' Biodiversity—essentially a measure of the value of a city for and through biodiversity (*Figure 1*).[144]

Greenwich Peninsula Tidal River Wall, London, England

In 1998, renewal of the river wall along the Greenwich Peninsula was a requirement of urban regeneration works. Rather than merely being renewed, the old river wall was cut back and an inter-tidal terrace was created and filled with substrate similar to that of the foreshore before being planted with native species. The majority of the river edge, where space was limited to around seven metres, was reformed as stepped terraces, but at the tip of the peninsula a 'folded edge' was created, incorporating a continuous slope 'jack-knifed' over a wider ten metres terrace. The terraces have since formed into an excellent analogue of a semi-natural vegetated river edge, and have become an important Sea Bass nursery. It is now an exemplar in London for the progressive greening of the edges of the tidal River Thames, 60 per cent of which is still sheet piled and only one per cent natural. Continued efforts of this kind may help to restore fish populations in the North Sea.

FEATURE OR SERVICE	TARGET	RESULT AFTER 10 YEARS
BIODIVERSITY/ ECOSYSTEM SUPPORT		
PRIORITY HABITAT INTERTIDAL BRACKISH MARSH	Creation of ca. 0.7ha of stable analogue tidal marsh along just over one km of river edge with over 90 per cent plant coverage.	Habitat established. Stability excellent. Plant coverage achieved except in one short section where substrate settled below the required optimum level.
INTERTIDAL PLANT COMMUNITIES	Survival of over 50 per cent of planted species and colonisation by others.	Achieved. But over-expansion of Common Reed *Phragmites australis* due to lack of rhizome barriers and management. Excellent natural colonisation by Sea Aster *Aster tripolium*, occasional Sea Club-rush *Bolboschoenus maritimus* and Grey Club-rush *Schoenoplectus tabernaemontani*. Nine other species at rare occurrence (two naturally colonised). Nine other species planted did not persist (these were more characteristic of other river reaches).
INVERTEBRATE COMMUNITIES	Assemblage comparable to those at similar tidal levels in more semi-natural stretches of the river.	Achieved. Colonisation by 24 macrofaunal and 11 meiofaunal species in only six months as compared with three taxa on the former sheet piles.
FISH COMMUNITIES	Regular use of new habitat by all the key fish species in the adjacent riverine reach.	Terraces a major nursery for Sea Bass *Dicentrarchus labrax*. Also used by the European-endangered Smelt *Osmerus eperlanus*. Stepped terrace areas used by all except demersal fish—Flounder *Platichthys flesus* and adult Common Gobies *Pomatoschistus microps*—due to their unwillingness to rise up submerged step. This finding informed new national design guidance—favouring continuous slopes in a folded sequence (as at the peninsula tip) over stepped terraces.
PRIORITY VERTEBRATE SPECIES Smelt *Osmerus Eperlanus* (EUROPEAN ENDANGERED)	Regular use of new habitats.	Present on the terraces at certain times.
PRIORITY VERTEBRATE SPECIES— Reed Bunting *Emberiza Schoeniclus*	Regular breeding presence of one or two pairs.	Breeding pair on terraces in most years (with two pairs of Reed Warbler *Acrocephalus scirpaceus*).
REGULATING/SUPPORTING		
FLOATING DEBRIS	Functional trap.	Achieved by accumulation at back edge of terrace behind Common Reeds where readily removable by maintenance.
WILDLIFE DISPERSAL	Corridor aiding colonisation of wider peninsula by invertebrates.	Achieved. Dragonflies disperse peninsula-wide in summer; shelter provided by reeds etc.
PROVISION		
SEA BASS AND COARSE FISHERIES	Significant feeding/nursery function.	The terraces are now an important Sea Bass nursery in the context of the southern North Sea. The terraces permit fish to feed and reduce energy use in holding their position against the ebb and flow of the tides.
SOCIAL/AMENITY/CULTURAL/ EDUCATIONAL		
AMENITY	Highly positive reaction by public to landscape aesthetic.	Survey showed theoretical willingness of even those members of the public passing occasionally to contribute financially (actually over £40 per year) from their own resources to retain the feature if it (hypothetically) had to be maintained by public donation.
EDUCATIONAL	Permanent education of public on river system and biodiversity.	High-quality signage conveys key messages of the tidal nature of the Thames and its high water quality and abundant fauna to the public immediately adjacent to the feature. Much visited by schools.

*Intertidal terraces and
environmental signage at the
Greenwich Peninsula, London.*

Ralph Erskine's Greenwich Millennium Village Park created on former derelict land included an ecology park, designed as a 'wetland within a 'wetland' (the inner wetland being accessible only when wardens are present). Given the upmarket urban context there was considerable focus on maintaining the highest possible water quality. Elements of this included low phosphorus top-up water from chalk borehole, water circulation, water aeration, water filtration through a constructed reedbed·and phosphorous scavenging pit, and occasional water treatment with bacterial phosphorus scavengers. The wetland was also occasionally electrofished to maintain balance. Targets were either attained or exceeded in nearly all instances. The site is now close to being nationally important in terms of its dragonfly fauna and supports an impressive assemblage of other wildlife. It is now an important educational and amenity feature in a Borough context. One of the authors (MW) was the ecological designer of the park.

ECOLOGICAL FEATURE	TARGET	RESULT AFTER 10 YEARS
BIODIVERSITY/ ECOSYSTEM SUPPORT		
2.3 HA WETLAND MOSAIC *INCLUDING: Open Water With Floating And Submerged Aquatics, Temporary Ponds, Lake Edge Reedbed, Treatment Reedbed, Biodiverse Marsh, Wet And Dry Grassland, Wet Woodland, Ruderal Sward, Vertical Deadwood Habitat, Artificial Refuges For Invertebrates, Birds And Bats.*	Stable communities with healthy plants and balanced faunal assemblage.	Habitat established and stable.
INVASIVE ALIEN SPECIES	Absent or readily controllable.	Colonisation by *Typha* has been controlled—and invasive alien aquatics so far excluded. Breeding Canada Goose *Branta canadensis* controlled. Brown-tailed moth *Euproctis chrysorrhoea* outbreaks controlled manually.
PLANT SPECIES	No net loss of species-richness from over 70 species planted.	More than 70 species present, some new species replacing some of the planted species.
TROPHIC STATUS BASED ON DIFFERENT INDICATORS	Mesotrophic (*based on measurements of Total P, Oxidation/Reduction Potential, DO. Secchi disc readings etc.)	Occasional algal blooms readily addressed. Water quality generally high on most parameters. Temporary colonisation for one season by Stoneworts *Chara* spp. (probably brought in by birds). These are indicators of very high water quality, so even their temporary presence is considered a success.
LEPIDOPTERA (Butterflies)	Good assemblage for London for a site of c. two ha.	Achieved.
ODONATA (Dragonflies And Damselflies)	Good assemblage for London for a site of c. two ha.	Achieved fairly quickly. After seven years—14 species. An outstanding assemblage in southeast England is 15 species.
Fish	Largely absent	Control of fish introduced by the public and as eggs on the feet of birds achieved by electrofishing and natural predation by e.g. Grey Herons, Common Terns and Cormorants.
Little Grebe *Tachybaptus ruficollis*	1–2 breeding pairs	1 pair
Mute Swan *Cygnus olor*	1 breeding pair	1–2 breeding pairs
Mallard *Anas platyrhynchos*	2–3 breeding pairs	2–3 breeding pairs
Moorhen *Gallinago chloropus*	3–4 breeding pairs	4 breeding pairs
Coot *Fulica atra*	2 breeding pairs	3–4 breeding pairs
Blackbird *Turdus merula*	2–3 breeding pairs	3 breeding pairs
Wren *Troglodytes troglodytes*	1 breeding pair	1 breeding pair
Dunnock *Prunella modularis*	1 breeding pair	1 breeding pair
Common Tern *Sterna hirundo*	1–2 breeding pairs on two rafts	3 pairs—increased further in subsequent years with further addition/modification of rafts
Woodpigeon *Columba palumbus*	2 breeding pairs	2 breeding pairs
Sedge Warbler *Acrocephalus schoenobaenus*	1 breeding pair	2–3 breeding pairs
Reed Warbler *Acrocephalus scirpaceus*	3 breeding pairs	4–5 breeding pairs
Reed Bunting *Emberiza schoeniclus*	1 breeding pair	1 breeding pair
Great Tit *Parus major*	Breeding (numbers not predicted)	2 breeding pairs
Blue Tit *Cyanistes caeruleus*	Breeding (numbers not predicted)	3–4 breeding pairs
Carrion Crow *Corvus corone*	1 breeding pair	1 breeding pair
Pied Wagtail *Motacilla alba*	1–2 pairs	0 pairs—too few open areas
Song Thrush *Turdus philomelos*	1 pair	0 pairs—in keeping with a national decline
Blackcap *Sylvia atricapilla*	1 breeding pair	0 pairs—inadequate quantity of thorny shrub?
Chiffchaff *Phylloscopus collybita*	1 breeding pair	0 pairs—woodland quantum possibly too small, edge to interior ratio perhaps too great and lack of nearby mature woodlands.

ECOLOGICAL FEATURE	TARGET	RESULT AFTER 10 YEARS
REGULATING		
WATER QUALITY	Wetland system to maintain high water quality for public amenity.	Achieved (see above).
URBAN TEMPERATURE	Temperature below that of areas of comparable urban density.	To be assessed. Anecdotal accounts suggest this to be the case.
PROVISION		
REED AND WILLOW	Harvested for use in other urban reserves.	Significant annual production is harvested and some of this is used elsewhere in London reserves.
SOCIAL/AMENITY/CULTURAL/EDUCATIONAL		
AMENITY	Amenity feature to become of at least Borough Value.	Possibly Metropolitan Value. Over 10,000 visitors per year. Visitor books almost completely lack negative comments and are full of praise.
SOCIAL	Positive interaction from nearby residents and involvement of volunteer groups on long-term basis.	Trust for Urban Ecology (TRUE) charity moved headquarters to park lodge and facilitates events and social involvement. Park now the social focus of the village. Large parties of volunteers assist with management works year-round.
EDUCATIONAL	Significant use by schools and colleges.	Extensive use by schools. Many hundreds of school visits per year. TRUE's expert educational skills sustain this. Several urban ecological studies by university students and amateur natural historians have been undertaken.

This is due to be finalised in November 2010. It aims to combine ecological summary metrics of eco-system health and biodiversity content with scores relating to eco-system services which include carbon storage, educational and recreational services and measures of community involvement and activism.

For each currency of value, a further important quantification involves estimation of the geographical scale at which the newly created viable ecological feature is likely to be significant, either on its own or in combination with other existing or proposed ecological features. That might just be within the context of the development site itself, or the context of the wider neighbourhood, region or of the whole nation. Some designed features of sufficient scale might even be able to accrue international value in time.

To do this requires a prediction of the value of different sizes and compositions of habitats and/or species populations that might colonise or utilise the designed site. Two examples which demonstrate the value of quantitative targets and monitoring, one involving tidal river wall habitats and the other an ecology park in an urban village in London are presented on pages 24 to 27.[145,146, g]

Crucial to this assessment is the place of the new ecological features within a wider network. Here the concept of the Urban Biosphere Reserve is key, where the best urban and peri-urban habitats can be linked into functional reserves that show complementary provision of nature conservation, environmental education, research and monitoring in the context of sustainable urban development.[147]

The green designer should then try as far as possible to quantify the functional performance of the designed eco-systems in terms of possible provision of eco-system goods and services in the urban realm.[148] Full data on the functional performance of ecological features are never available. Nonetheless,

qualitative or semi-quantitative assessments of some functions can generally be made.

DEFINING CONDITIONS FOR LONG-TERM VIABILITY OF DESIGNED ECOLOGICAL FEATURES

Having listed the relevant targeted ecological features and described them as fully as possible, including predicted/desired areas/population sizes, etc., the conditions and parameters that would be associated with the viable long-term presence of the feature should be defined. This means defining the conditions or properties that are likely to be associated with the existence of a species population or habitat at a 'favourable conservation status' or with a proposed eco-system that has 'integrity'.[h, i] In essence this means ecological features that are healthy and likely to survive long-term in a variable environment as recognisable and functional entities.[149] A recent review draws the following key conclusions on the assessment of eco-system health: [150]

- Several metrics are needed at each eco-system level and at different eco-system levels
- Both physico-chemical and biotic metrics are needed.

There is a need for the practitioner to draw on the fast-growing literature on urban eco-system functionality to maximise the chances of design success.[151]

Any degree of quantification reduces the risk associated with qualitative assessment and overlooking a potentially very important eco-system service. It hence increases the likelihood that informed professional judgement will make sustainable design choices. The examples on pages 24 to 27 illustrate some of these principles. A further good example of frequently used but sometimes ill-conceived interventions of green design is the 'wildlife corridor'. The green designer should:

---

g Two of the authors (MW and AC) provided ecological design input to these habitats.

h IEEM (2006) provides definitions as follows: For habitats, conservation status is determined by the sum of the influences acting on the habitat and its typical species that may affect its long-term distribution, structure and functions as well as the long-term survival of its typical species within a given geographical area.

For species, conservation status is determined by the sum of influences acting on the species concerned that may affect the long-term distribution and abundance of its populations within a given geographical area.

i IEEM (2006) quoting other guidance provides a definition for site ecology integrity as follows: The integrity of a site is the coherence of its ecological structure and function, across its whole area, that enables it to sustain the habitat, complex of habitats and/or the levels of populations of the species for which it was classified.

Table 1: A review of the ecological components of some selected urban sustainability accreditation systems: N.B. Because categorisations used are sometimes quite different between systems a degree of simplification and division/ grouping of weightings has been necessary to give some measure of comparison between approaches.

Countries have been placed in order of the overall weighting given to ecology in the overall sustainability score.

COUNTRY AND ASSESSMENT TOOL

PERCENTAGE OF THE TOTAL CREDITS AVAILABLE IN RELATION TO ECOLOGY, NATURAL SYSTEMS PROTECTION, HABITATS, VEGETATION AND SPECIES

	SINGAPORE GREEN MARK: INFRASTRUCTURE 2008	NETHERLANDS BREEAM: NEW BUILDINGS 2010	UK CODE FOR SUSTAINABLE HOMES 2009	CANADA LEED: NEW BUILDINGS 2009	UK BREEAM: OFFICES 2008	CANADA GREEN GLOBES: NEW BUILDINGS 2004	ABU DHABI ESTIDAMA PEARL RATING SYSTEM 2010	MALAYSIA GREEN BUILDING INDEX	GULF STATES³ BREEAM GULF: NEW BUILDINGS 2008	SOUTH AFRICA GREEN STAR 2010	NEW ZEALAND GREEN STAR 2009
OVERALL WEIGHTING GIVEN TO ECOLOGY (%)	12.3	12	12	11	10	9.5	8.8	8	7	7	5.5
AVOID SITES WITH HIGH ECOLOGICAL VALUE	○	●	●	○	○	○	M²	○	○	M	M
USE PREVIOUSLY DEVELOPED LAND	○		●	○	○	○	○	○		○	○
USE CONTAMINATED LAND	○	○		○	○	○	○	○		○	○
PROTECT VALUED FEATURES ON-SITE	●	○	●	○	●	●	M	○	●	●	●
MINIMISE BUILT FOOTPRINT	●		●	○	●			○			
AFTERCARE AND MANAGEMENT		○				○	M		○		
PROTECT OFF-SITE FEATURES						○	M				
HABITAT RESTORATION AND CREATION	●	○	●	○	●	○	●	○	●	○	●
ALLEVIATE HEAT ISLAND EFFECT	★			○		○	★	○			
INSTALL FOOD SYSTEMS							○				
INNOVATION¹	●						●	●			●

Key

○ 0–9.9%   ○ 10–19.9%   ● 20–29.9%   ● 30–39.9%   ● 40–49.9%   M 50–59.9%

★ Allocated elsewhere

☐ Absent from credits assigned to ecology

¹ Additional credits obtainable for innovation provide further incentives for imaginative design of green infrastructure.

² The indication of Mandatory in this row and later rows is caveated in that these metrics permit onsite mitigation or offsite compensation where habitat protection is impractical.

³ Gulf States covers: United Arab Emirates (except Abu Dhabi), Oman, Qatar, Bahrain, Saudi Arabia and Kuwait.

Table 2: Existing shortcomings of ecological aspects of ecology assessment in urban design project sustainability accreditation systems and some selected possible improvements/elaborations.

DESIGN ELEMENT	POSSIBLE ENHANCED DESIGN OF TARGETS: ASSIGN TARGETS AND CREDITS FOR...	
VALUED FEATURES OUTSIDE THE DEVELOPMENT SITE	Developments with least collateral adverse effects on nearby sites of value from development-related influences such as disturbance from residents, pets, movement,	light, noise, runoff, etc. This consideration should extend to avoidance of effects on mobile species from special sites at a distance (e.g. birds, bats, etc.).
CREATION OF SEMI-NATURAL HABITATS	Habitat creation based on the area of habitat created, its viability and similarity to semi-natural habitats valued in relation to local, regional and national priorities. Include concepts of habitat integrity. Accreditation systems should reward creation of full suites of	eco-system features, e.g. all functional stands in woodland, all trophic levels, crucial deadwood habitat, soils etc.—all part of developing eco-system authenticity and resilience. Estidama is by far the most advanced system available in this regard.
USE BY FAUNA	Realistically predicted colonisation by faunal species including predicted numbers and status (e.g. rarity, breeder or non-breeder,	migrant, etc.) and include the concept of favourable conservation status of populations.
CONNECTIVITY AND DEFRAGMENTATION	Contributions to improved connectivity and defragmentation in the wider landscape, especially for larger projects. Additional	credits should be assigned when significant contributions are made to the coherence of Urban Biosphere Reserves.
GREEN INFRASTRUCTURE GOODS AND SERVICES	The full range of functions of green infrastructure, e.g. heat island reduction, water treatment, air quality improvement and flood risk alleviation, psychological health and wellbeing and environmental education and (for larger projects perhaps) carbon sequestration and propose appropriate metrics and provision for biodiversity, reflected in the recent guidance for net biodiversity gain (after full mitigation) in 'Eco-towns,' which provides biodiversity-led design principles for green infrastructure for the first time in the UK [clix]. Additional credits should apply where enhanced eco-system services are provided by biodiverse systems.	Tree plantings should be differentially scored in relation to the eco-system services provided (the simple difference between large and small trees in this regard is not recognised in all existing systems) and adverse influences avoided (e.g. mass plantings of trees that produce high concentrations of Volatile Organic Compounds or particularly potent allergens).
VEGETATED ARCHITECTURE	Habitat creation on buildings, beyond mere greening, for the particular value this has in creating relatively undisturbed habitats and countering the effects of high urban densities. The level of sophistication of targets should extend, e.g. to favouring deep substrates for living roofs for their contribution to hydrological balance, cooling and habitat resilience. Living roofs and walls should universally be officially	recognised as part of Sustainable Drainage Systems by specific accreditation.
AFTERCARE, MANAGEMENT AND ENVIRONMENTAL EDUCATION AND AWARENESS	Different levels of involvement of existing organisations, communities in sustainable stewardship of created and existing ecological features. They should also significantly reward higher levels of commitment to horticulturally	and ecologically sophisticated management the provision for quality and security of long-term funding and environmental education and awareness.
MONITORING	Proper and scientifically controlled monitoring should attract specific credits. Monitoring should relate to a variety of taxa	both at a given trophic level and between levels.

- Investigate the precise requirements of size and composition of the corridor so that it is actually used by the target species[152–154]
- Realise that some corridors may actually *increase* vulnerability of valued ecological features by facilitating the movement of undesirable organisms
- Understand that many species disperse very well across large areas of inimical habitat without corridors[155]
- Refer to the very latest research findings.[156]

There will always be gaps in our knowledge of the behaviour of species that militate against success, but a scientific and professional extrapolative approach should always be applied to maximise the chance that any created wildlife corridor is truly functional.

One crucial element in long-term viability will be appropriate management. In many cases far greater management resources for biodiversity are available in metropolitan areas than in the countryside. In some cases, this has permitted urban semi-natural habitats to be managed as biodiversity 'arks' for species in recovery programmes.[157]

DEFINE SHORT-TERM/INTERIM TARGETS AND PREDICT MATURITY PATTERNS

Habitat creation generally involves elements of a 'scattergun' approach. More species of plant are generally seeded or planted than will be likely to survive in the long-term. For wetlands and wetland treatment systems simplification of the species lists to a half or quarter of the number originally planted is quite common and often such a poor result is accepted as the best that can be achieved. Initial failures of species may be due to inappropriate initial conditions in terms of vegetation context, and hence continued planting, seeding and substrate modification over time may be required. Careful design and planning, however, including greater attention to species autecologies, hydroperiods, competition dynamics and successional changes can greatly reduce loss of originally planned diversity.

It is also important to consider whether each created ecological feature is likely to change in the long-term through changes in other factors, such as climate. In landscape and ecological design in urban areas, the long-term view needs to be taken, and the likely

effects of both climate and social structure change on ecological features need to be considered. Approaches to habitat creation that allow for natural dynamism and later direct modification are likely to be ever more relevant to urban green design in a changing climate.[158] Finally, how the ecological features created might be moved to a new location at decommissioning, or compensatory habitat created, should be considered early in project development.

EXISTING AND EMERGING SYSTEMS FOR ORGANISING, RECORDING AND MONITORING PROJECT-LEVEL TARGETS FOR BIODIVERSITY IN URBAN DESIGN

Various systems for prescription of targets for ecology/biodiversity in urban design exist around the world as part of wider sustainability rating systems, several of which are reviewed in Table 1. The following key points are suggested by the data presented:

1. The weighting given to ecology in the overall sustainability scores of these systems varies between five per cent and 12 per cent. This may to some extent reflect different national priorities for development over protection of wilderness, though for some countries with the lowest weightings for ecology in the overall scoring system, the requirement to protect the most valued habitats is mandatory.

2. The other variations reflect differences in the historical, geographical and other conditions prevailing in the different countries, but also differences in levels of sophistication of thinking about green infrastructure and habitats.

3. The variation in emphasis given to habitat creation/positive ecological change is significant. The suggestion is that to some extent countries with the largest areas of remaining natural habitat perhaps place lower emphasis on habitat creation in the urban setting. The systems also vary notably in the level of sophistication of their approach to assigning credits for ecological enhancement. Estidama is outstanding in this regard, and invokes numerous metrics of eco-system functionality and monitoring that require deep ecological understanding to apply.

4. Long-term management and monitoring are in general poorly covered in these appraisal systems with the notable exception of Estidama.

5. Targets tying in the provision of green infrastructure/urban habitats to sustainable goods and services other than provision for biodiversity are far less well addressed overall (Estidama usefully introduces credits for food production systems). Design to ensure water treatment or air purification or general and psychological health and wellbeing may be covered indirectly elsewhere in some systems but is rarely linked directly to development of green infrastructure.

The last point may seem wishful with the many constraints on urban development budgets. Target setting, however, is pointless without an effective regime for monitoring the success of incorporated/created ecological features. This should be as simple and automated as possible. Baseline data collection should be undertaken in keeping with the planned future monitoring protocol. Data gathered should be widely disseminated, including both positive and negative results. New targets can always be introduced as long as we have not too readily abandoned efforts to achieve our original goals. Biodiversity targets are, therefore, to be regarded as clear ambitions, but ones that may be reviewed in the light of habitat development, succession and social responses.

CONCLUSION

Biodiversity is an important element of green infrastructure, which must be appropriately, sensitively and holistically designed if we are to address some of the key threats caused by our own environmental degradation of planet Earth. Advanced green design should set and monitor detailed targets associated with the maintenance or creation of robust ecological features that will combine to form new green infrastructure to greatly enhance the sustainability of urban areas for all life. The resultant biodiverse urban realm can potentially bring real economic, social and environmental benefits and contribute significantly to reversing biodiversity loss.

To achieve success in this endeavour requires the different urban design disciplines to develop a deeper shared understanding of the functional characteristics of urban green infrastructure and to work together in more synergistic collaborations than is often currently the case.

The various systems in use for sustainability accreditation around the world vary in their quality and sophistication as regards the setting of ecological design targets, the most recent and in most ways the best being the United Arab Emirates' Estidama system. However, notable improvements can be envisaged for all systems in use to enhance results both in terms of biodiversity per se and the urban goods and services it provides.

ACKNOWLEDGEMENTS

The authors wish to thank Professor David Goode, Dr Lincoln Garland (Biodiversity by Design), Ben Dewhurst (TRUE) and Oliver Prudden (Biodiversity by Design) for comments on earlier drafts. Thanks are also extended to the Environment Agency and Trust for Urban Ecology for use of material.

BIOMIMICRY

MICHAEL PAWLYN

Biomimicry is a rapidly developing discipline that finds inspiration in the startling solutions that natural organisms have evolved over the course of the last 3.6 billion years. Proponents of biomimicry contend that many of the solutions that we will need during the sustainability revolution are to be found in nature: super-efficient structures, high strength bio-degradable composites, self-cleaning surfaces, zero waste systems, low energy ways of creating fresh water and many others.

Typically man-made systems and products involve using resources in linear ways. Often the resource extraction is energy intensive, then used inefficiently and ultimately ends up as waste. While some benefits can be derived by looking at each of these stages separately, it is worth remembering Einstein's maxim that problems are not solved by thinking within the same level of consciousness that created them. Biomimicry offers completely new ways of approaching design such that the whole system can be optimised and radical increases in resource-efficiency can be achieved.

The application of peak oil theories to resources other than just oil has revealed the extent of transformation that will be required during the next few decades. If future generations are to enjoy a reasonable quality of life then we urgently need to redesign our buildings, our products and our systems to be completely closed loop and running off current solar income. While no-one would suggest that these transformations are going to be easy, biomimicry offers a vast and largely untapped resource of solutions to such problems. There are countless examples of plants and animals which have evolved in response to resource-constrained environments and much can be gained by treating nature as mentor when addressing our own challenges. Biomimicry can be conveniently divided into three strands, deriving inspiration from natural forms, natural systems and natural processes. This essay studies each of these in turn and outlines some of the potential that this approach presents.

INSPIRATION FROM NATURAL FORMS

The challenge when designing the Eden Project (by Grimshaw Architects) was to radically re-interpret an established building type, producing a botanical enclosure that was fit for the twenty-first century. We also had to contend with the client's demand for "the eighth wonder of the world" which added a certain amount of pressure to the design process! To make matters more difficult we had a site that was still being quarried so we had no way of knowing what the final ground levels were going to be. The approach that we adopted was to conceive the building as something that would inhabit the site rather than the site being shaped to suit the architecture. We designed the building as a string of bubbles, the diameters of which could be varied to provide the right growing heights in the different parts of the building, and to connect these along a necklace line that could be arranged to suit the topography. We explored lots of different iterations of this bubble string and set them into 3-D terrain models of the site. By cutting away everything that was below ground, we arrived at the first images that resembled the final scheme.

The next challenge was to strive for the lightest possible structure. We knew from a whole series of natural examples—from carbon molecules and radiolaria through to pollen grains—that the most efficient way of structuring a spherical form is with a geodesic arrangement of pentagons and hexagons. Richard Buckminster Fuller pioneered the technology and even has a form of carbon molecule (the "Buckminster Fullerene") named after him. We started with conservative structural assumptions and then set about refining the system. The most significant move in this process was in trying to maximise the size of hexagons so that we could increase light penetration. Glass would have been a serious constraint both in terms of its unit sizes and weight, so we explored a material which had been used on some much smaller and more conventional buildings and showed great potential.

Ethylene tetrafluoroethylene (ETFE) is a high strength polymer that can be formed into an ultra-lightweight cladding element by welding the edges of three layers together and then inflating it for strength. The great advantage of this was that it was a fraction of the weight of glass and could be made in much larger 'pillows' than the biggest available sheets of safety glass. A combination of wind tunnel exploration and thorough material testing allowed us to tune the design of the enclosure to the specific conditions of the site. We found that we got into a positive cycle in

which one breakthrough facilitated another: with such large pillows it meant there was less steel, which in turn admitted more sunlight and reduced the amount of heat that would be needed in the colder times of the year. Less steel also produced substantial savings in substructure. It was a satisfying example of how a process of refinement, analogous to evolution, resulted in a scheme that used a fraction of the resources of a conventional approach and cost one third of the normal rate for a glasshouse.

In contrast to many of the historic precedents we studied, the biomimetic approach resulted in a much more sympathetic relationship with the landscape. Examples such as the Palm House at Kew—a highly symmetrical building on a flattened site—can be read as an expression of the view of nature that prevailed at the time, as something that could be dominated by man. The Eden Project biomes accommodated the existing form of the site with a minimum of excavation and suggest a more respectful reconciliation between humans and the natural world.

Taking inspiration from various natural forms including soap bubbles, Buckminster Fullerene molecules and pollen grains, the scheme that resulted was a highly original piece of architecture that achieved a factor 100 saving in its envelope design at a third of the cost of a conventional approach. Towards the end of the project we calculated that the steel, aluminium and ETFE superstructure of the Humid Tropics biome was lighter than the air that it contains. With a slightly bigger budget we would know how to make it even lighter still.

Janine Benyus, author of *Biomimicry—Innovation Inspired by Nature*, has described eloquently how natural forms are being used by scientists and designers to develop forms of adhesion based on a gecko's feet or a mussel byssus, colour effects without dyes using principles of 'structural colour' found in butterflies and bird feathers, self-cleaning paint finishes inspired by lotus flowers and many other revolutionary new designs.

To date architects have only mimicked nature to a fairly limited extent and often the results could be more accurately described as biomorphism rather than biomimicry. The distinction is between an approach that copies natural forms and one that

learns from the principles that lie behind those forms. The opportunity therefore exists for architects to learn from a vast resource of design solutions, many of which will have evolved in response to resource-constrained environments. Within nature one can find examples of incredible efficiency that can point the way to more sustainable solutions: examples using shape and tension membranes rather than mass to achieve strength, using passive ways to control internal temperatures and making use of what is locally abundant rather than transporting materials over vast distances.

One area in which the construction industry could potentially learn a huge amount from nature is the world of manufacturing. Aside from the energy required to operate a building, this is one of the most significant environmental impacts that the construction industry has on the environment. Nature generally makes materials with a minimum of resource input, at ambient pressure, close to ambient temperature and does so in a way that enhances the environment rather than polluting it.

Abalone shells are a great example of 'natural manufacturing' that produces a material twice as tough as hi-tech ceramics and highly resistant to crack propagation. The shells are a composite made from very tough discs of calcium carbonate glued together with a flexible polymer mortar. The combination of hard and elastic layers stops cracks from propagating and the shell behaves like a metal deforming elastically under load. Research into abalone shells may well lead to stronger and lighter windshields, bodies of solar cars or anything that needs to be lightweight but fracture-resistant.

INSPIRATION FROM NATURAL SYSTEMS

Technology that would allow manufacturing at a molecular level is clearly some way off but rapid prototyping represents a very promising direction. Rapid prototyping approximates molecular manufacturing in that it allows the material to be placed exactly where it is required. If we look at the way we build things at the moment, the technology is relatively crude. Steel tubes, for instance, are uniform along their length even though the bending moment varies enormously. If rapid prototyping were to become rapid manufacturing, we could create far more efficient structures with a fraction of the weight.

A number of organisations have looked at natural systems for ways in which man-made systems and products can be rethought to yield much greater efficiencies. Eco-systems are a wonderfully rich interaction of different species that thrive in exactly the ways that human civilisation will need to develop—closed loop and living off current solar income. In eco-systems, the waste from an organism always becomes the nutrient for something else in the system. While traditional economists have consistently denied that there are limits to growth, we are becoming increasingly aware of the finite nature of our resources and there is an urgent need to adopt solutions based on the densely inter-connected and cyclical efficiencies found in nature.

The Cardboard to Caviar project (also known as the ABLE Project) is an inspired example of how wasteful linear systems can be transformed into closed loop systems that produce no waste and yield much greater productivity. Initiated by Graham Wiles of the Green Business Network, the scheme started as a way of involving handicapped people in recycling cardboard. The waste material was shredded so that it could be sold to equestrian centres as horse bedding.

At every stage of the project Graham Wiles applied the biomimetic principle of seeing waste as a resource with which to feed another process. So, when the equestrian centre asked what they should do with the soiled cardboard, he offered to collect it and established a wormery composting system. A deal was also confirmed with a firm that supplied angling bait to buy surplus worms, but when this fell through, Wiles decided to establish a small-scale fish farm to raise Siberian sturgeon. This part of the project involved working with former heroin users and has achieved huge success in getting addicts off drugs and involved in more productive pursuits. Since then many other elements have been added to the system:

1. The filtration system uses micro-organisms and watercress to clean the water while also producing a food crop.

2. It was noticed that the growth rates of the fish reduced dramatically in winter due to colder water temperatures so willow has been planted (using fertiliser from the adjacent sewage works) such that a biomass boiler can be used.

3. An area of land adjacent to the project is being cultivated, partly for the people that work on the project to learn about food, but also to produce food for the fish to supplement the diet of worms.

This year the sturgeon should produce their first batch of caviar demonstrating the potential to turn a waste material into a high value product

while yielding numerous social, economic and environmental benefits.

The Cardboard to Caviar project managed to transform a low value material into a high value product and earn money at each stage in the process. Others such as Gunther Pauli of *Zeri.org* have achieved similar alchemical transformations, creating man-made systems that mimic eco-systems. In one example Zeri reworked a brewery from a wasteful linear system into a highly inter-connected network that produces not just beer but fish, mushrooms, bread, pigs and gas, so with exactly the same quantity of inputs it is now producing far more outputs and virtually no waste.

Systems-thinking was a profound influence on the design of the Eco-Rainforest project while I was at Grimshaw. This had a number of similarities to the Eden Project—it was to be another botanical visitor attraction and it also had a challenging site. Its location was between two major conurbations (Liverpool and Manchester) and it was being used as a landfill facility. While the client's expectation was that

we would ignore the mound of landfill and design something to sit alongside it we decided to respond to this aspect of the site's history.

Inspired by the resourcefulness of the Cardboard to Caviar project and the schemes by Zeri we decided to design the building so that it could be made from and heated by waste. We proposed that the walls could be built up out of rubble waste, stockpiled during the remaining period of the landfill site and then loaded into gabion wire baskets. The roof would be a south-facing ETFE structure so that for a lot of the year the building would be self-heating using passive solar gain and a lot of thermal mass in the heavy walls. Within the walls we proposed to incorporate large vertical bio-digesters that would produce heat from the decomposition of biodegradable waste. These would be connected to the internal surfaces of the walls with heat exchangers so that during the colder times of the year we could draw heat from the decomposition process and use that to heat the building. The potential existed for the scheme to handle most of the biodegradable waste from a whole city and for various other waste streams to be handled

By contrast, man-made developments are often destructive on a number of levels and even the concept of 'sustainability' implies merely maintaining a basic level of existence. The real challenge before us is to go beyond 'sustainable development' to achieve solutions that are actively restorative. This is one of the preoccupations that we are addressing in our next project.

INSPIRATION FROM NATURAL PROCESSES

The Namibian Fog-Basking beetle lives in a desert and has evolved a way to harvest fresh water in this arid environment. This example of a natural process has inspired innovations in a number of fields of design including architecture. Grimshaw Architects' Las Palmas Water Theatre is a carbon neutral desalination plant that takes the form of a stunning outdoor amphitheatre. The Sahara Forest Project (by the Bellona Foundation, Bill Watts, Exploration Architecture Limited and Seawater Greenhouse Limited) is a proposal for restoring large areas of desert to agricultural land while producing large quantities of fresh water and clean energy. It combines two proven and commercially viable technologies in a way that produces significant synergistic benefits.

A major element of the proposal is the Seawater Greenhouse, an ingenious technology that creates a cool growing environment in hot parts of the world and is a net producer of distilled water from seawater. Designed by Charlie Paton, with versions built in Tenerife, Oman and the United Arab Emirates, the scheme essentially mimics the hydrological cycle in miniature. Seawater is evaporated from cardboard grilles at the front of the greenhouse to create cool humid conditions within the greenhouse and is then condensed as distilled water at the back.

When we think about nature we tend to think of it as being all about competition. While this is an important factor there is a growing consensus amongst biologists that it is not as significant as we once thought. If you look at mature eco-systems you are just as likely to find striking examples of symbiotic relationships in which organisms have hooked up for mutual benefits. So, applying a similar principle through biomimicry, we looked for other technologies

on site in a way that transformed a big problem into valuable opportunities.

Our idea for the exhibit that would be contained within the greenhouse was a replica of an Amazonian rainforest and the focus of the educational message would be all about eco-systems. This allowed us to pursue slightly different themes to the Eden Project as we had no wish to duplicate their approach, which was primarily about man's dependence on plants for a range of uses including food, medicine and shelter. For the Eco-Rainforest, we had an opportunity to explore the complex inter-relationship of species in natural systems. As the project developed it became clear that there was an interesting parallel between the exhibit and the way that the site was operating: one was to be an actual eco-system and the other was to be a man-made system reconceived on the principles of natural systems, creating more value out of the same resources and approaching zero waste.

A striking characteristic of natural systems is that they tend to enhance their setting and, as they mature, create increasing opportunities for further organisms.

The Namibian Fog-Basking beetle.

that could work in synergistic ways. The one that we settled upon was Concentrated Solar Power (CSP) which involves concentrating the heat of the sun to create steam that drives conventional turbines to produce zero carbon electricity.

The two technologies have very promising synergies that will make the economic case even more attractive. Both CSP and the Seawater Greenhouse work extremely well in hot desert conditions. While the former produces large quantities of surplus heat, the latter can make use of this to evaporate more seawater. The Seawater Greenhouse produces large quantities of pure de-ionised water which Concentrated Solar Power plants need for the turbines and cleaning the mirrors to maintain maximum efficiency.

The scheme has the potential to produce more fresh water than it needs for the plants in the greenhouses, so this surplus could be used to grow further food crops outside. While bio-fuels have been the subject of some concern recently, Jatropha is an energy crop that is not considered to be contentious as it can be grown in very dry soils that would not support food crops. The Sahara Forest Project would grow Jatropha to produce bio-diesel for transport purposes and to maintain energy generation at night. The electrical energy would be distributed to local users and, via a DC connection, to other parts of Europe with minimal loss.

Within recorded history large parts of the Sahara, and other deserts, were vegetated with forests of desert cypress and other drought tolerant vegetation. The process of desertification has reduced the amount of vegetation on the planet and threatens to exacerbate climate change, potentially creating a positive feedback that will further accelerate desertification. This project has the potential to

reverse that trend, returning areas of desert to biological activity and sequestering large amounts of carbon in plants and soil.

A further principle of biomimicry that we referred to above is applying systems-thinking to transform waste into opportunities. Given that the scheme involves evaporating large quantities of seawater it will produce significant quantities of salts. The calcium carbonate, sodium chloride and other useful compounds resulting from the evaporation of seawater would also be exploited to beneficial effect. Seawater contains nearly every element of the periodic table in varying quantities—including gold and uranium. While it will not be commercially viable to extract those that are present in very low concentrations it should be possible to extract many useful elements from seawater to fertilise desert soils, countering the trend over the past century of a steady loss of minerals from the land.

The project represents a very significant new development in the way that it combines two proven technologies in a new way to produce multiple benefits: producing large amounts of renewable energy, food and water as well as reversing desertification.

CONCLUSIONS

Janine Benyus has made the valid point that the typical involvement of an ecologist in the construction industry is as a consultant who does the body count when the scheme has been designed. Clearly there is a much more constructive relationship that is possible and we are likely to see an increasing number of ecologists working with industry and designers, introducing biological thinking into the earliest stages.

Biomimicry offers enormous potential to transform our buildings, products and systems. For every problem that we currently face—whether it is generating energy, finding clean water, designing out waste or manufacturing benign materials—there will be precedents within nature that we can study. All those examples will be running on current solar income, and they will be closed loop in their use of resources.

HOW TO THINK LIKE A FOREST

BERT GREGORY

"The time has come to link ecology to economic and human development. When you have seen one ant, one bird, one tree, you have not seen them all."
EO Wilson

INTRODUCTION

Imagine if cities were like forests; plenty of shade, diverse, rich in variety while offering abundant fresh air and daylight, with access to clean water, surrounded by living things—an integrated natural system in balance. Like a forest, urban sustainability begins with a healthy watershed, encouraging storm water use, re-use and delivery back into the eco-system. Operating to maximise efficiency of energy to renewable strategies. Extracting energy from waste, appropriate biomass and waste heat. Creating more compact, mixed-used neighbourhoods with buildings, streets and parks linked to mass transit. Providing healthy, liveable habitat for all living things.

As Mithun's practice has grown and evolved over the last 60 years, our designs have increasingly explored natural light and ventilation within buildings, conscious, site-sensitive use of water and the creation of vibrant yet comfortable spaces for people to live and work. We're privileged to have played a part in designing some of North America's greenest buildings and campuses—a new retail concept, environmental education centres for schoolchildren, urban condos and the restoration of a century old pier along the Seattle waterfront. Through this journey, we've evolved as well: adding landscape architecture, interior design, urban planning, even an ecologist to our core competencies as a firm. In turn, this has forced us to think more holistically, to begin to see our designs—inside and out, materials, energy, transportation, people and nature—as an integrated whole, interconnected.

We continue to seek new design strategies and technologies to make our green buildings consistent with LEED, ASHRAE 90.1 and other emerging standards. Our tradition has been to be aggressive with energy demand reduction strategies and try to exceed those targets. It has become clear that American engineering, and probably engineering throughout the world, has moved to a point where every design element is aimed at perfection. And nature really is not perfect. Going outside can mean different temperatures, different breezes and different humidity according to the time of day and season. Sometimes it rains and sometimes it does not. So it is important to ask the client on each project: What band of tolerance do you have in your space? Will this need to be a 'one sweater' space or a 'two sweater' space? That idea—of design tolerance, of active and passive approaches, reminding us that engineering does not have to be perfect—continues to inform every one of our designs.

THINKING BEYOND THE BUILDING

In Portland, Oregon Mithun came to a new understanding of space—particularly the interconnectedness of a building and its surroundings—with the design of Stephen Epler Hall. This six-storey residence hall for Portland State University takes full advantage of natural ventilation, rainwater and sun while carefully integrating energy conservation and increasing students' awareness and learning opportunities about natural resources. A mixed-use project, it features classrooms on the ground floor and very small studio apartments on the upper floors. It is also a very simple building, where aggressive energy strategies led to demand reduction of approximately 50 per cent below average. Site orientation was key, as were a series of simple cooling strategies making it possible for the building to operate without air conditioning.

Epler Hall's most distinctive feature is its stormwater management system. Portland has a very mild climate, actually perfect for natural cooling, but it does rain often. Therefore, dealing with water is important here. The city's watershed is degraded and toxins have moved into the river. Enter Portland's Big Pipe: over two metres in diameter and 1.5 kilometres long, it was constructed to divert stormwater and minimise sewer overflows into the Willamette River and, ultimately, to protect the river's salmon habitat. An emphasis on size, namely bigness, characterised many approaches to similar design problems in the twentieth century.

Using the Big Pipe as our rallying point, Mithun and PSU approached the city for funding to support an alternative strategy on site that would fix the top of the pipe instead. Using our design, rain would

flow from the rooftop through downspouts to river rock splash boxes, then through 'rainwater runnels' across a shaded pedestrian plaza and into planter boxes, where water is aerated before entering an underground cistern for re-use in toilets and on-site irrigation while reducing water demand. This installation became the first in the State of Oregon where it was legal to use rainwater to charge a toilet. Economics were critical to this proposal—in this case, costing about $90,000 (2006) and generating an expected five per cent internal rate of return for the university. So with a cheque from the City of Portland, we achieved a 64 per cent internal rate of return on this stormwater scheme—able to contrast modest funding of $79,000 with a $6 billion pipe.

At Epler, we recognised the importance of trying to fix the top of the pipe, allowing rainwater to move down to a rain garden, filtrating naturally back to the aquifer and recharging the city itself. We also began to understand that the balance of nature is no longer in balance in many of our urban areas—that we need to create cities that elevate the human spirit: beautiful cities, cities that feel like a walk through the forest.

REDISCOVERING, RECONNECTING THE PRIVATE/PUBLIC REALM

Simultaneous with our work for Portland State, we were invited to participate in a re-envisioning of Seattle's urban open space. Known as the Blue Ring Strategy, this long-range masterplan represented the city's first real attempt to connect its downtown core with the waterfront. Inspired by the Olmstead Brothers' 'Green Ring' network of parks and parkways, the Blue Ring would create an interconnected system of private and public open spaces for the city centre. Unlike that earlier plan from 1903, there are no large parks within the downtown core: Seattle's primary open space is Lake Washington. The city includes three watersheds which, of course, are somewhat disorganised as a result of myriad stormwater systems constructed over time. We also discovered that 38 per cent of the city was in common ownership: the streets, sidewalks, parks—all of it in the public realm and outside property lines.

Despite the lack of necessary funding to purchase large blocks of land for a new park, we felt it would still be possible to improve the quality of that space.

Closer examination of this pattern of private and public property led to recommendations for revising the city's street design manual and providing more pedestrian connections. This strategy resulted in a 100 year vision for urban liveability. It remains an important element in Seattle's approach to area planning while tying together several key redevelopment projects for the public realm at the city centre.

The Blue Ring Strategy served to inform much of the design thinking behind the South Lake Union Neighbourhood Plan. Located at the northern edge of downtown, South Lake Union was planning for growth with a mix of retail, housing and office space expected to bring a large number of new jobs and new households over the next 20 years. This comprehensive plan update would reflect a new vision for the neighbourhood as a liveable, walkable and sustainable community which recognised its maritime and industrial past while embracing its future as an urban centre for innovative thinking. One centrepiece for this re-emerging area is South Lake Union Park, a 12 acre site adopted by the Seattle Parks Foundation as its first major park project. Through a series of joint land acquisitions by the City of Seattle and Vulcan Real Estate, the neighbourhood developer, the park has become a reality and a stunning waterfront gathering place. Along with San Francisco's Hargreaves Associates, Mithun explored innovative ways to connect people with the water while considering how to continually improve that public realm. For the first time, we recognised the streets and sidewalks and parks could be used in many different ways at many different times—so how could we capitalise on the space, use it multi-functionally and wisely to have a positive ecological impact?

Seattle is much like Portland and benefits from a very mild climate, yet many of its buildings rely on air conditioning. Ensuring that we can cool the streets becomes very important, as hot streets mean higher outside temperatures and more energy consumption to cool spaces with air conditioning. With natural cooling and ventilation, a cool exterior environment helps keep the interior of a building cooler. Preliminary designs for the South Lake Union Guide focused on vegetation. This meant neighbourhood streets became a critical part of the public realm

rather than just thoroughfares for cars, and using the land helped channel stormwater runoff through rain gardens for sidewalks and bio-swales for streets.

Our big opportunity to put these ideas into action came through an urban redesign project known simply as Taylor 28. Within the boundaries of the South Lake Union neighbourhood is a 1.2 acre site of mostly concrete and asphalt bound on all sides by busy Seattle streets. This neglected stretch of Taylor Avenue had been completely left out of the neighbourhood planning process. The challenge for most American cities is that they cannot keep up with the changing demands of urban density. Seattle can be very wet, particularly in winter, and, as more people migrate into the city, more toilets are flushed and waste water flows into the combined sewer system, reducing its capacity. As climate change produces heavier, more frequent rainstorms, that stormwater flushes out and contaminates the bay with toxins.

Mithun's initial charge from the client was to design a new residential, mixed-use market-rate apartment development. Then one of our planners suggested we create an element of the Blue Ring Strategy right there, transforming that piece of the public realm into a greener, more liveable space. Through a radical new streetscape design, the site has been transformed into a plaza street, complete with a wide pedestrian zone and outdoor seating. By 'unplugging' the street from the sewer system, Taylor 28 relies on natural infiltration through a collection of rain gardens, trees and native plantings and becomes the first leg of a linear park to extend the length of Taylor Avenue.

SETTING A NEW PRECEDENT: LLOYD CROSSING

Following our work on the Blue Ring and South Lake Union plans, the Portland Development Commission (PDC) invited Mithun to lead urban design concepts for a 35 block urban district across the river from downtown and PSU's Epler Hall. Designated Lloyd Crossing for its proximity to the intersection of Portland's light rail and bus networks and a planned streetcar line, this inner city area included several large 1960s and 1970s office buildings with extensive surface parking, yet the neighbourhood itself lacked

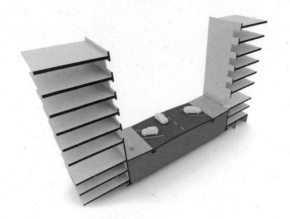

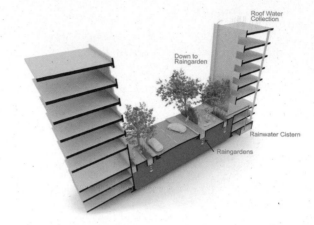

any distinct identity. Given only rough urban design parameters, we quickly discovered there were no natural boundaries for the neighbourhood and no access to the water. PDC clarified that our task was to create a model, a catalyst, to help them more fully understand the scope and requirements of achieving a truly sustainable urban development for Portland. So our journey through the complexities of the private and public realms continued.

The city had already expressed support for a five-fold increase in development of the district while quadrupling its population by the year 2050. Our design statement for Lloyd Crossing posed an intriguing question: how to turn the neighbourhood into a vibrant, attractive and highly desirable place to live and work while simultaneously reducing its net environmental impact over time. We faced several challenges, beginning with the Big Pipe. Once again, in this mild, wet climate our strategy focused on reducing the combined sewer overflow moving into the Willamette River. Another challenge: with 73 per cent of Portland's energy production generated by burning coal (quite astounding, since Seattle relies primarily on hydroelectric power and carbon offset strategies), what would it take to shift from coal to clean energy sources?

At that time, no metrics had yet been defined for this neighbourhood plan—no benchmarks against which we could measure the area's ecological or economic performance, nor compare with future sustainable development. Our goal went beyond LEED Platinum. After much searching, the design team finally arrived

at a series of "pre-development metrics" for the project, essentially using as our baseline the pristine, mixed-conifer forest that existed 200 years ago on the same site. Metrics within the study area would focus on tree cover, precipitation and water flows, solar energy input, materials, carbon and release of oxygen. Still, we asked, could we match the environmental footprint of a 35 block neighbourhood that would add 70,000 square feet over several decades to the native Northwest forest, and what were the barriers for us to overcome?

Through careful choices about open space and infrastructure, we believed the district could actually reduce its water, energy, habitat and carbon dioxide footprints to pre-development levels. Ultimately, the Lloyd Crossing Sustainable Urban Design Plan envisioned a series of key strategies to be phased in over time. We excluded only transportation planning, since the city had already factored this into its very aggressive management model for the district. Among the plan's key recommendations were:

- **Habitat** Restore habitat and tree cover by integrating a mixed-conifer forest into the urban streetscape through green streets, pedestrian streets, bio-swales and public open space
- **Water** Live within the site's rainfall budget (of 64 million gallons per annum) by employing a water conservation strategy through use of efficient fixtures, rainwater harvesting and black water re-use
- **Energy** Live within the site's solar budget by balancing carbon and the use of incident solar energy through building efficiency upgrades,

thermal transfer between buildings, use of renewable energy and purchase of carbon and wind offset credits

- **Placemaking** Preserve urban density through a combination of strategies for street-level and upper-level land use, street hierarchy, open space, landscape and habitat, ground-level building character and tower setback requirements.

- **Materials** Achieve carbon balance through a process of evaluating and selecting construction materials based on long-term energy efficiency and low embodied CO_2 content.

Although intended as a sustainable urban model, the Lloyd Crossing plan's ultimate success would mean each strategy could be measured and quantified against an achievable goal. This called for understanding and harvesting the district's potential solar energy input as our ultimate energy strategy. As a first step, we recommended pursuing aggressive energy efficiency measures and retrofits for existing buildings, then demand reduction, green power and any remaining carbon offsets. Energy sources would also require a creative shift from coal to natural gas, combined heat and power and wind en route to a much more aggressive carbon neutral plan: by 2050, Lloyd Crossing would be a carbon neutral operational neighbourhood.

Water is another vital theme for this model. As in most climates, a certain percentage of stormwater runoff is necessary to maintain a healthy eco-system and these 35 blocks receive more than 64 million gallons of rainfall annually. Per zoning code, this neighbourhood would need to import 160 million gallons of water during its development, resulting in 56 million gallons of stormwater runoff and approximately 144 million gallons of wastewater—a negligible aquifer recharge. The Lloyd Crossing plan made it possible to alter some of those statistics dramatically: a 28 million gallon demand reduction in potable water, a stormwater reduction of 37 million gallons and a waste water reduction of 92 million gallons. Simple strategies—rain gardens, landscape elements that help lift the human spirit, a pattern at each intersection—form an urban design strategy for the district to ensure that every section would have a green space and integrated, neighbourhood-scale water treatment.

Finally, economic analysis played a critical role at Lloyd Crossing as well. Accordingly, our design team included an economist along with landscape architects, engineers and a creative agency to brand the neighbourhood. Through this process, we gained a better understanding of the gap between society's goals and what the free market can bear. While a tenant and owner focus on their building, the city's responsibility lies in regional water, sewer, electricity and other systems. As a result, we chose to create an intermediate entity able to manage the district resources in a cohesive, integrated fashion: a Resource Management Association (RMA). As an intermediate step, this solution offered the long-term view of society while comprehending the short-term needs of most developers. As established, the RMA could make capital investments for energy retrofits, even for very aggressive net zero energy buildings requiring long-term paybacks.

Based on a novel premise, the creation of the Lloyd Crossing Plan established a new path for urban sustainability: that it may be possible to increase density, expand wildlife habitat and connections to the larger landscape, aim to live within a site's rainfall and solar budgets and achieve carbon balance—all whilst developing renewable wind and solar energy systems to ensure that these improvements are self-supporting.

URBAN RE-VISIONING: AUSTIN, BALTIMORE AND THE SUSTAINABLE CAMPUS

Several years after completing the Lloyd Crossing Plan, we were given a unique opportunity to put many of its design principles and planning concepts into practice—further south, in Austin, Texas. Designated "Project Green", Mithun won a developer-led competition to transform five city blocks into a dynamic, transit-oriented neighbourhood that included 2.5 million square feet of office, hotel, residential and retail space. Crucial to this masterplan was walkability, based on the reintroduction of the city's historic grid as well as new pedestrian alleys, bike trails, civic plazas and courtyards. Along with a renewed focus on urban food production, Project Green linked pedestrian, transit and bike routes to a series of flexible outdoor spaces while creating new venues for Austin's thriving music culture.

The plan's focal point lay at the intersection of Second Street and Shoal Creek in downtown Austin. Here, in the footprint of a decommissioned water treatment plant, the new masterplan set out a series of strategies to achieve both water and carbon neutrality by the time the build-out was complete. With several aspects of this project aspirational in nature, it was also important to clearly define what carbon neutral

meant: energy, transportation, the materials within each building, new or old. Energy elements—both passive and active—for this hot climate included natural cooling, solar thermal collectors, double skin membranes, solar screens, hydronic heating and cooling and solar hot water. Energy efficiency and demand reduction were critical components, yet Project Green also proposed a concentrating solar plant, in partnership with Austin Energy, to generate electricity and waste heat for hot water. To become a water neutral development, the plan recommended a grey water treatment plant to lower potable water demand and irrigate landscaping and park space throughout the neighbourhood.

Mithun has also enjoyed a long and productive relationship with higher education institutions. Since Portland State's Epler Hall and a previously completed student housing complex for University of Washington, we have learned valuable lessons through sustainability planning for a growing number of university campuses, in a sense microcosms of the larger urban environment. At Seattle University, the administration desired a campus masterplan, coupled with its Sustainable Masterplan, to advance best practices and create both vibrant and sustainable campuses. SU became an early supporter of the American College and University Presidents Climate Commitment, with the goal of achieving climate neutrality. Covering SU's entire 48 acre site, this comprehensive sustainability plan will help the University achieve this goal while implementing design strategies that address energy, carbon, water, ecological systems and human wellbeing.

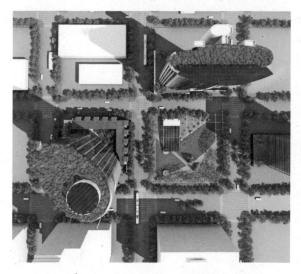

In addition, Mithun is supporting Ohio State University's Framework Masterplan to identify synergistic solutions to create a more sustainable campus consistent with the University's mission and climate change targets. Sustainability planning for both schools relied on Lloyd Crossing as a basic framework but further explored public and private realm issues—the ideas and analysis are more comprehensive, with greater detail and academic rigour than our earlier work in Portland.

Seattle, Portland, Austin, Columbus, Ohio—Mithun's designers have embarked on a number of exciting opportunities to push the limits of sustainable masterplanning. Now, a new plan for Baltimore known as State Center offers what may be our biggest challenge yet to see the ideas of Lloyd Crossing actualised. At the intersection of a crime-ridden housing complex and a restored historic rowhouse district—and not far from Maryland General Hospital, Symphony Hall and the Baltimore Armoury—is a challenged neighbourhood, a place virtually without a soul. Rather than the classic 1960s urban renewal tactics once used to consolidate so many of the Maryland state offices, this project focuses squarely on sustainability and smart growth principles. In fact, State Center's proximity to surrounding neighbourhoods as well as light rail and subway stations could make the area a national model for transit-oriented development. Plans for this 28 acre district could also make it one the most attractive arts, entertainment, retail and residential districts in the city.

Upon completion of its first phase in 2014, the project will include state-leased office buildings (400,000 square feet), a 1,000 car parking garage, 150 units of affordable housing, 50,000 square feet of retail space and later, a 120,000 square foot private office building. Located nearby will be a new 120,000 square foot headquarters for Maryland Transportation Authority. State Center's goals are lofty, but certainly achievable—to support human capital through a healthy workplace, system-based infrastructure and an integrated process that results in environmental, economic and social benefits to the community, government and developers as part of an innovative public-private partnership. The deep green design of this unprecedented, multi-use development began with sustainability analyses to focus on energy and water consumption, greenhouse gas emissions, the ecological function of campus landscapes and a reduction in impacts from purchasing decisions, food systems and waste flows.

At State Center, two key aspects of the masterplan bring us closer to making the concepts of Lloyd Crossing a reality. The first is an integrated strategy for district water and energy. Here, designers will "do the math" in demonstrating radical efficiencies for the site's office buildings, comparing code-level construction with alternatives that include LEED Silver, a 50 per cent below ASHRAE 90.1 design and a 70 per cent below ASHRAE 90.1 design. Essentially, this exercise more fully explores lease rates, capitalisation costs and other economic factors in relation to a 70 per cent efficient building with a much lower environmental footprint. Secondly, the project presents a new opportunity to put in motion creative financing mechanisms like those first unveiled at Lloyd Crossing. Once again, a Resource Management Association model allows us to better understand the real estate, regulatory and financing barriers to meet the leasing and short-term payback requirements of a market-based economy while supporting the broader societal and environmental goals of this neighbourhood over a 25 to 30 year period.

CONCLUSION

What began more than a decade ago on the US West Coast and now brings us east to the historic city of Baltimore are simple, but powerful, truths about transit, placemaking, resources and the importance of finding—and implementing—new strategies for growth and revitalisation while respecting the best of our urban traditions. We need twenty-second century approaches to open space, economic development, affordable housing and low-impact design, water and carbon neutrality for the built environment and the seamless integration of private and public interests. The opportunities are endless, the challenges often daunting, but if we are to protect the earth, we must create great sustainable cities made of compact, complete and connected neighbourhoods. The future of urban sustainability lies in learning from nature, in making buildings and public spaces that lift our spirits, and perhaps most of all, in designing each city to perform, even to think, like a forest.

SUSTAINABILITY

STEFAN BEHNISCH

What does the term "sustainability" mean? There seem to be as many definitions as the number of people one asks. Over the years in which architectural sustainability has been widely discussed, confusion has been caused by the fact that there are such very widely divergent views on how to achieve it.

In architecture the term is relatively new, although in the German language it has been used in relation to forestry since the early eighteenth century. Good practice is to never fell more trees than the number which can be re-established within a given time span. This ensures that stocks are continually replenished and is as such a very sustainable working dictum. Every three seconds the world is burning fossil fuels which the planet will need 24 hours to replace. Mathematically, this is not a sustainable approach.

Many architects and engineers think sustainability is a mere issue of mathematics. Their method is to apply technical means in order to produce sustainable architecture at the other end of the building process. In my view, sustainability has to be redefined on each and every project in relation to its cultural, social, geographical, topographical, climatic, geopolitical and local political context. Sustainable architecture cannot be achieved if the culture in which it stands is ignored.

One of the biggest misunderstandings, I think, of twentieth century modern or contemporary International Style architecture is that architects thought they could build the same buildings all over the world, ignoring all cultural and physical contexts. It was possible, but it required a massive input of energy. So long as this energy was available, architects could afford to ignore all the very different locations in which they were building. As architects and planners we have a broad sphere of power and influence when it comes to the built environment.

In Germany, when we discuss sustainable architecture, we often narrow the subject down to purely quantitative aspects: annual kilowatt hours/square metre. Of course energy is important, but it is not the whole story. At the moment the standard energy consumption for a bank office building in Frankfurt am Main is between 600 and 800 kilowatt hours/square metre annually, but now we are discussing being able to achieve annual values of just 100 kilowatt hours for

future projects. These empirical standards are important and technically feasible but they are not everything, because we are not measuring other values which also contribute to good architecture. All the energy saving standards could be incorporated in a building and still result in bad architecture that nobody would want to use.

There are other factors. We should be considering annual working hours related to energy, building users' annual occupation times related to energy. We should be considering each person's carbon footprint while in the building. When we start investigating these qualitative aspects of working and living in buildings our ways of calculating start getting more difficult, more fuzzy and imprecise. We see this as no longer just a matter of mathematics.

I am trying to understand the fears we architects have when we think about designing sustainable environments. We talk about the renaissance of urbanity, the metamorphosis of our societies, including changes in organisations and lifestyles, new ways of integrating work and home in so-called loft spaces, made possible by new communications technology. How can we create a good urban fabric, a public realm setting, with these new processes? We often forget that not only do our buildings affect the lives of those who occupy them, but also the lives and attitudes of those who experience them from the outside, while passing in the street. Buildings are the walls of everyone's "public living rooms".

The most prominent cultural asset we have is architecture. Architecture is the measure of our cultures. Why are we interested in visiting ancient and modern cities? Because we are fascinated by the way in which they are built. Architecture is a powerful motor driving our social and religious organisations, and our body politic both influences, and is influenced by, architecture. Architecture helps us define places in their geographical, cultural and historical context. So architecture is the human artefact that culturally defines space and time.

Then there is our responsibility for the choices we make and the way in which we use materials. We have to exercise value judgements in relation to nature, which leads us to think about recycling and life-cycle systems. We have a much wider responsibility for the environment enveloping our architecture—the air, water, earth and climate—before we even start moving into the buildings and considering internal conditions.

Let's consider some of the aspects mentioned in my introduction.

URBANITY

On the subject of urbanity we have learnt a great deal from working with Jan Gehl Architects, who are excellent city planners from Copenhagen. The city of Oslo built a magnificent opera house and when it was finished they realised they had forgotten to consider the building's setting, its urban surroundings. So they held a competition, which we won with Jan Gehl Architects and Transsolar. In Stuttgart for example, the city where I come from, a political decision, once reported in the media, becomes irreversible, but Oslo is much more flexible.

Our design had to solve the problem of how the city approaches the opera house, or how the opera introduces itself to the city, which involves enhancing the harbour and the waterfront. It was a presentation by architects for non-architects, and that is when we do our most interesting work, because we cannot presume anything. We detailed the presentation together with Transsolar, so the design solutions had very strong sustainable aspects. We worked on the typology, but most importantly we addressed the public realm. How could we make the city livelier? How could we create a mix in this city's quarter? It was a challenge because the measure of a landmark opera house is that of Sydney in Australia, where the surroundings do not compete with the focal structure, but still have an outstanding, matching, quality.

The public realm is what makes our cities lively entities. Architects have a tendency to overvalue the appearance of buildings, but as you walk through a public space your sphere of awareness is actually limited to a few metres in height. Anything further up you see only as a blur. Anyone in a city craning their neck to look at details high up on building facades is probably an architect or an architectural student. Facades influence the distant view, but in the public realm it is much more subjective.

What makes for a lively public space? Activities. Most city planners think this is reduced to shopping, but shopping is only one form of activity. Other important factors are protective structures against adverse weather elements and crowd management. Masses of people, unless on the Champs Elysées, are not usually very attractive, but density is. People are attracted by other people.

REDUCING ENERGY USE

I come from a very densely populated country, where most of what we see as "nature" is actually cultivated. How can we preserve it, but also take advantage of it for the people? Our first international project in the 1990s was the Institute for Forestry and Nature Research in Wageningen, Netherlands, a country even more densely populated than the western states of Germany. It was a European pilot project for a humane, user-friendly and energy efficient building. Today it would be classified as a sustainable project. The building is still being monitored and, interestingly, we have never achieved a result as efficient as this. The reason is simply explained. The building users are scientists working for the Dutch Environmental Agency. They make the difference. They helped us in the design and have taken the project to heart, finding ways to use it as efficiently as possible.

It was a great research project designed with the help of the Fraunhofer Institute. The brief was for a flexible and sustainable energy saving building but we had no data to work from. We had to start from scratch, calculating life-cycle costs, life-cycle energy use and making lists of primary energy materials. The site was formerly highly fertilised agricultural land. Our client, the Dutch Building Department, wanted us to remove the top metre of soil and replace it with new topsoil from an uncontaminated source. It was not possible to remove more than one metre because if we excavated any deeper we would disturb the ground water level. To us, the idea of transporting so much contaminated material, probably across the world to a dump, and also having to find an uncontaminated source and transporting that to the site, seemed a very energy-consuming and unsatisfactory proposal. We decided to work on an in situ solution with the help of botanists and biologists, using appropriate plants and fauna to clean the soil and water. The lake is artificial,

filled by rainfall and ground water, with a circular pump system for irrigating the landscaping. We estimated that the rehabilitation of a sustainable life cycle, the establishment of frogs, birds and insects, might take a decade but it took only three years. Today the landscape is like a jungle. It was certainly a cheaper and less aggressive solution. Within the building there are also pocket gardens with their own sustainable micro-climates.

For the building itself we discovered that the most efficiently produced materials were factory made, the kind of components bought at building materials suppliers. Industrially produced elements optimise the use of materials and energy in the manufacturing process. We used greenhouse units, made for growing tomatoes, and every other conceivable off-the-shelf type of element, except in the construction of the reinforced concrete structure. Originally we wanted a timber structure but that was beyond our budget. We used wood off-cuts for the facades. There is a natural ventilation system, operated by simply opening windows, the facade is shaded from strong sun and we have enough water to cool the air. Then the Fraunhofer Institute, who were analysing the systems for us, suddenly became cautious and said we should provide earth channels with ventilators for the atrium air quality. They thought it might be necessary as a back up system.

EMBODIED ENERGY

The key is to recycle and re-use materials. In previous ages builders used what was to hand. Not only was that easier and less time-consuming, but also more efficient and energy-saving. In Toronto we were asked by Ryerson University to convert a former power station into a venue for ice hockey games, with a conference centre and exhibition halls. We examined, together with Transsolar Climate Engineering, the embedded energy in the existing structure and discovered that to demolish and rebuild the same volume would be equivalent to the annual consumption of 30,000 American homes, or almost the annual carbon dioxide emission of 40,000 American cars. If you demolish an existing building with the idea of creating a more sustainable alternative, you need to use the replacement structure for ten years before you have compensated for the loss of the demolished structure's primary energy. Sustainability means stepping back and examining the whole balance sheet, which may include incorporating existing buildings and altering them to make them more efficient. This strategy has great potential.

There is a similar project in Stuttgart, which my father designed in 1968. A motorway was planned through the city, so the building's facades had been totally closed, with mechanical ventilation and

air conditioning. Just 18 months after the building was completed, the city decided to make the area a pedestrian zone, for which the building design was totally unsuitable. 30 years later the client returned to us and asked for a sustainable refurbishment, using the original structure but without air conditioning or mechanical ventilation.

SUSTAINABLE CULTURE

Ozeaneum, the German Oceanographic Museum in Stralsund completed in 2008, is an example of architecture as a cultural asset. This Hanseatic city in northern Germany is a World Heritage site, a trading city with ferries, a harbour and many landmark buildings and they wanted a new aquarium. A competition was held in which 400 architects took part. Many of the submissions were brick buildings. Most of the entrants had thought this material, similar to that of the existing historical structures, would be most acceptable. They failed to understand that a city might not want to be condemned to adopt this same image for eternity. A site outside the city limits might demand a contemporary solution. Brick is also highly inappropriate for the spans over the volumes needed for an aquarium and for the larger dimensions of a public events building. The scale of a brick is also out of proportion. An architectural design using brick would have had to be brickwork on steroids.

In contrast, our design consisted of four free forms with facades constructed from steel manufactured at a nearby shipyard with experience of spherical forms for supertankers. Soon after we won the competition, Stralsund's client representatives went to Paris to ask the World Heritage Organisation for approval of the design. It was given without a problem.

Ozeaneum is not only for public entertainment but also includes a research institute. They do not show particularly spectacular exotic fish, but those from the region, like herrings. In the first three months Ozeaneum was open, it had over 10,000 visitors, which proves that people are actually interested in seeing what a herring looks like.

CARBON DIOXIDE EMISSIONS

We won a 2006 competition to design the Science Center in Harvard, Massachusetts and managed to complete contract documents and start on site before the world financial crisis. Completion will be in 2012. It is our largest and most expensive project to date, with a usable floor area of 110,000 square metre. Our first task was to analyse Harvard as a university complex and then suggest the form of a new campus. Harvard is a strange collection of architectures, none of which matches the intellectual and research standards of the buildings' users.

The traditional image of a well-respected university is that of brick and ivy. Universities like Harvard are even known as Ivy League institutions. In reality, the buildings are a patchwork of timber, limestone or concrete. Our proposal created a courtyard-quadrangle ringed by four mixed-use buildings containing childcare facilities, a restaurant, lecture hall, conference centre and shop units. The upper floors are state of the art laboratories and offices with architectural features such as bridges, atria and wintergardens as connectors between functions. The energy saving windows are triple-glazed with a fourth extra skin, plus sun shading devices. They are far too heavy to be manually opened, but we didn't want to depend solely on mechanical ventilation, so the glazed areas are fixed and we made openings like 'windows' in the stone walls.

Our goal was to reduce carbon dioxide emissions by 60–80 per cent. This is only possible with a reasonable budget and a great deal of design effort expended in redefining comfort levels. Our analysis of energy consumption in a typical American laboratory building revealed that the interiors are heated in summer. Incredibly, they consume a third of the heating they use in winter. This unsustainable state of affairs is due to the fact that the air conditioning is set to the highest demand, and it becomes necessary to reheat the air. In other areas this is clearly an energy-wasting exercise. Our solution was to create five different climate zones in the laboratories, offices or winter gardens where people take their coffee breaks. Each zone has a tailor made air quality specification, related to functions in that volume. This strategy alone saved a huge amount of energy.

We also held the theory that while research processes had changed over the last 40 years, laboratory layouts had not kept up with these developments. We therefore carried out shadowing studies, following scientists around the whole day with stopwatches. The first day's findings could be ignored as people acted too self-consciously when they knew they were under observation. After a week they began to act more naturally. The study showed that the laboratory bench is only used for 20 per cent of a person's working time. By separating laboratory areas into three different climate zones we were able to use energy more efficiently and even introduce natural ventilation into some of the laboratories. Previously it was thought that laboratories needed high rates of air exchange to protect against dangerous substances. Nowadays, however, not so many dangerous materials are used, so air changes can be reduced. Without any technical innovations and by tailoring the services according to function, we were able to cut energy use by 33 per cent. With more sustainable systems, geothermal and thermal mass, we could make further reductions.

DAYLIGHT

An example of developments in the use of daylight come from the Genzyme Centre in Cambridge, Massachusetts. We won the competition in 2000 and the project was awarded a LEED Platinum Seal of Approval in 2005. It was a developer's architecture competition, but the tenant immediately commissioned us for the tenant improvement.

Using daylight is a problem in cities where street layouts are based on colonially influenced grid systems. Either the grid is orientated in the wrong direction towards the sun or the city building blocks are too deep and too tall in relation to the narrow streets, so that very little natural light is able to infiltrate the interiors. To correct this, we punched a hole in the building block and placed seven heliostats on the roof, mirrors which reflect daylight into the depths of the building, 13 floors down.

We are now designing light enhancing systems in projects for Boston and Germany. Having tracking mirrors is like dealing with canned light, which can be turned on and off and directed at will. It plays with daylight and sunlight to bring changing conditions of time, weather, season, and colour into interiors, connecting people inside buildings with the external world. It is not just a matter of introducing natural light deep into the architecture, but also controlling the quality. Cold light combats heat and harsh sunlight, so these light enhancing systems are even more useful in the southern hemisphere. Tracking mirrors and ceiling mounted prisms are just some of the hardware which can be programmed to precisely guide the different types and intensities of light into spaces, or block light in order to shade and cool areas. A further development has been the hanging of chandeliers in the atrium space so that light reflected from their surfaces is made visible and mobile as the chandeliers rotate in the air currents generated in the atrium. Motorised louvres, which seem to randomly change position, reflect and deflect light, adding to the subjective experience of the space.

DISTRICT HEATING ENERGY SAVINGS

As a footnote to the Genzyme Centre story, there is also something to be learnt from the use of existing local heat sources. During design, we discovered that a nearby power station was expelling hot water into the nearby river. We requested that a loop be constructed to feed this hot water into the Centre so we could use it with absorption chillers to cool air in summer and to heat in winter. This diversion has paid back its capital costs in four years. Now the Centre is saving $500,000 per year, compared with what its bills might have been without this form of district heating.

The annual publicity budget at Genzyme is vast. The CEO of Genzyme, Henri Termeer, told me that with all the energy efficient systems and improved qualitative measures, the building had completely paid for itself over five years, and almost solely out of his publicity budget. As built theory, the project is its own best publicity.

ENERGY SAVING LED LIGHTING

Hamburg's Chamber of Commerce, housed in Germany's oldest stock exchange, wanted to triple its internal floor area without changing the building's historic envelope and interior finishes. This was equivalent to constructing Chinese boxes, building a building within a building in the dark.

We won the Haus im Haus project in 2003 with the idea of a transparent structure in glass. In the detailing phase, when fire protection, fittings and structure were added, the design became less and less transparent. Another restriction was that all building components had to access the hall through existing doors, as the historic structure was not to be touched.

Our solution was to change from transparency to an emphasis on immateriality, which is more an illusion, a trick of the light.

The historic trading hall is circa 400 square metres, while the new insert has a total of 1,000 square metres stacked over four levels. The illusion of immateriality is created with LED light sources and reflective elements, making for a very even light coverage and surreal atmosphere. 180,000 LEDs on the ceiling can be animated to produce the illusion of clouds scudding across a non-existent sky. Reflective surfaces make the visitor continually aware of the extreme contrast between the ornate plaster, carved woods, marble and stone of an historic building and an ephemeral space age pod, fitted out and furnished with high quality contemporary designer furniture.

The most revolutionary aspect of this lighting system is that the whole building uses only 2.7 kilowatt hours for lighting, about the amount used by a big dryer. Although the project was only completed in 2007, the LED system we used then is already three generations old in comparison to what is now available. LED technology has fast tracked at a rate similar to computer technologies in the 1990s. Every year LEDs are doubly efficient and half the price.

In Harvard we are specifying only LEDs, not only because it is more energy efficient but also because it has a ten year life expectancy. In a laboratory one doesn't want the building janitor frequently climbing on to the benches to change light bulbs.

Here I have described some of the different concepts which can convince clients that it is worth paying for sustainable architectural solutions. Convincing clients, for their own good, can be a hard fought battle but clients are usually open to reason, and success is always convincing.

THE NEXT GENERATION: TRANSFORMATIONAL BUILDINGS FOR TEACHING AND LEARNING

DAVID LLOYD JONES

CHANGE

Change is always with us, but the scale and pace of change increases exponentially in response to cultural evolution and technological development, and it is the speed imposed on change that results in economic disruption and social conflict. The current situation has taken us to a new watershed. We are now faced with the aftermath of unprecedented economic meltdown, worldwide sectarian violence and catastrophic climate change.

The notion of sustainability has been appropriated, bandied about and misapplied by so many vested interests that it has all but lost its currency. However, its three underpinning tenets—economic benefit, social well-being and environmental protection—remain and form the basis for any move to improve conditions here on earth. These three tenets, not surprisingly, closely mirror the three current areas of global fracture.

Brundtland's seminal 1988 definition of sustainability—"Development that meets the needs of the present without compromising the ability of future generations to meet their own needs"—uses the welfare of future generations as a measure of the impact made by preceding ones. It is the next generation that architects in the UK and other countries are addressing in the most direct way possible. This is illustrated here in the design and building of new schools in the context of a transformational approach to teaching and learning and a pioneering reappraisal of sustainability.

In the UK, the Socialist government set up a programme for rebuilding and re-equipping the entire stock of primary and secondary schools. This was the biggest public investment programme ever seen, amounting to approximately £90 billion over ten years. Although the manner in which the schools are being procured is far from perfect, there is a concerted attempt to transform pedagogy as well as physical setting. Also in place in the UK Schools Programme is a review process aimed at ensuring design excellence. Furthermore there is, in parallel with this process, a procedure for ensuring that the designs comprehensively address sustainable measures.

The need for new schools is driven as much by changed learning and teaching attitudes as by inadequate, worn out and energy-profligate buildings. Although successive governments have constantly tinkered with school curricula, teaching standards and methods of learning assessment, schools by and large have been stuck in a Victorian legacy of exam-focused instruction. Only recently has it been broadly recognised that learning technologies and social upheaval have forced the scope, setting and span of education to a position that is vastly different from that of a couple of decades ago. The school no longer sits within a community serving as the prime dispenser of child enlightenment, inculcating useful skills with, maybe, a little adult learning when it can be fitted in.

Prospective work opportunities and the type of work are also changing. Teachers now have to prepare students for jobs that may not yet have been conceived where they will be using technologies that, as yet, have not been invented in order to solve problems of which we are so far unaware.

Although teaching and learning was never solely confined to schools and education institutions, there was a sense that you went to school to learn and to register the extent to which you have learnt by taking examinations. Now, with the pervasiveness of cybernetic technology and the exploration and investigation opportunities it provides, the value of self-learning and small-group learning has become as important as family learning and learning in the classroom. Video games are woven into this generation's lives as television was to those of their predecessors. In most developed countries 80 per cent of children between five and 15 have access to the internet at home. 40 per cent of eight to 11 year olds and 71 per cent of 12 to 15 year olds say they browse the web unsupervised. If MySpace were a country it would be the eleventh largest in the world. Neither is printed word on the decline: 3,000 books are published each day. Pat Kane in *The Play-Ethic* says that "play will be to the twenty-first century what work was to industrial society—our dominant way of knowing, doing and creating value".

Digital access and communications has changed everything. It has changed the way we work, where we need to work, the timeframe in which effective learning can take place and the compartmentalisation of curricular disciplines. Despite all this, or perhaps because of it, it appears that place and physical setting—places both of congregation and introspection—remain extremely important. Richard Florida in *The Rise of the Creative Class* says "the death-of-place prognostications simply do not square with what I hear from the countless people I have interviewed, the focus-groups I have observed and the statistical research I have done. Place and communities are more critical factors than ever before… the economy itself increasingly takes place around real concentrations of people and real places."

AN ARCHITECTURAL RESPONSE

So what do these new school spaces need to be? It is increasingly clear that they need to be designed around a smaller group unit; a group of, say, five rather than a class of 30 or more. There needs to be the possibility of bespoke space configuration. There needs to be excellent ICT provision. There needs to be a practical and life enhancing relationship between indoor and outdoor space. There needs to be the imposition of significant architecture: a physical order that holds everything together, giving the building identity and a sense of place.

One aspect of our belief in the significance of architecture is the notion that, for better or worse, we are different people in different places—at home we are one person, at work another and in a restaurant yet another—and the conviction that it is the task of architecture to render vivid to us who we might really be. Of course, at school age our persona is incomplete and in flux, so the interplay between the student and his school building and landscape is particularly potent and formative. At a recent CABE workshop attended by architects and other specialists associated with school design the opening gambit was to ask all those present to sketch on a flip chart what they remembered of their school buildings. The level of detail that most retained was far higher than expected and the descriptions subsequently related were unusually graphic.

In considering the design of new schools, the accommodation of a transformational approach to pedagogy goes hand in glove with the current transformational approach to sustainability. It is, of course, right to stress the need to design buildings that use precious resources economically and effectively and that avoid environmental degradation.

Since the beginning of the last century, architects and engineers have increasingly disregarded the historic precept of designing in harmony with nature. Real effort is needed to redress this situation and, indeed, real effort is now needed to address the inevitable and largely irreversible consequences of environmentally profligate design. Our goal is to ensure that all designers reach an understanding of the issues and the measures for avoiding and countering degradation of our planet. We need to reach a point where we think no more of designing a building sustainably as of designing one to stand up. When it comes down to it, sustainable building design deploys the same tenets—cultural, technical and climatic—as does all good design.

The incorporation of sustainability in terms of environmentally effective measures in the design of schools, as usual, raises conflicting needs. Wherever possible, teaching and learning spaces need to be day lit and naturally ventilated and, because of the size of the spaces, this usually means daylight and ventilation from two opposing sides. This in turn means relatively generous ceiling heights and penetration of floors with light and ventilation shafts. Schools are often located in noisy, urban settings and they are themselves noisy at times. The reconciliation of daylight penetration, effective air movement, sound attenuation and prevention of fire spread is a major conundrum in environmentally sensitive school design.

Another dichotomy in sustainable design, but this time more to do with social performance, is achieving a balance between visibility and privacy. We have found that quite focused activities requiring a high degree of concentration can be visually overlooked by those not taking part and actually gain benefit by being on display, provided that disturbance from noise and outside activities taking place in-the-line-of-sight are avoided. Generally speaking a school gains from their essential activities being on view. A collaborative dynamic and sense of common purpose can be engendered by being visible and open, attributes that are far more difficult to realise in a school of furtive, enclosed and boxed activities.

Design of schools, like the design of most buildings, is studded with such intractable issues, but many apparently insoluble conflicts fade into relative

*Top: Townley Grammar School for Girls: the performing arts space looking toward the public entrance and bleacher seating.
Bottom: Townley Grammar School for Girls: performance in progress.*

insignificance—or maybe just fall into place—if they are being addressed within an all-embracing architectural vision: one imbued with a sense of inevitability, a rightness sustained by a concatenation of valid and mutually interdependent pedagogic, sustainable and physical solutions carrying all before it.

ENGAGEMENT

Embarking on a new school, or a school extension, to an environmentally sustainable and educationally transformational brief is a very significant learning opportunity in itself. With the right organisational structure and the active support of the community and the school, the processes of design, construction and building operation can become revelatory and often support school curricula, providing a valuable learning experience for students.

Furthermore, engagement of parents, staff and students in aspects of design and project implementation inevitably draws them into the workings of their future school and allows them to

influence the result so that when the school is finally ready it is already familiar to them and they have taken ownership of it.

A LIFESTYLE PARADIGM SHIFT

The economic downturn has an upside. It forces people to question their lifestyles and review their role in preventing environmental depredation. The

*Classroom of the Future:
external view showing from
left to right: classroom,
observatory and conservatory.*

financial value of conventional property development in many areas has vanished or been much diminished. Old and now demonstrably flawed investment criteria are, at least temporarily, on hold and under review. At the same time the adverse financial consequences and implications of development that does not take on board sustainable measures has been clearly demonstrated. The questioning of pre-credit-crunch values and processes, together with new financial measures designed to avoid or mitigate climate change disaster are forcing commercial change and beginning to encourage businessmen to switch support from profligate development and manufacture to investment in sustainably beneficial initiatives. The construction industry—one of the most destructive of our environment—in responding to this shift has paradoxically discovered a new benefit. In being cajoled and forced to adopt sustainable measures—the use of sunlight, daylight, natural ventilation and the fostering of biodiversity—it is finding that these are the very same attributes that promote stimulating, rewarding and healthy settings. It is, of course, these settings that are now increasingly attractive to a refocused, more selective market.

PROJECTS

Studio E Architects has completed and is currently engaged in many educational projects both in the UK and overseas. All take the issues of pedagogy and sustainability very seriously and some can be regarded as truly pioneering. Four contrasting projects are illustrated here: St Francis of Assisi's Classroom of the Future, Townley Grammar School for Girls, The City Academy in Hackney and the Abu Dhabi Education Council Model School.

St Francis of Assisi's Classroom of the Future, Kensington

The Classroom of the Future is one of 20 projects funded by the DCSF and distributed throughout the UK with the aim of challenging conventional primary school building design and informing the Building Schools for the Future programme. The project is focused on a single classroom. Each school was asked to identify a particular subject around which the classroom could focus. St Francis of Assisi opted for astronomy, and accordingly the project boasts a small observatory containing a telescope.

The telescope is largely symbolic since astrological observation is somewhat restricted in the middle of London. However, the School is linked to a network of observatories around the world, so it is a small matter to patch into a more powerful, better placed observatory, view and appraise the results.

The classroom is fitted out with leading-edge tablet-based wire-free ICT and also includes membrane mounted photovoltaic power generation and a conservatory with an ETFE inflated roof. The schoolchildren were closely involved in the design and the building's alien form resulted both from the idea of space ships and, more cerebrally, from the notion of a cranium encasing grey matter.

Townley Grammar School for Girls, Bexley

A school that has vibrant performance at the heart of its activities is usually a happy school. Performance cuts across, and sometimes highlights, ethnicity, class, age, gender, sexual orientation and personality. It is not factional and competitive, like sport usually is. It makes connections between conventional school disciplines and is a catalyst for communal expression, drawing from concealment latent ideas, concepts and expression. It can be as cathartic and fulfilling as any race won. It can bind the school together and it can also give it identity and recognition within the community.

The corollary to this is the need for a responsive, spacious and versatile performance space. It needs to be part of the school, but also separate. Key to securing a suitable new space for performance is ensuring that all possible aspects are covered early on and built into the design brief. In designing a totally new school, performance space is often undifferentiated from the 'assembly hall' requirement, with performance coming second best to the more conventional needs of school gatherings, examinations and concerts. So careful consideration of the answers to the what, who, when and how of a building brief is crucial. This new space has been a resounding success, catering for hugely diverse and demanding needs, from professional string quartets through dance, the spoken word and media-based studio work to full blown musicals.

The performing arts space is one component of the new building. It also provides new science

laboratories, a sports hall, fitness centre, art galleries and a computer suite: a real renaissance mix.

Laid beneath the concrete slab of the performing arts studio floor and surrounded by sand and cement fill is a series of 500 millimetre diameter concrete pipes running the length of the building and connected at each end by header ducts. In summertime, or when the heating load of the art studio requires, air from

outside the building is forced through this labyrinth of pipes where it takes up the chill from surrounding ground mass and passes into the studio space. Warm air is extracted at high level. Air can be circulated in this way as the heat load requires during the day and at night, when air temperatures have dropped, to lower the temperature of the ground mass and the building structure so that the following day the studio space can be cooled again. During winter, when the studio needs to be heated, the same system is used, but with the air being tempered to 18°C. Perimeter radiators are located along the western wall of the studio to provide top-up heat as and when required. Heating is supplied by a modulating gas fired condensing boiler.

The City Academy, Hackney, London

The City Academy, sponsored by the City of London Corporation and KPMG, opened its doors to its first year intake of 210 students (of its eventual 1,140 pupils) in September 2009. It was delivered on time and to budget by a fully partnered team led by the City of London's City Surveyors Department, Studio E Architects and Willmott Dixon, the building contractor. The challenges of a tight programme and a complex, physically split and noisy site were successfully met, whilst implementing an exemplar programme of "young client" engagement with the participation of the Sorrell Foundation.

A strong sustainable approach has driven a concept that has reconciled aspirations, site issues and environmental performance. This includes passive environmental measures that rely on high standards of daylight and natural ventilation. A glass secondary facade assists dealing with noise generated by heavy traffic along the street frontage. A strong sustainable strategy delivered a BREEAM rating just short of 'Excellent'.

The imprint we leave on young minds of their new world is at least as significant as the physical presence of the buildings they inhabit. We offer our building projects as locations for successive investigation, giving young people hands-on experience of understanding issues that affect their environment. We elicit these insights through planned engagement. It commences at project inception and follows a programme of workshops, building visits, design days at consultants' offices, specialist talks, site visits, project related learning projects and eventually building performance monitoring. Students thereby embrace the sustainable design concepts and become the conduit through which knowledge is disseminated to the community at large.

This grass roots engagement could not succeed without the full commitment of all stakeholders. We work closely with local authorities, sponsor organisations and central government, who welcome our sustainable approach to project design and delivery, and who, increasingly, mesh with our activities through their own initiatives.

All the characteristic, conflicting issues of daylight penetration, cross-ventilation, noise control and prevention of fire spread come together in this school. Their reconciliation can most easily be seen in section. There are four floors. The ventilation of the ground floor is supplemented by mechanical systems. The upper three floors rely for comfort entirely on natural light and natural buoyancy, this despite fronting onto a busy high street and the adoption of fully glazed partitions between the classrooms and the access concourses. A secondary glass facade is placed at a distance from those south-facing external walls facing the main road. This shields the ventilation openings from the noise while allowing daylight to pass into the building, securing views from the building and creating a ribbon of translucency and colour flowing along the length of the building.

Abu Dhabi Education Council Model School

The dispensation of education is a universal and enormously valuable international commodity. A good education for their children is the one item that is essential to aspiring families. And good education is not necessarily available where they are. The UK has been fortunate in its educational heritage and is particularly fortunate in having English as its mother tongue. It has been exporting its particular brand of education for generations and each year the UK receives millions of visitors clamouring for academic accreditation.

Abu Dhabi Education Council received more than 27 proposals from international firms in response to a design competition to produce model school designs for their expanding multi-racial population.

Studio E Architects along with local partner Tawreed and environmental consultants Max Fordham were one of three consortia selected to develop model designs through the summer of 2009. The schools will include seven Cycle One (Grade KG-five) schools, seven combined Cycle Two and Cycle Three schools (Grades six–12), two Cycle Three schools (Grades ten–12), and two KG-12 schools. The programme will provide learning environments of the highest quality that support current teaching methods and new curricula while supporting the population growth of the Emirate.

This model will be used for seven Cycle One schools and features defined learning communities set around a series of leafy courtyards. Designed to achieve a three pearl rating in the Estidama Sustainability Rating, the proposed new schools will contain features not seen at schools in Abu Dhabi before: innovative learning environments which are flexible and conducive to transformational teaching methods and personalised learning, teaching facilities equipped with state of the art technology and a generous array of support spaces including swimming pools, gymnasia, libraries, auditoria and dining areas.

POSTSCRIPT

At the Green Design: from Theory to Practice Conference held in Jerusalem in January 2009, 12 students aged between 12 and 15 representing ten different nationalities, including a Palestinian, Russian, Chinese and Jew from the Anglican International School in Jerusalem were asked to design their ideal school. Working closely as a team they came up with a carefully conceived project that not only provided formal teaching space, but 'encounter' spaces with no specific designation, but highly serviced, in addition to a comprehensively developed low carbon emissions strategy. They presented this scheme with the aid of drawings, a model and a computer fly-through to 500 professional delegates.

REFLECTIONS ON SUSTAINABLE ARCHITECTURE: ECOLOGICAL CONDITIONS AND INTELLIGENT ARCHITECTURE

THOMAS HERZOG

When an architect wants to successfully coordinate a building as a whole, he has to have the largest overview possible over subsystems such as the load-bearing structure, skin, interior equipment and installation based on the current level of building technology.

It is essential for him to understand all the main subsystems in depth. Anyone who tries to make the energy systems of buildings more efficient than they used to be needs to know that energy consumption is a matter of the arrangement of the rooms and the details of the structure, including choice of materials, the individual colours and surfaces, the degree of exposure of the building, the organisation of the floor plan, the section and overall shape of the facade construction, the dimensions and proportion of all parts of the system.

The masses of the building's load-bearing structure directly correlate to the active energy that is needed for heating, cooling, lighting and ventilation. In the light of this, it seems obvious that it is not possible to create anything along these lines without knowing more or less how these individual dimensions react with one another (a doctor cannot operate without knowing how to keep the patient's metabolism stable during the operation). All this means that the architect himself must keep the structural system in his mind as an entity. This is an integral part of the architect's work, which is based upon the state of the art, the technical knowledge of his time.

Considering the global tasks of today, i.e. usage of resources and consumption of fossil fuels, the guideline should be "sustainable design has to be knowledge-based"! Creating architecture along this line does not mean to first postulate a form or even a style but to necessarily develop structures to a complex shape as a result.

It was a serious mistake for so many architects to follow the pied piper antics of the post modern era. It resulted in their losing from sight of the fact that architecture really is not just about the aesthetic or even the literary dimensions of building, but all about the three classical categories that Marcus Vitruvius Pollio defined: the functional efficiency, the correct technology and the beauty of the building.

We are currently building up our own experience in taking over the planning in its entirety, and are striving to improve co-operation with engineers who, being highly specialised, cover only one or two aspects such as load-bearing structure, technical equipment in the building, energy technology, acoustics, sound protection or daylight technology.

If the architect is to take responsibility for the integration of planning as, per definition, one of his chief activities, he has to understand enough about the whole system as well as all the details of said areas, otherwise he is in his work as composer just as totally exposed to these specialists as he is exposed to companies on the building site without the technical knowledge to coordinate the construction work.

ECOLOGY IN BUILDING

Ecology originated in system theory. It is a sub-discipline of biology, and concerns itself with nature's 'budgets'—the give-and-take that keeps everything in balance. For this reason the term "ecological architecture" is questionable: it could even be said it is a self-contradiction. The most one can say is that the architect has to take ecological aspects into account. Every building is interference, a change, and starts with destroying something but at the same time has the chance of creating something new and better.

However, the building work being done in our civilisation is not in itself an ecological process. We see a large amount of abuse of the term "ecological design". There is no relation between the free forms and undulating shapes of lowland forests, unregulated waterways and intelligent, highly efficient building structures. In this context, Renaissance buildings and gardens serve as a positive historical example.

Architecture must define itself in terms of its primary tasks, and each individual building must express its essential being as a physical and visual interpretation of it. These primary tasks include the creation of a good indoor climate through the sensible use of energy in general and the locally available environmental energy. 35 years ago we started to seek answers to the question of how one can use renewable energy in the operation of buildings. More and more questions about the consumption

Top: Mountain Rescue Bavaria State Centre for Safety and Education. Bottom: Hall 26, Deutsche Messe, Hanover.

of primary energy in the production process arose, how the choice of building materials, including regrowing ones, can be optimised and whether there is such a thing as renewable raw material. We have successfully collaborated with landscapers, engineers and scientists. One still current and interesting contribution to this is the last chapter of the book *Solar Energy in Architecture and Urban Planning*,

1996. In this publication, amongst others, very competent authors reflect on timber applications.

There is also the question as to how we should handle water—this is an area in which we ourselves have not yet made much progress. There is also the matter of the transition from the building to the outside. For many years we have been collaborating with Peter Latz: it was he who observed that "ecology is not curved". What he means is that it is wrong to start by looking for romantic or 'organic' images—instead one should start by trying to understand the structures and logic of a complex subject.

FUNCTIONAL FORMS

It is not until one has understood the essence of a matter not just in one's head but in one's feelings as well that one can find forms of expression for it, and I think this should, if at all possible, be a 'performance form' (citation from the great theologian Romano Guardini), as we call it. In particular cases it can then even become a 'symbolic form' or even a 'type'.

So far the largest building we planned according to this maxim is Hall 26 for Deutsche Messe AG in

Top: Administrative
Extension for the
Supplementary Pension
Fund of the Building Industry
(SOKA-BAU), Wiesbaden.
Bottom: Guest Building for
the Youth Education Centre
Windberg, Niederbayern.

Hanover. Furthermore there was the building complex for SOKA-BAU in the dimension of a large town block.

Let us compare architecture with examples taken from nature, with such totally functional things as a tree, a root system, a fish or an insect, where the outward appearance changes as soon as the function varies. The diversity of nature in all its aspects is the best proof you could have of the fact that functionality in the sense of optimisation is the motor of evolution and is accompanied every step of the way by relevant forms of expression, which really reflect the performance form.

This is what we are actually attempting to do in our work. We are not imitating nature, but we are filled with astonishment and deep admiration the more we understand about its interactions, as we do when we study bionics. It might sound rather odd comparing the facade, the outer skin of a building with, for instance, the function of the feathers of a water bird: heat insulation, flight, swim, role indicating. The bird's body is perfectly streamlined in the water and in the air and yet, despite the high functionality, there is a vast variety of types.

INTELLIGENT BUILDINGS

We have been trying for some time now, in our work on buildings, to lay the weight more on the 'reactive'

components. The aim is that the external climatic fluctuations should have a controlled effect inside the building as far as keeping it within the parameters of what one would call "comfortable". This means that one ought to be able to react to changing outer weather conditions within the skin of the building.

The alternative to that is to say that the envelope of the building is a fixed entity and everything inside the building has to be modified, that the implemented

technical equipment has to serve that purpose, which of course means that an input of energy is required. However, the form and structure of a building have to be able to do more than that, and this is a primary responsibility of architecture.

Just as "ecological architecture" is a fashion-word, people are also using the term "intelligent building" somewhat thoughtlessly. Intelligence actually means the ability of a living organism to 'read between the lines'. If in the future the control systems inside buildings register fluctuations of the weather more effectively than they used to, and react by changing something inside the skin of the building automatically, without the user of the building having to do anything, this is a process that might be called intelligent as a cybernetic embellishment.

Some architects, engineers, scientists and producers increasingly see this as a new ideal and promote its development. I am sceptical towards any further extension of technological control to run buildings up to a full automation. In large buildings nowadays the central technical control rooms take up a great deal of space and account for a remarkable proportion of the construction costs. The intentions of those, particularly in the industry, who encourage this trend is to save human beings the need to take any action and to replace this with technical systems. It is no longer desirable for people to pull the outside Venetian blinds up as soon as a thunderstorm approaches— which has been a very sensible and normal matter for some decades now.

It is questionable whether one should be able to switch on an oven by giving a telecommand like touching a screen or pressing a button in the car on the way home. I consider that many of the aims and potential future uses of automatic machines of this kind are superfluous and senseless—ultimately sensually and intellectually a loss. In a large part of our lives, and to a growing extent, we are dependent on technology, and particularly high technology, working properly.

In many areas we have long passed the limits of the necessary. One example: we will obviously have problems in designing office buildings if on the one hand we use maximum daylight in the depth of the rooms and on the other hand prevent glare, and

thirdly want to ensure that the recommended low degree of brightness is attained for working with computers. Fourthly, we intend to use solar energy in winter, and fifthly want to avoid overheating in summer. At the same time, however, we insist on having a constant temperature everywhere throughout the year because we choose our clothing on the basis of the totally dysfunctional dictates of fashion and expect the building to give us mild, early summer weather all the time instead of moderately modifying the clothes we wear. These problems can be easily solved by closing all the apertures in the building and working by artificial light with full air conditioning. However, that would mean losing all contact with the outside world, making us totally dependent on energy supply and virtually blocking the use of solar energy as an aesthetic tool. A bunker. Aesthetically and physiologically a disaster.

We think we should change course and make the users of buildings aware of the facts, but then mainly leave it to them to take action. One argument in favour of the so-called "intelligent building" is that users' behaviour is totally wrong and leads, for instance, to undesirable effects in energy consumption. It is after all only possible to reduce fossil energy consumption if everybody sticks to the rules. Anyone who does not do so is placing arguments in the hands of those who insist on automation. As a permanent solution this is an entirely unnatural attitude. I suggest a different approach: people must be aware of the consequences of their actions. It would be important to implement an information system in buildings that indicates wrong behaviour. If someone leaves a window open directly above a thermostat valve, resulting in heat being wasted, the same thing should happen as when a warning appears in a car's instrument panel: "boot lid open"—or, in this case—"heating system wasting energy". Actually, anyone who is taking a shower or a bath using water not heated by environmental energy ought to have to insert money, just like a parking metre , so that the user really pays at the time of consumption. In 90 per cent of cases, the user does not know the connection between his own behaviour and its effect. By the time he receives his heating bill months or even a year after the last heating period, he cannot recall the individual occasion when he acted in a way that caused high energy consumption.

CAUSE AND EFFECT

Everyone is used to adapting their behaviour in a car in line with the information given by the instruments, with consumption level and other service indications given by technical equipment. The otherwise aesthetically 'neutral' cubes of domestic appliances and home electronics work because people act correctly, millions of times a day, in response to information from instruments.

Therefore the main task of the moment is to get people informed about the inter-relation of cause and effect. This calls for intelligence both in the quality of the information supply and in the way instruments are established in buildings, and does not call for any additional technology—only for us to use the equipment we already have for these purposes and to make it understandable.

We have been accumulating relevant experience for 20 years at the Extension of the Youth Education Centre at Kloster Windberg, a monastery in lower Bavaria, where we put up a display board in the main entrance area, illustrating the technical systems of the building. The monitoring system includes little displays from which one can read off the current temperature in the various parts of the building: What are the collectors doing? What is going on in each storage area? How hot is the outside of the south façade behind the translucent heat-insulation? How high is the surface temperature? The training centre has now made this part of its educational programme, and the young people are very interested in it.

It seems to me that society's ideal at the moment is to envision a house as a wonderful, highly sensitive technical system that coddles the user in a constant indoor temperature of a minimum of 20°C and 50 per cent atmospheric humidity. That is just absurd and, due to the lack of changes needed to stimulate the human body, even can be critical for one's health. Let people do things for themselves so that they can learn how to be sensible. Most of them have enough time at home, but they know little or nothing about the ecological and economic effects of their immediate actions.

We therefore have to take a new look at the tasks. The whole point is to create awareness, and not to let the experts take over the whole responsibility, which would be counter-productive. The more

sophisticated the technology, the more one has to rely on it. Increasing automation in operation makes buildings less and less robust, the users more and more ignorant and dependent. And we should not regard this as being just a technical problem. The experts who understand most about technology are usually those who understand least about people. The whole issue calls for a human design in the field of interaction between humans and machines. As a reminder, 'industrial design' had its origin in military technology, in aircraft, submarines and tanks, where good handling of levers and switches in a confined space and the quick awareness of facts was a prerequisite. A perfect information system was necessary, ergonomically and anthropometrically, things had to be haptically correct. It was a matter of survival.

Many tasks in a house are much simpler today and so the positive effects of implementing these guidelines can be enormous. None of us nowadays wants to waste energy. However, it is happening, and on an enormous scale. We, as architects, are endeavouring to show that, in the light of the new aims, new buildings can be built that are equally functional and beautiful.

As about 40 per cent of fossil energy is consumed to run buildings, the question of how they can be modified and new concepts developed is very important on a social level. Since that also involves applying the latest knowledge in science and technology, and since our office has always been highly interested in opportunities for new purpose-oriented design concepts, we see in the developments of the last 30 years a major step in the evolution of modern architecture. This is documented in the "Charter for Solar Energy in Architecture and Urban Planning", which hopefully will serve more and more as a means of orientation for architects.

THE FIFTH ELEMENT IN SUSTAINABLE DESIGN

JOSEPH CORY

INTRODUCTION

In the ancient theory of classical elements and alchemy we can find five elements—Earth, Water, Air, Fire and a fifth element which is more mysterious, heavenly, non-material and therefore less defined than the others. These elements were discussed in both Western and Eastern cultures and set the first direction towards classification of the world's phenomena and scientific breakthroughs. Eventually modern scientific theories replaced this simplified way of thinking, but the echo of this tradition is still around. Tradition is a gradual build-up of knowledge. The sustainability era is still in its infancy, so it is closer to tradition than science, even though we use modern tools in it. So if we want to think in sustainable terms, what will each element represent in the way we approach the design, and can we find the fifth element in sustainability?

Putting theory into practice is a challenging process, as it was described during the seventh Jerusalem Seminar in Architecture in 2009, chaired by Dr Ken Yeang. I was privileged to be on its Organising Committee. In the following text, I will discuss the design approach and principles for the EcoBuilding project that manifest the way to move from theory to practice as a case study. The EcoBuilding project (designed by my office, Geotectura, together with NC Architects and Axelrod-Grobman Architects) won the competition to erect the first LEED Platinum building in Israel.

Good architecture can be achieved more easily when we have great clients with a vision. Dame Shirley Porter founded the Porter School of Environmental Studies in 2000. It has since become the leading school of environmental studies in Israel under the direction of Dr Arie Nesher. The School brings educational opportunities in many fields including architecture, renewable energy, waste water treatment, ecology and much more. Tel Aviv University's Porter School of Environmental Studies (PSES) is offering interdisciplinary degrees in environmental studies and unites researchers from different fields under one sustainable canopy. The School was established in response to the pressing need for greater academic knowledge in Israel on environmental issues. It promotes new areas of interdisciplinary environmental research, introduces novel teaching programmes and places

environmental issues on the academic and public agenda. So we have a strong theoretical platform to begin our journey.

The vision of Dame Shirley Porter included a sustainable building to host the research activities. A competition was held to design the most ecological building for the school. In 2008, PSES embarked on the process of constructing its own building to house the School's growing activities. The selection process for the design team comprised two stages: in the first, the selection committee shortlisted seven teams from the 39 leading Israeli firms. In November 2008, our architecture team was chosen to design the Porter School of Environmental Studies building. We shared from the beginning a passion to follow the vision and design the greenest building in Israel. Vision is essential for a pioneering project like a faculty for environmental studies. In her guiding vision for the Porter School of Environmental Studies, Dame Shirley wrote "Climate change is one of the greatest and most pressing challenges facing the planet today. It is a challenge that crosses all boundaries of race, creed and religion and it is only by working together that we will find solutions that are so vital to our survival. Israel must play its part and I am determined that the new building for PSES will demonstrate this commitment by providing real and practical applications of green technologies that may become a benchmark for sustainable development not only in Israel but across the whole region."

The University understands that green buildings are being demanded by the patron and will shortly be demanded by students as well. TAU President, Professor Zvi Galil said in reply "The construction of the PSES green building at Tel Aviv University emphasises the great importance TAU places on the environment in general and green architecture in particular. The establishment of the facility is another important step towards developing TAU as the largest green campus in Israel."

We felt during the design process that the early questions and uncertainties voiced by the University administration were superseded by the notion that this was an appropriate path for present and future 'green' design. Designing an LEED Platinum project is very challenging in Israeli architecture, as there are only two other LEED green buildings and neither is

Platinum. The lack of case studies in Israel emphasises the need for a location to study sustainability and showcase it to the public.

This paper analyses the local conditions (wind direction, orientation of the sun and the acoustic problem from the nearby highway) and resulting environmental solutions. The parameters are classified according to the ancient elements. We will further explore the strategies and dilemmas of the design team and will discuss the different solutions and conclusions for this important milestone in the sustainable architectural legacy of Israel.

THE FIRST ELEMENT—EARTH

Brownfield, Orientation, Transportation, Minimal Footprint, Urban Fabric

Earth is always a good starting point for a sustainable project. It reminds us that before we even start to dream we face a reality that keeps our feet on the ground. It is no accident that the LEED System starts with the site as well.

In the EcoBuilding project we started by collecting all available climatic data for the site, which informed the design process and the first mass concept. From the first survey, we found the site had many disadvantages. A soil survey determined that underneath the site (currently a parking lot), pollutants existed as a result of the disposal of construction waste.

Orientating the building mass was another major early decision. The climatic data and early site orientation led us to place the long facade towards the south. The architect can reduce energy consumption of the building with a few passive decisions that don't impact on the overall cost. We were also asked to provide underground parking for the development, but we convinced the client to do without it and encouraged students and faculty members to use nearby public transport and bicycles instead.

We are part of the earth and as designers must be committed to minimal impact with our buildings. Respect for the earth is declared once again by maximising the open space in the entrance lobby.

This will be achieved by placing the mass of the building on pillars and having translucent curtain walls. Underground works are limited to minimal excavation only around the auditorium and mechanical rooms. The symbiotic relationship between the building and the landscape will be manifested in the second phase of the project, which will transfer the promenade into the green roof of the new addition.

Green design means looking beyond the building. We examined the broader connections between the building and the landscape, the building and the campus, even the building and the city. The connectivity of the campus is getting better because the building is a generator for a green belt around the University that will connect it with the city. Landscape architects Braudo-Maoz are developing functions such as a pedestrian connection between the railway station and the University extending as far as the sea-shore as part of a promenade for cycling and recreation. The environment surrounding the building should be a demonstration of ecological design according to the landscape architects and it is all part of the dialogue between the University, the architects and the municipality of Tel Aviv. The dense urban location on one side of the campus does not overshadow the strong impact of nature in this location, where the building is on the edge of a hill, next to a zoological garden and a wide highway with a stream in the middle.

The complexity of the topography, which forced us to gather data to inform important decisions, is the reason that a 'traditional' architecture team is not enough in sustainable design. We had to put together a multi-disciplinary team of experts, including advisors for specific ecological issues.

THE SECOND ELEMENT—WATER

Green Roof, Grey Water, Stormwater, Low Water Consumption and Plants

The landscape architects, together with the drainage engineers and ourselves, examined different water treatment options with green roofs and constructed wetlands, grey water treatment and vertical green walls to meet LEED standards, reduce heat island effect and deliver water efficient landscaping.

The landscape architects' objectives included the use of captured rainwater and grey water for irrigation, stormwater management, paving from recycled materials, low water-consumption plants, shade, purification of the air and much more. Stormwater penetration will be used for experimental and educational studies as well.

50 per cent of the roof area will be a green roof, with local and water efficient vegetation that will moderate the temperature beneath it during summer and winter. It will also serve as a learning centre and an open classroom for the students.

The aim of the drainage systems consultants was to save water and energy through the use of sanitary fixtures with water-saving devices and two separate sewage systems—a drain water system, known as grey water and a sewage water system (black water). The grey water system, that was to be treated in biological pools and re-used by the irrigation system, was subject to the approval of the Health Ministry, which is against grey water in general in Israel. We convinced the Health Ministry of the legitimacy of the grey water system and it will be an important precedent for future ecological buildings in the region. This is a great example of how design can act as an educational and influential tool in raising awareness and updating our design principles.

The building acts as a cup for the water—the walls and roof direct it to different locations—all water is welcome! Rainwater, dew, moisture, grey and black water are all being tested, collected and exhibited. Water goes hand in hand with the landscape outside

but also with the interior of the building. It is being handled with care as a scarce resource and is at the forefront of the design process.

Things have evolved since water was associated with intuition. In a sustainable design, intuition has less impact.

THE THIRD ELEMENT—FIRE

Energy Saving, Energy Production, Natural Light, Efficient Artificial Light

Fire is energy. A sustainable fire should be energy efficient. The design approach for the Porter School, conceived by Assa Aharoni Consulting Engineering,

was to embed the energy concepts early in the design process.

In order to increase the energy savings potential, the engineers recommended the use of active chilled beam cooling, which is energy efficient and provides many temperature control zones. An absorption chiller system with dedicated solar heat collectors will eliminate the high incremental cost of electricity and the solar heat source will provide the energy to run the cooling system. The absorption process has no moving parts and is powered only by heat. It has other benefits such as low noise levels, low operating and maintenance costs and long product life.

A 50 kilowatt photovoltaic system will be installed next to the building in order to produce energy and sell it to the electric company. Two years ago, the PV business in Israel was almost non-existent. Once the government understood the potential of green energy, it helped open up the market. It is an important reminder that sustainability is saving us money in the long-term and we need help in order to make it available to as many sectors as we can in our society. The electrical report for the Porter School presented the green principles of electrical, lighting and communication design. The objective was to reduce the energy consumption of the building according to LEED standards. The lighting design is based on lamps with high levels of output throughout their life, giving higher energy efficiency. Photocells will measure lighting levels inside the rooms and dim according to specified lighting levels (used in daytime) and motion detectors.

Daylight simulations and glare control for all windows were examined and influenced the design of the rooms and furniture layouts. This important aspect improves the working and learning environment and saves a lot of money. The lighting presentation on the skin of the capsule (the beating heart of the project) gives information to those outside the building on the nearby highway and promenade about the energy production/consumption level or the amount of air pollution on the highway below. We had new data requirements that the University was never asked for before, including total energy consumption, water consumption and waste production of the campus buildings and landscape. The data gathered will help other design teams to design better buildings on the campus in the future.

THE FOURTH ELEMENT—AIR

Acoustic, Wind, Air Pollution, Simulation

The nearby highway is causing acoustic problems and air pollution and so the building mass responded to the need to overcome these. A barrier was conceived to absorb all the noise and pollution from the southeast and it makes the building more iconic.

In order to optimise the building form, we took into account the climatic conditions around the site, including wind velocity and direction and noise from the highway. Although Israel is a small country, the climatic conditions vary greatly from one location to another and it is very hard for planners to source accurate information about local climatic conditions and therefore harder to move from theory to practice. We were able to compare wind conditions with and without our building mass and choose where to locate a wind turbine and a calmer spot for the cafeteria.

The ecological consultant proposed a natural ventilation strategy that complemented the energy efficiency concepts set by Assa Aharoni Engineers. Good communication between the architect and client effected a reduction in energy losses as well as the efficient generation and utilisation of energy. Eventually, the project will incorporate passive solar building design (maintaining interior comfort levels while reducing the requirement for active mechanical heating and cooling systems), a high performance envelope with optimised insulation techniques and building energy performance simulations such as CFD (Computational Fluid Dynamics).

The fact that a 'green' building is more complicated than a regular one means that communication between consultants is essential. All team members are working with the Building Information Modelling process (BIM)—they share the same 3-D model of the building with access to and total synchronisation of all the data. This integration and streamlined process is an important tool for a sustainable design.

THE FIFTH ELEMENT—EDUCATION

Adaptable, Dynamic, Eco-Global, Innovative, Creative

Environmental solutions to acoustic problems, wind and sun exposure, meteorological data, soil categories, passive energy saving, positioning of the building and so on were analysed over and over again during the work flow, as we saw in the other elements. But what does it take to step beyond a green checklist and achieve something that is above all that?

The Eco-Wall in the south facade is an iconic ever-changing display window for the other universities and visitors and serves as a constant socio-educational contributor. The building will serve as a platform for ongoing experiments. The Eco-Wall is a unique concept allowing researchers to conduct several experiments in the eco-pods. The Eco-Wall is a window display for the rest of the students and outside visitors (from different universities in Israel around the world, schools, kindergartens and so on). The innovative idea is the ability of the wall to absorb changing technologies over time and not become a static monument to sustainable architecture. The kinetic wall represents the technological frontier of the faculty and our generation as well.

The project is designed to perform as a living laboratory of ecological and social values for the community and the environment. It tells the story of the complex sustainability concept and simplifies it for the public strolling along the Eco-Wall, the ground floor and the green roof, all of which showcase current research into energy, water, soil, vegetation, materials that they can see, touch and learn. The fact that the building will be like a living laboratory for sustainable ideas means that the design process and all the researchers' results are available to the public. In many green buildings, public access is limited and therefore they have less impact. In our case, because the client is a school of environmental studies, the whole process is dealing with future educational values of the building itself.

Architects should lead and be involved in wider aspects of the design in order to be able to meet the complicated challenges of sustainable design. In the architecture team, we share strong connections between the academy and the practical world. We teach sustainability as well as build in a sustainable manner, so it was the most fitting project for us to win and share our knowledge. Education is not just for future students: the design process is educating the entire team all the time, forcing us to be creative in response to the challenges and turning us all back into students.

CONCLUSION

In ancient times people tried to explain the complicated universe in simplified terms of the five elements. People knew they were part of nature and had to relate to it in some way. But theories without practice are not reliable. Only when we test our theories can we rely on them more. On the other hand, practice without theory is problematic and might suffer from disorientation and a lack of

judgement as to what is more suitable in the design, so if we build only according to green regulations or the four modern elements or changing seasons, it will not be enough!

We follow environmental aspects during the design process, but must not neglect the values of good architecture that go beyond checklists. Our building has a deeper meaning besides being green— it is aiming to be a beacon to Israel and the world for green design and to make people believe in what they will see and touch and to fight scepticism and ignorance of the subject. Using green principles gave the project a solid platform to make architecture with meaning.

Even though we aspire to LEED Platinum for the Porter School, it does not mean we cannot improve our designs in future projects. In the near future we need our buildings to produce all their energy, and we might need a strong government to ask for it and finance it for fragile sectors in society. We need to aim towards zero-carbon design as well. We will have to track performance and improve our design bit by bit. The cost and return on investment of the Porter School was less of an issue, because the building needed to educate first and be efficient second, but in regular projects efficiency might be more appropriate. We should ask ourselves how we can create green buildings with minimal budgets, how we can reduce bureaucracy, consider the urban and natural fabrics and so on.

We competed against many talented architects who included the four sustainable elements in their proposals, but we were able to make the integration between the ecological values and the aesthetic values in an educational way—the fifth element. The Porter School will be first of all an educational model for a sustainable design. Education is not alchemy—it is the starting point for moving from theory to green practice.

THE HUMAN DIMENSION IN PRODUCT AND PROCESS MODELLING FOR GREEN BUILDING DESIGN

KHEE POH LAM

INTRODUCTION

There is little doubt in most peoples' minds that planet earth is experiencing an unprecedented scale and rate of climate and ecological change. This has potential consequences which can threaten the security and stability of human existence globally if not seriously and urgently addressed. This is in part brought about by the phenomenal expansion of the built environment, particularly in Asia and the Middle East. The World Business Council for Sustainable Development recently published their first report on Energy Efficiency in Buildings.[1] It states that buildings are responsible for at least 40 per cent of energy use in many countries, mostly consuming energy derived from fossil fuels. Energy use is increasing by an annual rate of more than three per cent in the US alone, and is growing rapidly in countries such as China and India. Worldwide energy consumption by buildings is expected to grow 45 per cent over the next 20 years.

The concern is not just about the sustainability issues related to dependency on non-renewable energy sources, but equally if not more importantly, the impact of by-products of energy production systems on the environment and their effect on climate change. The manufacture of some basic building materials such as cement, which accounts for five per cent of global CO_2 emission, is further exacerbating the problem.[2]

A critical contributory role that the building industry can play is to adopt an ecological and holistic performance-based building delivery approach to the entire process—from the macro scale of urban planning to micro level of individual building design. Design professionals should be challenged to create energy efficient and high performance buildings at the project inception, when the client meets the architect for the first time to formulate the design brief.

THEORY AND PRACTICE OF GREEN BUILDING DESIGN

In discussing the process of human involvement in the creation of our built environment, four fundamental human-related elements should be considered: theory and practice, knowledge and experience. These elements are always present, but the degree of engagement varies individually as well as collectively within the building design team.

Theories can be regarded as analytical tools for understanding, explaining and making predictions about a given subject matter. Theoretical constructs are particularly helpful when dealing with complex systems involving multi-dimensional and multi-domain interactions. It should be noted that a theory is syntactic in nature and is only meaningful when given a semantic component by applying it to content (i.e. facts and relationships of the actual historical and physical world as it is unfolding).[3] Green building design is a good case in point.

Green building, also commonly known as sustainable or high performance building, is the practice of creating structures and using processes that are environmentally responsible and resource-efficient throughout a building's life-cycle, from siting to design, construction, operation, maintenance, renovation and demolition.[4] This practice expands and complements the classical building design concerns of economy, utility, durability and comfort. There are many 'traditional' theories that relate building design with its environmental as well as human occupant performance within those buildings.[5,6,7]

A specific example of a performance-based approach to design is a well established model based on the concept of Total Building Performance and Diagnostics (TBPD) *(Figure 1)*.[8] This concept was originally advocated by a research team at Carnegie Mellon University, USA in the early 1980s. TBPD is an integrated and holistic knowledge-based framework for conceptualising, specifying, designing, analysing and commissioning a building project. It can provide a comprehensive brief for the client and the project team who are committed to quality and high performance goals throughout the project duration, from inception to completion, and can even extend to post-occupancy management and maintenance. It can facilitate optimisation of the design performance, avoidance of conflicts, elimination of omissions and abortive work, and wastage of resources.

It embraces six principal performance mandates, namely spatial, acoustic, thermal, visual, indoor air quality and building integrity. Each mandate comprises a set of performance targets and diagnostic tools. The targets are occupant-oriented deliverables

BUILDING DELIVERY PROCESS

TBP DESIGN AND PROCUREMENT

STRUCTURAL SYSTEM | ENVELOPE SYSTEM | INTERIOR SYSTEM | MECH & ELEC SYSTEMS | EXTERNAL/LANDSCAPES

TOTAL BUILDING
PERFORMANCE
MANDATES

PHYSIOLOGICAL | PSYCHOLOGICAL | SOCIOLOGICAL | ECONOMICAL

TBP COMMISSIONING AND POE

Framework ensures comprehensive and integrative design consideration for high performance and sustainable solutions

SPATIAL
THERMAL
INDOOR AIR QUALITY
VISUAL
ACOUSTICAL
BUILDING INTEGRITY

Diagnostic methodology for measuring building performance, evaluating impacts and establishing benchmarks

KNOWLEDGE-BASED DESIGN

←——→

KNOWLEDGE PRODUCTION

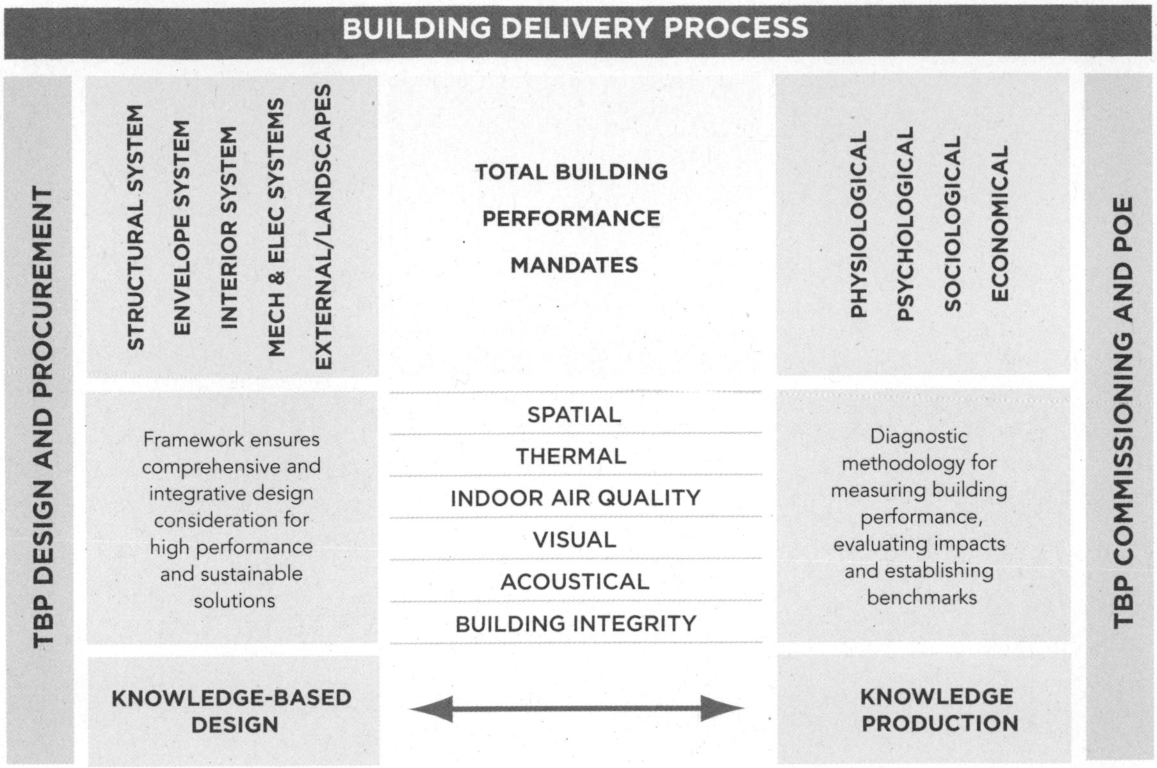

that pertain to the environmental or physical attributes of the building which impact upon the physiological, psychological, social and economic well-being of the occupants. The diagnostic tools are methodologies developed for the appraisal of the building design in terms of various performance indices.

TBPD is not just about the application of 'hi-tech' building systems and/or materials. It seeks to rationally and systematically exploit the synergy of the various technologies and management know-how to bring about desirable building performance at a reasonable cost. Knowledge and experience of an integrated team are clearly essential within the strategic framework. The ultimate success of a sustainable and high performance building may be assessed by considering how well it meets four principal criteria: occupant satisfaction, organisational flexibility, technological adaptability and environmental and energy effectiveness. In this regard, the TBPD concept has been applied successfully in practice to projects (some award winning) in North America, Europe and Asia (e.g. the Robert L Preger Intelligent Workplace at Carnegie Mellon University, Laboratory of Design for Cognition, Electricité de France, Paris, as well as the Urban Redevelopment Authority Building and the National Library Building in Singapore).[9–12]

KNOWLEDGE AND EXPERIENCE IN GREEN BUILDING DESIGN

Louis Sullivan defines architecture as the crystallisation of the thoughts and feelings of a civilisation. There is a long tradition in the architectural world of tracing and documenting the changes in building design over the ages and in different geographical, climatic, socio-cultural and political contexts. Such efforts in the realm of history and theory of architecture tend to focus predominantly on the arts and human aspects. Literature that rigorously records building related sciences and the technologies of the time is comparatively rare. Occasionally, we get a glimpse of the work of the ancient master-builders and the incredible technical ingenuity that created architectural masterpieces that are 'sustainable' in every sense by today's (re)definition of the term. Knowledge and experience are produced, preserved and transmitted through the generations, often by long-suffering apprenticeships. Arguably, life was simpler and the palette of options was limited in

COST OF INADEQUATE INTEROPERABILITY BY STAKEHOLDER GROUP AND COST CATEGORY (NIST 2004)

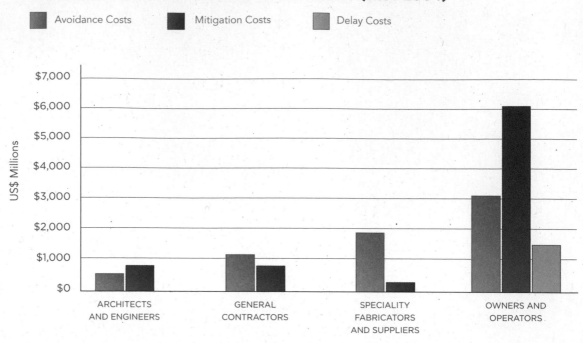

comparison with the modern world, but that was not necessarily a disadvantage and certainly did not hamper the creative and innovative spirit that existed during those past milieu.

Even as we witness phenomenal advances in science and technology, the building industry at large remains very slow in responding to or capitalising on the tremendous potential and opportunities offered compared with other industries. Building performance related research is not particularly valued by the industry or society and consequently, support for such endeavours is dismal. Despite the circumstances, there have been research activities that generated a significant body of knowledge over the past three to four decades, way before green design became a contemporary buzzword. However, this knowledge is invariably lodged within highly technical publication archives that continue to serve the academic and research communities but rarely touch the practical world in any meaningful way. As the knowledge base continues to expand, it is inevitable that the chasm between what is known and what is done becomes increasingly wide. Recognising this state of affairs, the building industry then attempts to ameliorate the consequences by simplifying the inherently complex relationships and interactions

between humans and the environment in the form of prescriptive solutions that get codified into standards and regulations. Simplification and prescriptive approaches are not inherently bad in themselves and they do provide a cost-effective means of setting certain critical performance benchmarks in building. However, there are always limits of applicability and embodied assumptions that are not often immediately apparent to designers who increasingly operate in a globalised practice.

This leads to the final human element of experience in this discussion. Even in this realm, the building industry is unbelievably weak in 'professionalising' this valuable human resource. Medicine and the law, two diametrically different professions, share a common unifying practice of systematically and meticulously documenting their 'experiences', both good and bad, as well as success and failure. These become the tangible and valuable industry assets that society has come to accept and somehow has to pay for. Whether it is attributable to the educational system and/or a deeply entrenched business structure, the building industry is highly fragmented and often adversarial rather than collaborative in nature. For fear of professional and financial liability, cases of failure are often buried through private settlement. Experiences

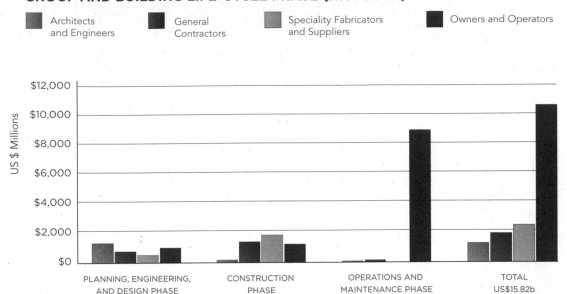

COST OF INADEQUATE INTEROPERABILITY BY STAKEHOLDER GROUP AND BUILDING LIFE-CYCLE PHASE (NIST 2004)

gained from such events reside only with the parties involved and are not generally accessible for the industry to share and learn from. Even if there is no catastrophic encounter, there is currently no widely adopted practice of monitoring and measuring the performance of buildings in use and comparing the empirical results with the predicted design performance targets. Much can be learned from such provisions and they can also open up new innovation pathways into the field of real-time intelligent sensing and predictive optimal building control. Unless there is some fundamental paradigm shift in professional practice, especially to address the specific challenge of green building design and operation, the industry may well be condemned to the 'Sisyphean task' for a long time to come.

PREREQUISITES FOR PROCESS AND PRODUCT MODELLING

An effective process of green building design requires engaging the elements of theory, practice, knowledge and experience through integrated inputs from multi-disciplinary professional teams. Effective communication through information exchange is an important factor. A study from the US National Institute of Standards and Technology shows that 30 per cent of the construction cost is due to the information interoperability problem within the building delivery team (*Figures 2* and *3*).[13] There is national interest in the USA to strategically address this issue, which affects the quality of buildings being designed and constructed as well as causing productivity loss in the industry.

A multi-pronged strategic approach has to be adopted to revolutionise the building industry and to change the 'business-as-usual' mind-set. It must concurrently address the processes and products involved in green building delivery and the nature of the hardware, software and human resources associated with the respective functions. Education is perhaps the most critical starting point from which to address the fragmented infrastructure as illustrated by Mattar and effect lasting change (*Figure 4*).[14] While architecture is traditionally regarded as 'the art and science of building', architectural education around the world is still seeking the balanced curriculum that provides a firm foundation in both the qualitative and quantitative elements of design creativity. The sustainability movement has yielded new and widely recognised building performance standards (e.g. LEED) which are leading developers

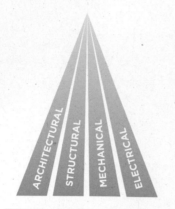

PRELIM. DESIGN

DETAIL DESIGN

WORKING DRAWINGS & SPECS

TENDER (BIDDING)

PLANNING & SCHEDULING

CONSTRUCTION OPERATIONS

COMMISSIONING

ARCHITECTURAL STRUCTURAL MECHANICAL ELECTRICAL

| PROFESSIONAL AND
TRADE RESPONSIBILITIES
FUNCTIONAL GAPS | BUILDING DELIVERY PROCESS
MANAGEMENT
DISCONTINUITIES | OPERATIONAL ISLANDS
INEFFECTIVE COORDINATION;
POOR COMMUNICATION |

to demand design teams to achieve such standards in order to remain competitive in the real estate market. Industry drivers are in motion to hasten the curricular and pedagogical change in schools of architecture and engineering.

The School of Architecture at Carnegie Mellon has a long-established reputation offering a programme that encompasses at least three curricular components that are needed to ensure 'systems thinking' critical to innovations in environmental performance: a building physics curriculum for total building performance fully linked to architectural design, a systems integration curriculum that merges architectural and engineering design disciplines and a curriculum on innovations in the building delivery process.[15] Graduates from such a programme are well-prepared with an appropriate collaborative mind-set and equipped with skill sets to effectively deploy the many design decision support tools in the modelling of green design processes and products.

Within the context of rapidly changing technologies, production processes and an explosion of knowledge, the capabilities of decision support modelling tools are expanding, but they still fall short of anticipating or challenging the logic of the rather static processes they are supposed to support. There is elaborate debate on the necessary conditions under which significant structural changes in the

building delivery process can evolve and the related implications for future development of decision support tools in Mahdavi and Lam.[16] It also considers the hidden potential of existing tools and proposes enhancements to facilitate effective knowledge transfer and process management. Since then, there have been significant advancements in building performance simulation, with new and improved computational tools that address the changing needs of design throughout the building delivery. However, there are still gaps to be filled in pursuing a coherent and systematic structured approach not just in dealing with the physical and procedural aspects of design but also to respond to the "human element" in the implementation pragmatics in industry.

CRITICAL ELEMENTS OF INTEGRATED PROCESS AND PRODUCT MODELLING

Building Information Modelling

As previously defined, green building necessitates a life-cycle approach to its creation and sustained operation. To support this process, a dynamic and robust information representation, management and exchange system is called for. In the USA, a National Building Information Modelling Standard (NBIMS) has recently been published. This standard is intended to provide the framework and foundation to encourage the flow of information and interoperability between

Figure 5: Dynamic Life-Cycle Building Information Model (DLC-BIM) in Support of an Integrated and Sustainable Building Delivery and Operation Process. (Architecture, Engineering, Construction, Operation—AECO—the "genetic DNA" of DLC-BIM).

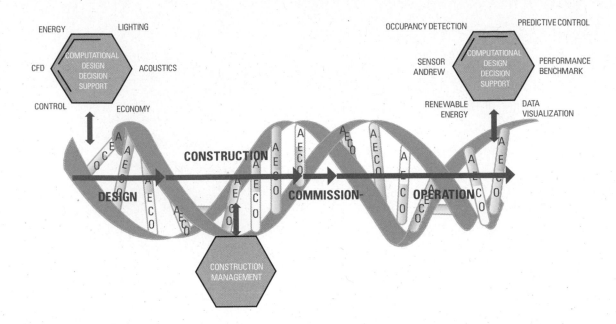

all phases of a development's lifecycle. It defines BIM as "a digital representation of the physical and functional characteristics of a development" and its overall scope is to facilitate "collaboration by different stakeholders at different phases of the lifecycle of the development to insert, extract, update, or modify information in the BIM to support and reflect the roles of that stakeholder".[17]

The key attribute of a BIM is its ability to organise and relate information for both users and machine readable approaches. However, to enable interoperability between applications and databases, the inherent semantics of the underlying taxonomy and ontology have to be unambiguous and non-redundant. One of the primary roles of the NBIMS is to provide the ontologies and associated common languages that will allow information to be machine readable across different but related domains. NBIMS presents an excellent conceptual model of information exchange in AEC industry. The question then is what approach can be adopted to develop an operative IT platform to realise and implement this conceptual model in practice. The Center for Building Performance and Diagnostics (CBPD) of Carnegie Mellon University has been researching this field for several years. Current BIM development work tends to be focused on the design and construction phases (and with minimal interoperability for integrated performance simulation support) but not yet extended

to consider ongoing performance monitoring and diagnostics throughout the life-cycle of the building. Particularly for complex buildings, effective operations have significant impacts on ensuring that the predicted design performance is actually achieved and sustained.

Therefore, a comprehensive Dynamic Life-Cycle Building Information Model for the 'Total Building Performance and Diagnostics' approach is advocated to address the entire building delivery process. The model structure is based on the Industry Foundation Class (IFC) schema (as endorsed by NBIMS) that will capture (a) 'static' building information generated during the design and construction process and shared amongst the design architects and engineers particularly to support building performance predictions using various simulation tools, benchmark evaluations (e.g. LEED) and advanced design optimisation; (b) 'dynamic' (operational) building information generated from large-scale occupancy detection and environmental sensing network for on-going commissioning, whole building performance monitoring and advanced adaptive controls based on occupant behavioural studies. This integrated model will also serve as a rich repository of comprehensive evidence-based case studies for on-going research and development as well as the education of professionals for the building industry in the long-term (Figure 5).

Building Performance Modelling

While the BIM development work continues, many well-established advanced 'stand-alone' performance modelling tools are readily available for use by design teams. The following discussion highlights some of the critical areas of input, especially from the architect working within the team. Whether or not the architect personally conducts the modelling work, these points for consideration are vital and must be clearly established. Otherwise, the age-old ugly truth of computing will prevail—garbage in, garbage out (GIGO).

Determining Occupancy Schedule

Building performance simulation aims to support sustainable design and the creation of healthy, comfortable and productive habitats for human activities while minimising resource utilisation and waste generation. Ironically, defining such human activities 'accurately' as factors in performance modelling remains the most complex and challenging task. For example, research has shown that for a variety of reasons, the actual occupancy rate in modern office buildings is frequently only 40–60 per cent of the design assumption. This has consequences not only for energy consumption but also the maintenance of comfort conditions in buildings. Mismatch between designed and actual operating conditions results in excessive provision of heating/cooling and difficulty in optimising control of building systems. This challenge lies squarely with the architect, whose responsibility is to thoroughly understand the client's operational requirements and translate that 'qualitative' brief into an architectural design solution, accompanied by appropriate quantitative parameters that can be communicated to the engineering design team members for producing concurrent technical solutions. Recognising this crucial communicative role should prompt architects to play a more proactive leadership role in building performance modelling.

Configuring Thermal Control Zoning

Architects and HVAC engineers typically have quite different notions about 'zoning' in a building. One views these zones as formal, spatial and functional demarcations which may be subject to certain design codes such as fire compartmentalisation,

while the other regards them as volumes that require conditioning according to a desired set temperature. The usual HVAC design objective is to size the systems and configure the layout so as to meet peak load conditions while minimising the number of discrete control zones to save cost. It is not uncommon to witness inadequacies and conflicts in operational control of the systems when there is a lack of cross-disciplinary understanding and communication during the design stage. Coupled with the uncertainties of occupancy schedule mentioned above, the systems may not be able to respond optimally, resulting in energy inefficiency and an uncomfortable indoor environment.

The theoretically ideal approach is to map the 'architectural' zones which are subjected to different location-based exposures according to orientations (e.g. perimeter versus internal core zones) with the thermal control zoning configuration. Possible design solutions can then be generated through parametric energy simulations and an 'optimal' decision derived through systematic analysis and evaluation of the results.

In reality, any simulation result is only as good and reliable as the assumed input values for the various parameters. However, if the model is constructed on the 'first principle' integrated approach mentioned above, there would be built-in capabilities in the systems for further fine tuning when the building is in operation. Looking beyond current practice, there are already R&D efforts to 'automate' such fine-tuning based on continuous concurrent sensing of the indoor environment and monitoring performance as well as micro-climatic conditions throughout the life of the building. The empirical data acquired is the 'real deal' and when used as input into a predictive control model, further realistic optimisation of the system can be achieved with even greater energy saving.

Concurrent Modelling of the Building and Surrounding Physical and Environmental Context

Traditional environmental performance modelling tends to focus mainly on active systems within a 'closed' building that rely completely on energy to provide some form of conditioning all year round. Green building design calls for a radical departure from that rigid approach and encourages the

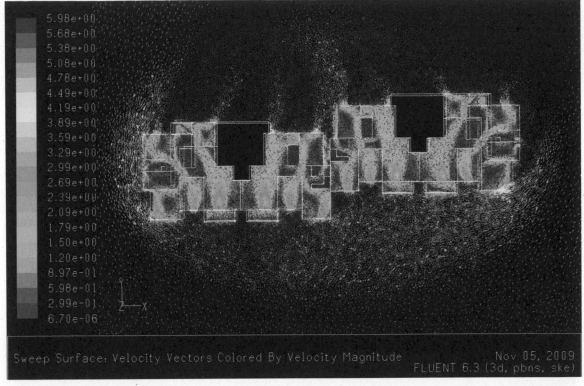

Scenario 1: All internal doors are opened.

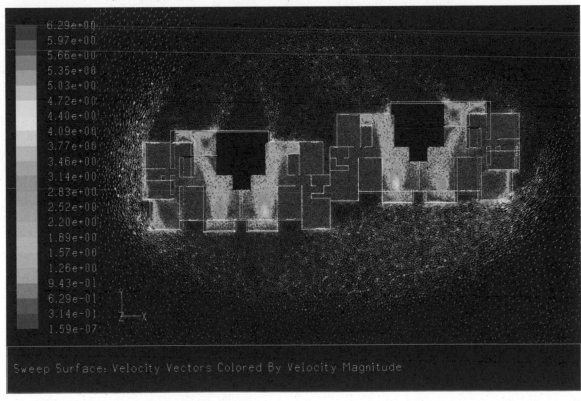

Scenario 2: Only the living room doors are opened.

exploration of multi-modal environmental control systems in buildings. These would include passive systems that require no energy for operation (e.g. sun shades for solar control, openable windows for natural ventilation, light shelves for daylight enhancement, etc.), the common active systems as well as mixed-mode conditioning that selectively combines the passive and partially active systems. Furthermore, the concern also extends beyond the performance of the building itself to its potential impact on the surrounding ecological and environmental conditions. The critical consideration for such a holistic design approach is that the design team should be fully cognisant of the physical and micro-level environmental conditions surrounding the proposed building, whether present or anticipated (to the extent possible) in the future.

The model should then include every object within the physical domain that will conceivably impact the overall performance outcome. Given that external climatic conditions are naturally dynamic, the parametric study should be carefully structured in order to provide design decision support performance data that sufficiently represent the probable occurrence under varying conditions over the year or even at a higher periodic resolution as each case may demand.

The results of modelling examples of building performance clearly illustrate the importance of considering not only the 'static' physical building layout but the inclusion of the 'dynamic' configurations under different in-use conditions (*Figure 6*).

Allocating Resources for Modelling in Early Design Stage

The predominant factor in the decision-making process in practice is cost, more specifically first cost. Traditional processes often ignore the operational and occupancy implications while emphasising first cost, despite the fact that tools are available for evaluating the cost benefits of a performance oriented approach to the building delivery process over the life-cycle of the project. Yudelson notes that increased economic benefits are the prime driver for change in green buildings. The business case for green development should be based on a comprehensive view of benefits, including economic, financial, productivity,

risk management, public relations, marketing and funding.[18] It is acknowledged that decisions at the early project phase can have significant impact on subsequent alternatives and design solutions, but unwillingness to invest in preliminary investigative design studies in order to keep costs low would invariably result in remedial or even abortive work, thereby increasing the overall costs towards the end of the project phase. The range and nature of existing design support tools that are being applied in practice clearly reflect this scenario, whereby they are almost exclusively developed for the back-end of the design and construction process. It is therefore of strategic advantage to re-assess the relative importance of early conceptual design within the whole and to allocate adequate resources to this stage of work, also to utilise the potential of computer-aided information processing tools to support a more comprehensive design/construction strategy.

CONCLUSION

Simulation tools will continue to evolve to address, amongst others, two major objectives: firstly to make simulation tools more accessible to the architectural profession to support the open-ended nature of design inquiry and secondly, to enable effective 'real-time' sharing of design information between the entire team through a web-based infrastructure. The pervasive use of these tools will ultimately depend on how they can effectively support the design decision making process (providing a level of confidence on the predicted performance of the solution) while reducing project overheads such as time, manpower, training and computational resources typically associated with advanced performance simulations.

As a collaborative activity, the building delivery process relies heavily on the effectiveness of communication structures and means. While it was initially expected that the application of innovative information technologies would enhance the information transfer mechanisms within this process, this has not occurred, at least not to the desired extent. To facilitate better understanding of this evolving circumstance, continuous critical review of the status quo and thoughtful theoretical reflection on the complex relationship between process evolution and tool development is necessary.

MATERIALS FOR GREEN BUILDINGS

NADAV MALIN

Newcomers to green building tend to focus almost exclusively on materials, because they are the most tangible aspect of a building—the things one can see and touch. Yet when we consider all the ways in which a building affects the natural environment, the impacts of the materials used to make the building are typically less significant than operating energy, water use and, depending on the location, transportation demands.

Furthermore, even though the materials themselves are highly tangible, the characteristics that make them better or worse choices from an ecological perspective are generally not perceptible in the finished building. The characteristics in question have to do with upstream impacts, intermediate components, ingredients incorporated into the finished item and options for eventual disposal or re-use. So the environmental footprint of the materials is often both invisible and less important, overall, than other aspects of a building's environmental performance.

Materials and product choices grow in significance, however, when we consider how those choices might affect ongoing impacts from building operations on energy, water and other resources. Creating an energy-efficient and resource-efficient building requires a combination of measures, including choosing appropriate materials, designing and assembling them for optimal performance and operating the building effectively once it is occupied. The contribution that smart material choices make in this regard should not be overlooked, and can be considered separately from the environmental impacts or burdens associated with the materials themselves.

All these impacts can be viewed through different lenses or filters, depending on one's priorities, interests and on what data happens to be available. We'll first explore the specific topic of carbon emissions, then look at the more holistic view represented by environmental life-cycle assessment, and finally outline methods available to designers seeking to make environmentally informed material and product choices in their practice.

Because climate change is such a significant concern today, it makes sense to consider materials from a strictly carbon perspective, as one factor that might influence decisions. As an element, carbon plays a role in many common materials, on a timeframe that extends well beyond the human era. There are three distinct carbon-based classes of building materials found in the natural world. Two of these accumulate on a geologic timeframe: calcium carbonate (limestone) and hydrocarbons (fossil fuels). The third is cellulosic materials from plants, which have a timeline that is more human in scale.

Of the geologic-cycle materials, limestone is used as a building material directly but it is also the raw material from which cement is made. Limestone is created by the accretion of minerals from marine organisms over millennia. While most limestone is quarried today from dry land, its existence indicates that the area was once the floor of an ocean.

Fossil fuels also come from an accretion over millennia, but in this case it's an accretion of plant material, decaying anaerobically. They turn into peat and then coal, or into oil and natural gas, buried in the earth's crust. These hydrocarbons were traditionally used directly as pitch for waterproofing, but since the latter half of the twentieth century they have been converted to polymers and used in many different ways. The plastic used most widely in construction is polyvinyl chloride, also known as "vinyl" or PVC, which can be a rigid material in piping, window frames and siding, or, with the addition of plasticisers, as flexible flooring and wall covering. Other common plastics in buildings include polyethylene, polypropylene, polystyrene and polyamide (nylon).

In terms of their contribution to climate change, there is an important difference between these two discrete geological-scale carbon cycles: to make cement from calcium carbonate, the carbon is driven out of the mineral and released into the atmosphere, while in the manufacture of plastics and most other petrochemical products the carbon atoms are retained in the material. Globally, about five per cent of anthropogenic carbon dioxide emissions are from cement manufacture, and more than half of that comes from the mineral itself. A small fraction of that CO_2 is subsequently reabsorbed by concrete as it cures over time, but most remains in the atmosphere.

Fossil fuels are, of course, also burned to provide energy for the extraction, transportation and processing of building materials. This combustion represents another channel for the release of CO_2 into the atmosphere. In fact, much of the current concern about climate change is associated with the rapid extraction and release of carbon from the fossil reservoirs where it had been safely sequestered.

From this perspective, buildings represent a potential 'safe haven' where carbon-based materials can be put to use, thereby delaying the release of the carbon contained in these materials and keeping it out of the atmosphere. Buildings can function as sequestration sites for carbon from plants, whether used in their cellulosic form (as wood, bamboo or agrifibre), or as plastic from petroleum. There is one important caveat here, however, about plastic foam insulation. The foaming agent used for this type of insulation is often a hydrofluorocarbon (HFC) gas with very high global warming potential. So even though the plastic itself may be a good sequestration site for carbon, the gas, which can leak out over time, may be a big contributor to climate change.

When from marine organisms, the carbon can remain sequestered if limestone is used directly, but not if it is used to make cement and concrete. Regardless of the material used, if large amounts of fossil fuels are consumed in the process of preparing and using the material, the net impact is harmful.

ENVIRONMENTAL LIFE-CYCLE ASSESSMENT (LCA)

Climate change is not the only problem to emerge as our human population increases and consumes more resources, affecting the planet in ever-increasing ways. Depletion of resources such as fresh water and minerals, pollution in its various forms and destruction of eco-systems all loom as deleterious effects of our expanding impact as a species. The emerging science of environmental life-cycle assessment, or LCA, seeks to account for all these vectors of concern and provide for more informed decisions.

Thanks to the work of LCA practitioners, it is increasingly possible to quantify the impacts of various material choices and compare options across a range of environmental impact categories. The practice of LCA begins with defining the scope of the analysis, because it could, in theory, extend indefinitely (everything is, ultimately, connected to everything else).

Once the scope is defined, researchers describe the life-cycle of a product or material as a series of discrete processes such as raw material extraction, transportation, initial refinement, further refinement, manufacture and so on. For each of these steps, flows of energy, materials and water are identified and quantified, both as inputs to the process and as outputs or emissions from the process. These quantities are then enumerated as the "life-cycle inventory" for that product.

For building materials, it is while a product is in use that it will affect both the occupants directly (with indoor air emissions, for example) and energy or water use in building operations. This is the 'use' phase of the product's life-cycle, and it is typically the longest and often the most important of all the life-cycle phases. Not all materials affect either indoor air or building operations directly, but nearly all do indirectly, with the ongoing demand they establish for cleaning and maintenance, for example.

Having such an inventory is not the whole story, however, because each input and emission has a different environmental impact. The next step is to characterise these environmental impacts and turn the inventory into an impact assessment. The results of this life-cycle impact assessment are presented in the form of a value for each impact category, measured in units appropriate to that category. Climate change impacts are measured in terms of carbon dioxide equivalents, for example, while release of organic effluents into freshwater (eutrophication) is measured in terms of biochemical oxygen demand. With an impact assessment it becomes feasible to compare one material or product option to another based on a full range of environmental impacts.

However, even with this comprehensive level of information, challenges remain. One challenge is that, with the metrics for each category in different units, there is no easy way to combine them into a single summary score. Simplistic approaches, such as adding up the number of categories in which each product comes out better, don't reflect the fact that some categories are more important than others in terms of overall environmental impact.

Exactly how to rank the categories is ultimately as much a matter of value judgements as it is about science. For this reason, many LCA practitioners prefer not to combine the scores from different categories, but instead to allow the specifier or purchaser to view the results for the full set of categories and make a decision that includes both the scores and the values appropriate to the project.

A second challenge that remains, even with good LCA data, is the problem of highly toxic or hazardous compounds, the effects of which are not well understood and therefore not well represented in LCA methodology. Some such compounds don't even generate clear dose-response correlations, so very small doses may be just as problematic as much larger ones. This leads to special considerations for the assessment of hazardous chemicals in building materials.

POTENTIALLY HAZARDOUS CHEMICALS

When the US Green Building Council sought to explore concerns about the use of PVC as a building material and find out how it compared to other likely choices for the same applications, it convened a team of experts to review the available data and present their conclusion (the author was part of that team). This team determined that LCA alone would not be adequate for the task, and developed a methodology that combined LCA with hazard risk assessment approaches.

The risk assessment looked at potential human health impacts from activities such as occupational exposure to hazardous compounds used in the manufacture of both PVC and the alternatives. This sort of exposure is outside the scope of a typical LCA, but it proved possible to combine the results of this risk assessment with LCA results for those same human health impact categories, based on the common unit of disability-adjusted life years.

Even with this combined methodology there was a high degree of uncertainty in the results, but we found that for human-health categories in general, PVC products performed worse than many of their alternatives. For a broader set of environmental impacts, however, PVC products often outperformed the alternatives, leading to a conclusion that a blanket exclusion of PVC products is not as useful an approach as one that recognises that all products have drawbacks and seeks to identify the best option (or create new options) based on a full assessment of strengths and weaknesses.

This PVC-related research illustrates the difficulty of trying to assess the impacts of a product that may have hazardous chemicals in its life cycle, if not in the final product.

Chemicals of greatest concern are those that last a long time, that are passed from one species to another through the food chain, and that have serious health consequences. Compounds that meet these three conditions are often known as "persistent bio accumulative toxins" (PBTs). PBTs include both organic (carbon-based) compounds and toxic minerals or metals. The organic compounds on their own are sometimes called "persistent organic pollutants" (POPs) and have been the target of specific regulatory action in many places.

The effect of these PBTs varies according to the type of hazard they represent. Some are carcinogenic, others specifically harm reproductive systems or cause chromosome abnormalities. Among the most problematic are the class of endocrine disruptors, because they mimic hormones and can therefore cause a big impact with a very small dose. Finally, many heavy metals are neurotoxins that harm the nervous system.

There are both regulatory and voluntary programmes seeking to eliminate the worst of these chemicals from common products. Where regulations fall short, some groups have created their own 'red lists' of chemicals to avoid. Others argue for a more nuanced approach, targeting certain chemicals for special attention but taking care to evaluate the alternatives before choosing a blanket avoidance strategy.

CHOICES IN PRACTICE

In practice, as designers and advisors to the design community, we have to make product and material choices for projects all the time. In this context, environmental and human health considerations, including embodied energy, design for disassembly, and transportation impacts, take their place alongside all the conventional factors that inform these choices, such as:

- Function: will the product or material serve its purpose?
- Aesthetics: will it look and feel good?
- Cost: is it affordable?
- Availability: will the builder be able to get it, in sufficient quantities, and at the project's location?
- Durability: will it hold up for an appropriate length of time (very long for a structural material, not as long for interior finishes)?
- Maintainability: what will it take to keep it clean and functional?

Some of these factors are absolute—if we cannot afford a certain product, it does not matter how well it meets the other criteria. Others are more flexible, and have to be considered as part of the overall decision process. Selecting and procuring products that represent the best balance across all these criteria is challenging enough. Adding environmental and human health concerns to this list could be seen as an added burden. It could also be seen as an added constraint that might actually help with the decision-making process.

To the extent that design is a process of iterative problem-solving, constraints are useful and even necessary in defining the problems to be solved.

By eliminating certain options and making others less attractive, the additional constraints that green filters represent can support this process.

As an illustration of this dynamic, consider the dietary situation often encountered by vegetarians in restaurants. There are often only one or two choices on the menu that suit individual vegetarian preference. As long as those choices are acceptable, the selection process is easier for the vegetarian, who can quickly shift her attention back to relaxation and socialising, while the others are still deliberating their greater options.

If, on the other hand, the few vegetarian choices are not suitable, the vegetarian is at a disadvantage, and all they can do is prevail upon the chef to make up something special. Sometimes such a request to the chef can yield impressive results, but it is unpredictable. Often if the vegetarian preference is not catered for on the menu, it may not be accommodated by the kitchen, either.

Sustainable design criteria can have a similar impact on material and product choices. By eliminating certain known 'bad apples' such as wood from non-certified and potentially illegal sources, the choices are more limited, which can simplify the decision-making process. However, if the remaining choices don't fit within the project's cost constraints, do not perform well functionally or meet aesthetic goals, these additional constraints become a liability. The only option in those cases is the construction industry's equivalent of the vegetarian's request to the chef—a designer can call upon product manufacturers to make other options available.

If the project is big or influential enough, there is a strong incentive for the manufacturer to accommodate such a request. When specifying workstations for the headquarters of a large utility company, the designers were leaning towards one manufacturer, but they were unhappy with the vinyl edge-banding around the desktops. Because they were ordering 1,800 workstations and establishing a precedent for many additional purchases by the same company, they were able to convince the manufacturer to come up with an alternative. That alternative has since become a standard offering from the manufacturer, available to any project.

For smaller projects, however, or those without much lead time, compromise becomes necessary. It's still possible, however, to make the request in the hope that better options may be available for future projects.

The Living Building Challenge, a cutting-edge green building certification programme created by the Cascadia Chapter of the US Green Building Council, has institutionalised this process as part of its certification process. Unlike most rating systems which have both required and optional measures, the Living Building Challenge has only requirements. Among these requirements are two specific constraints on material choices: they must all come from within a specified radius of the project and may not contain any banned ingredients, as specified in the programme's 'red list' of compounds to avoid.

Each of these requirements alone is challenging, but together they represent an unworkably severe constraint on product and material choices. Recognising that difficulty, the programme provides for an option that allows project teams to fall short of a requirement as long as they can show that they've made significant efforts to find compliant products AND that they have contacted manufacturers with a request to make such products available as soon as possible.

CONNECTING PRODUCT SELECTION TO DESIGN SOLUTIONS

When designers simply add sustainable design criteria to a standard design and specification process, the result is usually unattractive compromise. Green products that work as well as their conventional counterparts and look as good might be available, but only at a higher cost, straining the project's budget. They might cost the same, but not be as durable. To avoid this sort of no-win trade-off, it's necessary to re-frame the design problem.

To truly optimise a design in combination with its material choices, designers have to step back and look at the goals they are seeking to achieve, both ecologically and functionally. Often environmentally preferable materials aren't as compelling when they are thought of as direct substitutes for their conventional counterparts, but they may have other advantages that can be exploited to good effect if those advantages are accounted for in the design process.

In some cases this is simply about aesthetic choices. Clear, straight-grained wood products typically come from old-growth trees that can only be harvested with significant ecological consequences. Younger trees, and trees of less well-known species, are often available without those adverse impacts on the forest. In some cases they even come from thinning operations that contribute to forest health. In the right setting and with the right construction methods, they can provide an attractive alternative to old-growth wood at lower cost—but the aesthetic choice to use wood with knots and other signs of 'character' has to be embraced.

In other situations there are functional advantages to consider. A concrete structure can be exposed in the interior of a building, and made with supplementary cementitious materials to reduce its cement content. Such concrete might require a more refined finish than typical structural concrete, increasing its cost, but it can save the project money in avoided demand for finish materials. If it can also contribute to energy efficiency with a design that takes advantage of the exposed thermal mass, the project as a whole benefits in many ways from this more ecological choice.

Similarly, added costs for energy efficiency upgrades can often be offset with savings elsewhere in the building, yielding a higher-performing building for no additional net construction cost. Upgraded windows and insulation in a building envelope, for example, can be paid for by the associated reduction in the size of heating and cooling systems, especially when those reductions include both central plant (boilers and chillers) and distribution systems (ducts and piping).

There are many aspects to products and materials that should inform the design process. If these environmental and human health considerations are applied to material choices alone, without considering the impact of ecological choices on fundamental design decisions, they are likely to lead to less-than-ideal compromises. Integrating the material options into the design process, on the other hand, often leads to better solutions all round.

THE DAWNING OF SOLAR ELECTRIC ARCHITECTURE

STEVEN J STRONG

The last two decades have brought significant changes to the design profession. In the wake of traumatic escalations in energy prices, shortages, black-outs, embargoes and war, along with heightened concerns over pollution, resource depletion, environmental degradation and climate change, awareness of the environmental impact of our work as building design professionals has dramatically increased.

In the process, the shortcomings of yesterday's buildings have also become increasingly clear. Architects with vision have come to understand that it is no longer the goal of good design to simply create a building that's aesthetically pleasing—buildings of the future must be environmentally responsive as well. These architects have responded by specifying increased levels of thermal insulation, healthier interiors, higher-efficiency lighting, better glazing and HVAC equipment, air-to-air heat exchangers and heat-recovery ventilation systems. Significant advances have been made, and this progress is a very important first step in the right direction.

However, it is not enough. For the developed countries to continue to enjoy the comforts of the twenty-first century, and for the developing world to ever hope to attain them, sustainability must become the cornerstone of our design philosophy. Rather than merely using less of the non-renewable fuels and creating less pollution, we must come to design truly sustainable buildings that rely on renewable resources to produce some and, eventually, all of their own energy and create no pollution.

It may still come as a surprise to many architects and their clients, but every building they are currently designing to rely on fossil fuel will become obsolete within its lifetime as the world's remaining reserves are drawn down and prices rise to the point that simply burning these resources for their thermal content can no longer be justified.

Petroleum geologists (who should know the subject) expect world extraction to peak within the next five years. After that will come the long and irreversible downward slide where demand will greatly exceed supply and prices escalate. The heads of Shell and BP have both stated publicly that the end of the petroleum era is in sight while

also calling for immediate action on global warming and climate change.

As the era of cheap oil and gas draws to a close, we must begin in earnest to develop other more sustainable energy options to power our buildings as well as transportation, agriculture, utilities and industry. When all is said and done, renewable energy will drive the coming energy revolution.

One of the most promising renewable energy technologies is photovoltaics (PV), a truly elegant means of producing electricity on site, directly from the sun, without concern for energy supply or environmental harm. These solid-state devices simply make electricity out of sunlight, silently with no pollution and no depletion of materials and virtually no maintenance.

Photovoltaics are also exceedingly versatile— the same technology that can pump water, grind grain and provide communications and village

The Adam Joseph Lewis Environmental Studies Center, Oberlin College, Ohio. The Lewis Center is fully powered by solar energy and features a roof-integrated PV array and a solar pavilion above the parking area. The two produce more power than the building requires, creating a surplus that is shared with the local utility company.

electrification in the developing world can produce electricity for the buildings and distribution grids of industrialised countries.

There is a growing consensus that distributed PV systems which provide electricity at the point of use will be the first to reach widespread commercialisation. Chief among these distributed applications are PV power systems for individual buildings, which are among the most attractive distributed applications, because:

- Buildings and the processes they house consume the majority of electricity
- The real estate to field the solar system comes 'free' with the building
- There are no site development costs—they are part of the building construction
- Reduced structural costs—the building itself becomes the PV support structure
- The utility interconnection already exists—just connect to the distribution panel
- On-site solar displaces kilowatt hours on the customers' side of the meter at the retail rate
- Provides utility demand charge reductions
- Delivers additional financial benefits under time-of-use utility rates.

The building integration of photovoltaics, where the modules actually become an integral part of the building, often serving as the exterior weathering skin, is growing world-wide.

- Building-integrated PV components displace conventional building materials and labour, reducing the net installed cost of the PV system
- BIPV can yield multiple benefits as part of an integrated design process
- The architecturally clean, well-integrated systems increase market acceptance
- Building-integrated PV systems provide building owners with a highly visible public expression of their environmental commitment
- Building owners can finance the PV as part of the overall project.

With reduced installation costs, improved aesthetics and all the benefits of distributed generation, building-integrated PV systems are a prime candidate for widespread adoption. Innovative architects the world over are now integrating PV into their designs and PV manufacturers are responding with components developed specifically for BIPV applications, including integral roof modules, roofing tiles and shingles, modules for vertical curtain wall

The US Mission to the United Nations, Geneva has multiple building-integrated solar electric applications. The southeast and southwest facades feature integral PV sunshades and vertical facade arrays. Much of the roof area is covered with solar generation and a sloped solar glazing system crowns the building.

facades, sloped glazing systems and skylights. A whole new vernacular of Solar Electric Architecture is beginning to emerge.

It is essential to appreciate the context within which solar electricity can best contribute to a building. PV systems are only a part of the solution. We must address both sides of the energy use equation—supply and consumption. To maximise the solar contribution, the building should be designed to use energy most efficiently. Energy generated from renewable resources will contribute a great deal more to an energy-efficient building.

A high-integrity thermal envelope with monolithic air and moisture barriers and superior, high-R-value glazing is desired. Further passive solar strategies which reduce heating and cooling requirements should be employed along with daylighting and energy-efficient equipment, systems and end-use loads. Advanced mechanical systems such as heat-recovery ventilation and geothermal heat pumps should also be employed. Solar thermal systems should also be considered for space and water heating. Only within the context of a comprehensive

energy-conscious 'whole building' design strategy can BIPV achieve its full potential.

Major changes in the world's energy use patterns and systems are upon us as the era of cheap oil and gas draws to a close. We see this played out in ever increasing energy demand, shortages of supply, economic disruption and conflict over resources.

Over the past two decades, PV has moved from the research laboratory to commercial applications and is now ready for widespread commercialisation. As architects and building engineers become more involved, PV is taking a progressively more sophisticated, elegant and appropriate role in building design, putting energy-producing buildings within our reach. As building-integrated PV becomes an integral part of the form and aesthetic of the built environment, these systems will contribute greatly to a more sustainable future for their owners, their communities and society at large.

INFRASTRUCTURAL ENGINEERING AND UTILITIES

SIMON WOODS

INTRODUCTION

The evolution of infrastructure systems and utilities in particular has been a major factor in allowing urban areas to develop relatively unrestricted compared with, for example, the nineteenth century when developments needed to be near an energy source. The introduction of national and international networks for the distribution of utilities, combined with the availability of carbon based fossil fuels such as oil and gas, has provided many more opportunities to construct urban developments how, when and where required.

In considering whether an infrastructure system is sustainable, there are a number of factors to take into account, including the following:

Resilience and Security

The vulnerability of infrastructure systems can be influenced by a number of factors including the physical disruption of lost supplies, the security of utility supply chains and political considerations.

Environmental

The environmental impact of infrastructure systems should be taken into account, including not only the operational efficiencies of the systems themselves but the whole life-cycle from construction through operation to the final decommissioning of the plant. In the case of nuclear energy, it is the disposal of waste fuel and plant decommissioning that provide the strongest arguments against the original development.

Futureproof

Infrastructure systems need to be designed with capacity for future extension and to embrace new technologies. Many current electrical infrastructure networks are unable to accept new renewable technologies.

Efficient and effective development of infrastructure systems can provide significant reductions in energy wastage and carbon emissions. A gas powered central energy system can have an efficiency of as little as 55 per cent by the time the energy is received by the consumer. The amount of CO_2 emitted can vary depending on the source of the energy inputs—for example, the carbon emitted by hydro-electric sources once constructed is virtually zero, although the energy and impact of the construction process must be taken into account as well as the embedded carbon.

THE PRINCIPAL INFRASTRUCTURAL UTILITIES THAT ARE REQUIRED IN URBAN DEVELOPMENTS ARE:

Energy

Typically in the form of electric power and fuel supplies for generation and heat such as gas or renewable technologies.

Water

Provision of a safe water supply for washing, cleaning and drinking.

Telecommunications

To enable rapid and effective transmission of data.

Waste

The discharge and treatment of rainwater/storm drainage and foul waste.

POLITICAL AND SOCIAL DIMENSION

Apart from the technical aspect that is discussed in more detail later, strong influencing factors on the choice of infrastructure solutions are the political and social dimensions.

Different countries and living conditions around the world require different solutions. The major issues facing humanity, such as climate change and poverty, have different priorities depending upon where in the world people live. What might be a priority in one country will not necessarily be so in another. Developed nations tend to take water and food for granted—we might complain about rising prices, but a typical family spends only 20–25 per cent of net income on food and drink, so this does not have the same impact as in other countries whose working population typically spends 95–100 per cent of net income feeding their families.

Developed nations are only just becoming aware of climate change and energy security issues, having lived off cheap and plentiful oil supplies for the past 40 years. Political and public awareness is focusing governments towards dealing with these issues, at the expense of food and water. The same could not be said for countries like India, where 56 per cent of the population does not have access to electricity. The general population of such developing countries is not as concerned with climate change, even though it is they who will be most affected in the future.

When looking at energy infrastructure opportunities around the world, our approach must be sensitive to different cultures and political agendas. A good example of this is a recent project in a North African country. A major issue is fresh water supply—the cost of a barrel of crude oil in the country is approximately $1, whereas the cost of an equivalent barrel of fresh water is approximately $7. An early proposal was to recycle water from a sewage works, which could have been treated and re-used. It was not realised at the time that local religious beliefs prohibited such re-use of water, hence the strategy had to be revised to use reclaimed water solely for irrigation.

Natural resources in any country vary considerably, as can population concentrations. This can affect the amount of waste generated by one particular community compared with another and potential energy from the waste. Another factor is the relative wealth of the households in a particular area: poorer areas produce significantly less waste than affluent ones, which again affects refuse-derived energy.

Legislation in a country can further influence energy strategies. An energy strategy for a city in Poland has recently been developed which recognised that waste collection and disposal is owned by the consumer and not by local government. This meant that each citizen could decide how their waste was to be disposed of, making a city-wide solution much more difficult to implement, because people could opt out of a central waste collection system, affecting predicted refuse volumes.

Political factors also play an important role in future energy strategies. At present, the UK government receives substantial revenues from transport fuel tax, and yet it is starting to give tax incentives for electric vehicles. This policy may well backfire if revenue starts to decrease significantly as electric car uptake increases.

The power and influence of the world's major oil companies is another factor affecting decisions on energy infrastructure. The military cost of protecting oil and gas pipelines and refineries is immense, and it is difficult to see how such companies are going to relinquish their control of oil products in our everyday lives.

Although recent conflicts, such as in Iraq, were reported as being unrelated to oil, it comes as no surprise that Iraq's proven oil reserves have been estimated at over 100 billion barrels, with 90 per cent of the country unexplored. One wonders why the same government and military intervention did not take place at the same time in the African sub-continent, where 15 countries who have little or no oil reserves are presently at war.

The influence of one energy controlling government over another is rising to the forefront of political agendas around the world. This was evident in January 2004, when Russian gas company Gazprom cut off supplies to Belarus, and in January 2006, where they cut off supplies to Ukraine, at least nine people dying as a result.

It is not always major infrastructure projects that are the answer to a country's needs. Localised solutions are often the best option: this is nowhere better illustrated than in India, where individual or localised bio-digesters generate bio-gas from effluent waste collected in large tanks. The bio-gas is used for cooking and electricity generation. In addition, local solar solutions are used in many developing countries where large regions are not connected to a national distribution system and it would be unfeasible to do so. In areas such as these, electricity is generated by solar panels which provide much needed school and medical facilities.

ENERGY GENERATION

As discussed earlier, the generation of energy and its location is influenced by a number of technical, environmental and political factors. This is exemplified by the number of energy solutions for the United Kingdom over the years in response to economic development challenges, and there are now serious environmental issues to address, in particular a reliance on fossil fuels and an ageing distribution system which has led to large inefficiencies and excessive carbon dioxide emissions.

Energy generation can fall into three categories, depending on scale:

Macro generation—International/National/Regional
Distributed Energy Systems—City/Region/Community
Micro generation—Domestic/Schools/Businesses

The current framework in the United Kingdom is macro generation, however the trend is likely to bring a system that is hybrid in nature with more localised energy production or a dispersed energy strategy as well as large-scale renewable generation. To make this possible, there must be a flexible infrastructure in place to allow technologies to feed into the grid.

It is often considered that the most sustainable power generation would be from renewable sources close to the point of use. To deliver systems that can provide secure, controllable and predictable power, an infrastructure that is not reliant on the combination of elements is required. Such solutions include large-scale hydro electric energy as well as geothermal energy.

To enable renewable sources such as wind and solar energy to be as effective as fossil fuels or nuclear power in delivering energy that responds to our needs, energy storage must be developed within the generation plant.

DISPERSED ENERGY SYSTEMS

One of the emerging strategies is that of dispersed energy systems (DES), which have many advantages, including the following:

- The production of energy closer to the point of demand reduces transmission losses
- They can contribute to wider environmental issues such as the treatment of waste in waste to heat and emerging bio-gas technologies. This waste would otherwise be transported to landfill
- They allow for a flexible solution that can incorporate a mixture of renewable technologies
- If incorporated into a wider network, they can export excess energy for use elsewhere
- Community involvement is possible in the ownership of the systems as well as in the provision of supply chains.

The development of DES strategies is encouraged by further developments in distribution design

and emerging technologies for storing the energy produced.

A significant development within dispersed energy systems is that of tri-generation. This involves the generation of electrical power and the use of waste heat to provide district heating or the conversion of the heat energy into cooling energy. Using waste heat products in this way enables much more efficient energy production.

The scale of this form of generation can vary, but it is most relevant to city and large community projects. Dealing with energy production on this scale enables the incorporation of low carbon and renewable sources, depending on the area. It also provides opportunities to introduce waste to energy schemes, linking waste disposal infrastructures with energy production.

The location of the plant would be subject to many planning considerations, including the following:

- Accessibility for input into the energy grid
- Local impacts on the environment, e.g. ecological and acoustic.

DISTRIBUTION AND NETWORKS

It is currently held that the world's long-term future energy infrastructure will be based around a de-carbonised electrical system. Significant research and development is presently going into smart grids and superconductor technologies which, when technically and commercially available, will significantly reduce or practically eliminate transmission losses. If this is the future, then should we be designing our present energy infrastructure around an all electric economy? If we did so, our transmission networks and generating plant, which presently suffer approximately 40 per cent losses, could not cope, leading to the blackouts which are presently being experienced by some North American and Canadian cities, where 50 million people in the region were affected by power blackouts in 2003. We need to provide energy systems which can satisfy demand and reduce reliance upon fossil fuels in transition to an all electric economy.

Networks developed to supply a city must be both affordable and flexible enough to accommodate growth in a sustainable manner. For the engineers developing systems that still serve some of our cities today, this involved sizeable overdesign. Much of the sewage system that was originally developed for cities such as London and Manchester is still operating well today. It is our electrical infrastructure systems that are often not adequate for the increasing demand of our city developments. The reinforcement of the electrical network can be a major cost, and developers often pay a substantial premium for network upgrades.

Another aspect to consider is the replacement of the physical parts of the network systems. The pipes that carry our water and gas have a limited lifespan and will eventually require replacement. If replacement is difficult and systems are allowed to deteriorate, prolonged periods of wastage can result.

The installation of systems with a suitable lifespan and future capacity will often depend on the cost at the time of original installation. The analysis of the routing of networks needs to consider the whole life-cycle environmental cost and in particular the decommissioning and removal of the service on upgrade or replacement. Also of growing concern is the embedded carbon aspect of the construction and infrastructure process.

DEMAND SIDE CONSUMPTION AND WASTE

When considering the holistic design of energy and infrastructure solutions for any new or existing developments, a hierarchal approach should be taken with the first step being the reduction of energy consumption and waste.

Current technologies incorporated into our buildings include smart metering to enable monitoring and control of energy consumption. Additional techniques for consumption control include principles of demand management now being termed "Dynamic Demand Management", involving the reduction of peak loads by allowing some systems to be shut off and reduce the need for large back up generation to make up the demand gap. This link between supply and demand is an area where technologies are currently being developed. If applied effectively, they have the potential to reduce the number of power stations constructed.

A reduction in energy demand can be brought about by efficient passive design methods. Local recycling of consumables such as waste water can reduce demand on the infrastructure and many technologies are now readily available, including rainwater harvesting and grey water recovery.

The need for demand side reduction and production of water is most prevalent in arid climates and has resulted in a number of innovative solutions. Solar desalination is a technique using solar energy to desalinate water and dates back to the early 1950s, when simple solar stills were studied for remote desert and coastal communities.

The treatment of waste is another process to have a considerable impact on infrastructure. A particular objective is the reduction of waste going to landfill. Responses to this include anaerobic digestion plants and bio-gas production which produce a renewable gas source that can either be used exclusively or fed back into the main gas supply to reduce its carbon impact.

The treatment of waste locally has also led to the introduction of composting machines into dwellings which accept food waste and speed up the process, allowing the resulting compost to be used locally.

Reed bed technology is also being incorporated into some new developments in the form of constructed wetlands. Constructed wetlands are artificial swamps (sometimes called "reed fields") using reed or other marshland plants to form small-scale sewage treatment systems. Water trickling through the reed bed is cleaned by microorganisms living on the root system which utilise the sewage for growth nutrients, resulting in a clean effluent. The process is very similar to conventional aerobic sewage treatment, except that the latter requires artificial aeration.

Constructed reed beds/wetlands can be of two main types, horizontal and vertical. Vertical beds are much smaller in area, and are most suited to a sloping site. Horizontal beds require considerable areas of land, but are simpler to construct. Usually the top surface is planted with reed, but, as one of the main treatment methods in a reed bed is filtration, a variation is to use unplanted beds that are simply sand filters. The depth of most reed bed systems is about a metre, as the reed's roots and rhizomes are rarely beyond 0.6 metres. Most contaminants are removed by filtration within the first metre of soil.

LOCAL AND MICRO GENERATION

Microgeneration represents the majority of installations at local level. In terms of financial payback, it is often difficult to justify the installation of these schemes. The motivation for microgeneration may include the need to meet local planning requirements or contribute to carbon reduction on a personal level. The principal microgeneration technologies include:

- Wind turbines
- Solar energy from photovoltaic or solar thermal panels
- Heat or heat and power generation from bio-fuels.

It is often technically difficult to provide independence from the main infrastructure networks, which requires a level of generation and energy storage that is not yet available. The advantage of wind or photovoltaic energy is its ability to feed the energy back into the main grid with good 'feed in tariffs', making the technologies financially viable.

An important advantage of local generation is that demand can encourage the development of new technologies that are both more economical and more efficient. This is best illustrated in the photovoltaic market, where there is a need to reduce the cost of the panels whilst increasing efficiency and lifespan. Typically a PV panel will have a lifespan of 25 years, and over that time the efficiency may drop by 85 per cent. The challenge in recommending PV systems is that often the payback can be well in excess of 25 years. One of the most interesting developments in this market is thin film technology, which offers the potential for integrated systems with reduced weight. This has encouraged traditional PV manufacturers to improve their product and develop more advanced systems.

The technology for small-scale wind turbines has also developed as demand has increased. One aspect that has previously hampered the introduction of wind turbines is reliability. Typically a uniform wind speed of over five metres per second will suffice, although the nature of each particular site should be considered. The number of turbines commercially available is now increasing, with vertical axis turbines popular in urban installations.

One project independent of the main infrastructure networks is Gibson Mill in West Yorkshire, which now operates as a tourist and visitor centre. Due to the mill's considerable distance from mains gas and electricity services, it was decided to use a combination of small-scale hydro electric power generation with photo voltaic panels on the roof to generate electricity. The site has a reservoir, providing a large store of potential energy that can be released on demand. This small-scale hydro electric installation provides a controllable energy source and a natural store of energy.

FUTURE TECHNOLOGIES DEVELOPMENT

Although there are short-term measures currently in use to reduce dependence on carbon intensive fuels, the long-term energy solution is all-electric. Contemporary sustainable solutions for producing energy on the scale that is required include wind and hydro electric energy. Others now being developed harness tidal and wave energy.

Hydrogen

The development of a hydrogen based economy also presents opportunities for a new infrastructure that stores renewable energy, the main by-product of which is water. In practice, the main barrier to a hydrogen economy and associated infrastructure is the capital investment required. However, it may offer a long-term solution working with other energy generation systems and infrastructure networks as the technology develops.

Energy Storage/Fuel Cells

Hydrogen fuel cells can be utilised not only for heating and power, but also transportation. Hydrogen buses are already a common sight in many city centres. The key to a successful energy infrastructure is to closely match supply and demand, so an element of storage is required. It is relatively simple to store heat or cool, but at present it is not easy to store electricity.

Other methods of storing energy are being developed, including the storage of energy from wind farms in underground silos consisting of gravel and argon gas. Another being developed is to save excess electricity as compressed air in an underground salt cavern. In essence, this technology works as a battery for excess power, storing power when the wind is blowing and releasing it again when the wind is not blowing. The technology works in combination with a gas power plant: thus power is generated on a mix of natural gas and air, which reduces CO_2 emissions.

Significant research and development is presently going into smart grids and superconductor technologies, which when technically and commercially available will significantly reduce or practically eliminate transmission losses.

TRANSPORT INFRASTRUCTURE

Visions of sustainable transport systems have featured heavily in theoretical eco-cities. Regional strategies have emerged as planners have realised how transport can have a large effect on environmental, economic and social sustainable development. An example of this is the visionary strategy developed by Will Alsop for the development of a network linking the north of England. Although this may appear to be rather abstract, there are many important features contained within the concept, in particular the adoption of transport nodes, accessibility and connectivity, important elements when developing a sustainable transport strategy.

There are now several simulation models available to demonstrate the effectiveness of networks as well as Geographical Information System (GIS) techniques which provide valuable tools to analyse transport and movement patterns. These are often used in the regeneration of existing urban areas to provide a measure of the effectiveness of existing transport systems as well as examining the potential for improving transport nodes and networks to encourage sustainable growth and development.

In terms of reducing the environmental impact of transport systems, recent technologies include bio-fuels and the use of hydrogen to provide the motive energy for transport. Private transport systems are being developed with either electric or hydrogen motive power, although these require an infrastructure to replenish the power and enable longer journeys.

Within the urban regeneration sector, the strategic implementation of mass transit systems that improve accessibility both to and within the city centre can provide infrastructure networks that promote sustainable development both of the urban area and linkages to other regions. The strategy also needs to promote integration with multi-modal public transport systems. Depending on the scale of the urban area, this may range from pedestrian to rail and air and include restrictions in car use to reduce congestion and traffic pollution.

In cities such as Manchester, these new transit systems have often resulted in the reinstatement of trams or the introduction of light rail systems providing vital links to regeneration areas. Such schemes need to be commercially viable and provide for a variety of travel patterns to justify the investment required.

TELECOMMUNICATIONS AND DATA

The increasing capabilities of telecommunications systems have immeasurable influence on every aspect of how we live, including how we work and socialise. In terms of physical infrastructure, the most effective and resilient method of data transfer is via hard cabled systems such as fibre optic systems, although the introduction of wifi technology has transcended the limitations of a wired network for day to day data transfer.

The development of Building Management Systems has enabled infrastructure systems such as security, fire alarms, CCTV and energy monitoring to be monitored and controlled both locally and remotely on world wide networks. For example, the operation and performance of a building in New York can be checked in London using data transfer by satellite.

Smart metering systems are now highly developed so that energy consumption within our buildings can be tracked to the extent that it is easy to detect whether lights in a certain part of a building are being left on or over-used. This technology can help to raise the building user's awareness of energy use and greatly reduce wastage.

Data infrastructure is now being used in the education sector to enable students to collect data and present it in a way that demonstrates their own energy use.

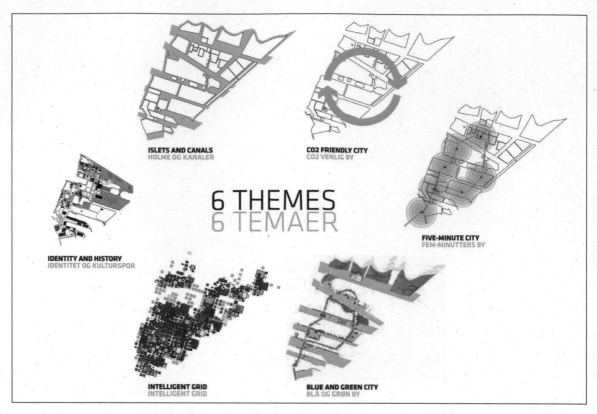

ISLETS AND CANALS
HOLME OG KANALER

CO2 FRIENDLY CITY
CO2 VENLIG BY

6 THEMES
6 TEMAER

IDENTITY AND HISTORY
IDENTITET OG KULTURSPOR

FIVE-MINUTE CITY
FEM-MINUTTERS BY

INTELLIGENT GRID
INTELLIGENT GRID

BLUE AND GREEN CITY
BLÅ OG GRØN BY

It can also show how their actions can influence energy use or the contribution that renewable energy systems can make.

CASE STUDY

Sustainable Masterplan—Nordhavn, Copenhagen

With its unique positioning and an area covering the size of 625 football fields, Nordhavn in Copenhagen is Scandinavia's largest and most ambitious city development project.

Over a 50 year period, Nordhavn is to be developed to accommodate 40,000 inhabitants and 40,000 workplaces. The scheme includes a CO_2 neutral energy system and a sustainable multi-mode transport network.

This new area creates an urban delta with 11 individual islets encircled by canals and water. The islets are planned as manageable units, small neighbourhoods each with its own identity incorporating the characteristics of its location and historic position as a harbour. It is easier to walk, cycle and take the Metro than use a car. Since transportation to and from work accounts for an increasing share of society's expenditure in terms of time, money and pollution, it has been recognised in the design that

an effective transport infrastructure makes a major contribution to reducing CO_2 emissions.

The scheme has prioritised an efficient public transport system with bicycle and pedestrian connections to transport nodes that tie the neighbourhood together with the rest of the city. The scheme includes an elevated Metro track and a bicycle network that together create a green artery. The track creates a linear park area and functions as a cover for the cycleway, enabling the people of Nordhavn the opportunity to cycle all year round in the dry.

The heating will be based on district heating and interconnected with the low carbon system in the Copenhagen region, which in a few decades will be CO_2 neutral. Buildings with cooling demand will be connected to a cooling network, combining free cooling with the integrated production of heating and cooling. Buildings will be designed for low energy demand with the incorporation of low energy passive design and efficient building engineering systems design. Local opportunities for geothermal energy, large heat pumps to utilise the fluctuating wind power, seasonal thermal storage and marine biomass are being considered.

DESIGN FOR DISASSEMBLY OF BUILDINGS

ELMA DURMISEVIC

BACKGROUND

The exponential increase in population and contemporaneous increase for many in standard of living will mean that demand for essential goods and services (transportation, cars and planes and also housing, materials, water and food) will increase by at least a factor of two in the next few decades (Natalis, 2007). If the need to support an additional three billion people and the effect of increase per capita in consumption is added, it is clear that the linear material flow (from excavation to disposal) present in the existing industrial system is not sustainable.

Many scientists speculate that if nine billion people have a Western life-style in 2050, we would need six Earths to provide the necessary resources to sustain the population. A point has been reached when the search for sustainable solutions for the resource feedback loops has become unavoidable. At a time of global climate crises and when natural resources are gradually depleting and becoming increasingly expensive, the durability of buildings and products is becoming a major issue. Issues such as adaptability, reconfigurability, re-use and recycling will be critical to building and product values in the future.

Some have suggested that industrial systems could use the metaphor and behaviour of biological systems as guidance for sustainable design. In an ideal case, one could adopt the following as goals: that every molecule which enters a specific manufacturing process should leave as part of a saleable product; that the materials and components in every product should be used to create other useful products at the end of the original product's life (Greadel and Allenby, 1996) and that the main structure of every building can accommodate different use-patterns during its total life. The aim is to close the loop of industrial processes and bring material and energy back into an industrial cycle while eliminating the concept of waste. Unlike car and product design, where the concept of industrial ecology (closed life-cycle of products) has been investigated and applied in the past, this approach is revolutionary when applied to building design.

The building industry has become the biggest polluter and waste producer in the world, with demolition and construction waste being an integral part of the construction process. A report by the World Resource Institute projects a 300 per cent rise in material use as world population and economic activity increases over the next 50 years. Landfill sites are filling up, forcing increases in waste disposal taxes and making waste management exceptionally expensive. The physical impact of increasing building mass in industrialised nations and the developing world has become undeniable in the twenty-first century and the construction industry has become a major player in achieving sustainable development.

If the construction industry is to play a role in sustainable development, current thinking regarding the performance and technical composition of buildings and construction materials need to be revised. Considering the focus on closing the material feedback loops in construction, the disassembly potential of buildings and their systems will become an important measure of their sustainability (*Figure 1*).

BUILDING CONSTRUCTION —GLOBAL PERSPECTIVE

In order to understand the overwhelming impact that the construction industry has, it is necessary to look at the sector from a global perspective. Construction contributes on average ten per cent of GDP and more than half of the capital investment in all countries. The construction industry is estimated to have 111 million employees worldwide, and is therefore the world's largest industrial employer (CIB, 2002). Nearly 50 per cent of the earth's land has been transformed for human activities, and more than 50 per cent of the human population currently lives in cities, with this percentage increasing (CIB, 2002). The impact of construction extends beyond the construction phase to include supply chain issues and the effects of post construction activities such as operation, maintenance and re-use of a building. The construction sector is directly related to other major sectors such as mining, manufacturing, agriculture and transport. Including all these, the sector accounts for 50 per cent of global greenhouse gas emissions (UNEP-IETC, 2002). making it the largest single contributor globally. In many countries, the construction industry accounts for up to 40 per cent of materials entering the global economy (CIWMB, 2000), 50 per cent of waste production and 40 per cent of energy consumption.

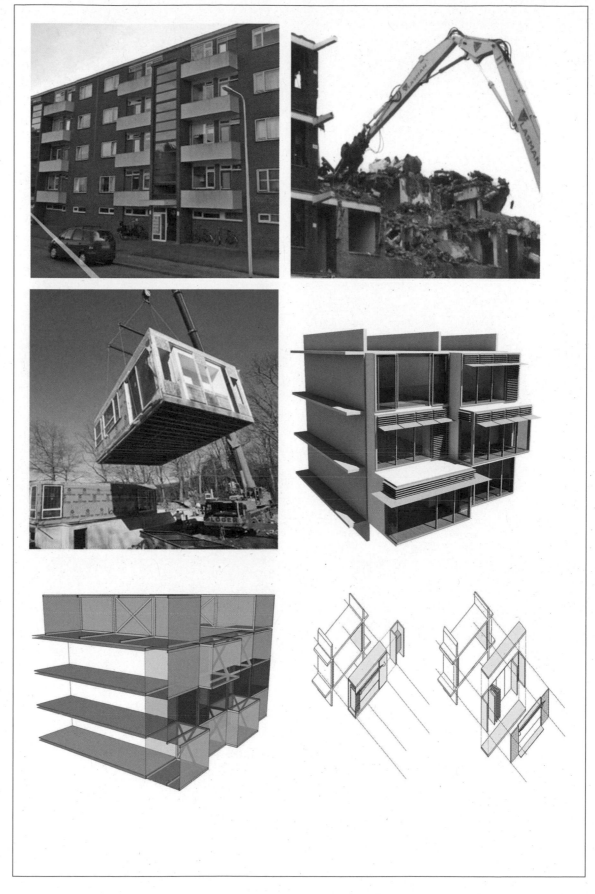

Figure 1: Transition from demolition to disassembly. In addition to new transformable structures based on the DfD approach, the concept can be applied to the transformation of existing buildings. By adding replaceable and flexible extension units to the existing housing blocks, spatial quality, energy performance and the architectural quality of existing apartments can be significantly improved and the life of the building extended.

Developers and real estate managers warn that there is a mis-match between existing building stock and the dynamic and changing demands in respect of the use of buildings and their systems. Use phases are becoming ever shorter, imposing frequent transformations of buildings and their surroundings. More than 50 per cent of expenditure on building construction in the Netherlands is on partial demolition and adaptation. At the same time, about 42 per cent of new construction is the replacement of demolished buildings. This gives an indication of the dynamics of activities around building stock that is not designed to adapt to market requirements. Until recently, investors considered that most financial risk occurs during the construction phase. However, investors who fund long-term projects realise there is even greater uncertainty in the operational phase of buildings. The lack of understanding of how often buildings change and why, also where intervention should occur, makes prediction of future costs unreliable (Clift, 2003).

Ultimately 'conventional' construction has become a burden on the dynamic and changing society of the twenty-first century. Buildings are not designed to meet the changing requirements of society. They are conceived as fixed and permanent structures although they are subject to daily transformation.

As a result, most building structures have to be broken down in order to be changed, adapted, upgraded or replaced. Their material flow is one-directional, starting from material extraction and finishing with landfill. Such building practices rely on unlimited consumption of diminishing materials and energy resources, as well as the use of rapidly filling landfills. Accordingly, conventional construction results in waste of materials and invested capital.

Rather than destroying structures and systems while adapting the building for new requirements, it should be possible to disassemble sections into components and to reassemble them in a new combination, to re-manufacture or recycle them. We must consider how we can access and replace parts of existing building systems and components, and how we can design and integrate building systems and components in order to be able to reconfigure or replace them later on. Considering the impact that material recovery options have on the environment, the sustainability

of design in the future will rely strongly on the disassembly potential of a building (Figure 1).

END OF LIFE OF BUILDINGS

One long-standing conviction held by many is that buildings and building components last longer when made of more durable materials. However, everyday demolition practice that results in material and energy losses proves the opposite. Buildings are designed to last 70–100 years, yet today buildings with an age of 15 years are demolished to give way to new construction.

Most modern buildings are made of prefabricated components designed to be mountable, but not demountable. For this reason, assembly of buildings can be seen as a complex sequence of connecting carefully designed components and materials, a process that may involve thousands of people and fleets of machines (Crowther, 1999). On the other hand, disassembly in the building industry usually involves a few bulldozers and some explosives. This is because buildings are not designed to be demountable: their components are not designed to be re-used or reconfigured and composite materials are often not designed to be recycled.

Such an approach ignores the fact that building components and systems have different degrees of durability. While the structure of a building may have a service life of up to 75 years, the cladding may only last 20 years. Similarly, services may only be adequate for 15 years and the interior fit-out may be changed as often as every three years. Nevertheless, it is quite normal for parts with low durability to be fixed in permanently, preventing easy disassembly. The way in which building parts are put together has a great effect on whether a part of the building or the whole is recycled at the end of its design life. This is independent of whether its materials were wisely selected. In other words, the composition of building configuration is responsible for the extension of the life-cycle of the building and its components and ultimately for the reduction of waste and use of raw materials.

If we recognise the potential of buildings whose components can be dismantled, reconfigured and re-used, it is possible to divert the flow of materials from disposal and save the materials and energy embodied in them by avoiding the demolition process. The design of green buildings runs the risk of being carried out on an ad hoc basis if the disintegration aspects of the building structure do not become an integral part of the design process.

DESIGN FOR DISASSEMBLY (DfD)

Disassembly is often seen as the last phase of a building. However, the influence of design for disassembly goes far beyond the technical and physical integration of the building. The two main indicators of disassembly are independence and exchangeability of building parts. Exchangeability of components relies on design provisions for physical connections, assembly sequences, connection techniques and the geometry of the components. Independence of building components relates to the functional composition and decomposition of the building, requirements for spatial flexibility and scenarios for building use as well as the hierarchy of components that correspond to the desired spatial use and maintenance strategy. If we are to design buildings that are flexible and reconfigurable and whose systems and components are replaceable and re-usable, disassembly strategy needs to be integrated from the beginning of the development stage.

A good understanding of the long-term purpose of the artefact is crucial in the DfD approach. Scenarios for the future use of the building and its materials have to be defined at an early stage. Every set of usage scenarios for a building or a system will result in different technical compositions and different configuration types. The aim of DfD is to find a match between long-term use scenarios (for buildings and materials) and configuration typology that will support transformations from one use scenario to another without having a negative impact on the environment.

The main characteristics of transformable/dynamic configurations based on disassembly principles are (i) separation of material levels which correspond to independent building functions, (ii) creation of an open hierarchy of distinct sub-assemblies, (iii) use of independent interfaces between individual components, (iv) application of parallel instead of sequential assembly/disassembly processes

and (v) use of mechanical connections in place of chemical connections.

In order to achieve this, a fundamental change in the architect's perception of buildings is needed:

- Conceiving the building not as a static but a dynamic and open structure that can easily adapt to changing requirements
- Extending the transformation capacity of buildings and systems by considering the whole life-cycle and seeing building as an ongoing process which does not stop at the end of the construction phase
- Treating building materials as long-term valuable assets throughout their life-cycle by utilising reconfiguration and re-use options at building, system and component level
- Considering waste and demolition as a design error
- Decoupling fixed function/material relationships in buildings by use/design of reconfigurable systems
- Involving the construction industry in the whole life-cycle of the building.

Design considerations for high transformation capacity involve:

- Setting the boundary conditions for transformation
- Specification of long and short term use scenarios
- Systematisation of elements according to functional groups
- Formation of a hierarchy of components that fits the desired functional decomposition
- Specification of base elements that fit the desired hierarchy of elements and functional decomposition
- Definition of assembly sequences that support desired functional and technical decomposition
- Definition of types of connections that support desired functional and technical decomposition
- Design of the geometry for connections that support the type of connection and technical decomposition
- Life cycle coordination that respects disassembly sequences, technical and functional decomposition.

Design for Disassembly can be summarised in six essential steps:

- Definition of the use performance through specification of long- and short-term scenarios

- Functional decomposition followed by initial specification of materials
- Development of a life-cycle coordination matrix for the proposed solution which indicates sensitive parts for disassembly
- A hierarchy of material levels that corresponds with the frequency of change of components for maintenance and function change
- Outline of the physical integration between parts which have different functional and technical life cycles
- Evolution of a knowledge-based model to match design solutions with desired performance indicators.

TOWARDS RECONFIGURABLE BUILDINGS

In general, demolition can be defined as the process whereby the building is broken up with little or no attempt to recover any of the constituent parts for re-use. Different functions and materials which comprise a building system are integrated (during assembly/ construction) in one closed and dependent structure that does not allow alteration and disassembly. The inability to remove and exchange building systems and their components results not only in significant energy consumption and increased waste production, but also in the lack of spatial adaptability and technical serviceability of the building.

The task for designers and architects is to replace established building configurations not designed for disassembly, adaptability and material recovery with open and dynamic configurations that can be reconfigured and whose parts can be easily disassembled. If this is the answer to durability of buildings and building materials, one should look at the transformation process itself, because the transformation of buildings, systems and components has to embody material recovery options.

The moment when buildings start to transform is the moment when structures can be reconfigured and re-used, or simply sent to waste disposal sites. At that moment, the technical composition of the building is crucial to its life-cycle and its materials. Thus it is not only the type and durability of material(s) but more importantly their arrangement

and hierarchy that determines the life-cycle of buildings and their products.

Green design should be the design of transformable building structures made of components assembled in a systematic order, suitable for maintenance and the replacement of various parts. This concept affects the design of all aspects of the functional and technical composition of buildings and accentuates the interdependent relationship between the transformation process and disassembly technologies. It also introduces three dimensions of transformation in a building: spatial, structural and material transformation. The key to each dimension (and ultimately to a 3-D transformable building) is disassembly. By adoption of the concept of design for disassembly, the spatial systems of a building become more amenable to modification and change of use. New standards in exploitation of structure by re-use and reconfiguration can be achieved, and conscientious handling of raw materials through re-use and recycling is encouraged.

LOOSELY COUPLED FUNCTION/ MATERIAL RELATION: A KEY TO DESIGN FOR DISASSEMBLY

Design for transformation, based on the disassembly potential of materials, addresses a moment of change in the purpose of the assembly. It addresses the moment when the rearrangement of functions and materials takes place. In order to understand and predict a building's behaviour and the re-use potential of its configuration at the moment of transformation, it is important to understand a life cycle duality present in each building and system structure. This duality has to do with the functionality of structures and their use life-cycle on one hand, and material type and technical life-cycle on the other.

The 'function/material' relationship is treated as an ultimate unity during the conventional design and construction process, which results in fixed relationships between materials and their functions and ultimately in closed configuration. If the functionality of an assembly changes, materials are disposed of and new ones used for the new function.

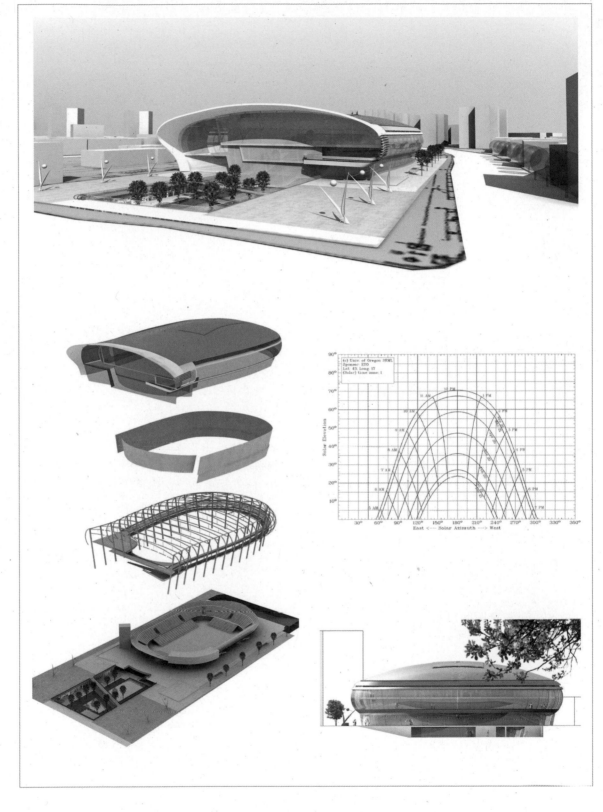

Figure 2: Multi-functional 45,000 square metre business-sports complex in Mostar under construction. As a result of careful design of the building configuration, providing a distinction between fixed and flexible layers, and analysis of climatic conditions of the site, a flexible and energy-efficient building has been designed as an icon for sustainable design in the region. The building structure can be adjusted to suit weather conditions and the requirements of four types of sport as well as providing entertainment, retail, restaurant and parking facilities.

Such a predefined end-of-life for each 'material function' relationship becomes a bottleneck for the transformation of assemblies based on disassembly.

The Design for Disassembly concept postulates that when the life-cycle of material levels becomes independent of the life-cycle of functional levels, the durability of building configurations can be extended and materials re-used for other purposes or recycled. This concept defines a building as a system of different levels of change (functional, technical, material levels, etc.). In such a system some levels dominate others. This dominance is defined by their rates of change. The dynamics of the system are dominated by slow rates of change. The ultimate task of Design for Disassembly is to reduce dependence between functional and material levels within building configurations.

Instead of designing one 'function/material' relational set at a time, it becomes necessary to design a flexible framework that allows reconfiguration of functions and materials without creating negative effects on the environment.

Therefore, Design for Disassembly addresses the breaking point for functional or material use. It addresses issues related to functional flexibility as well as the flexibility and physical integration of material levels. Decisions regarding functionality influence a number of material levels and the manner of their physical integration. At the same time, decisions regarding the hierarchy of materials and their physical integration have an influence on the independence of material levels and their functions. Thus, there is a constant interaction between the 'what' and the 'how' of design during a design for disassembly. If this interdependence is ignored at the beginning of the design process, it may result in a closed configuration with fixed material-function relationships.

Considering the growing number of requirements imposed on building design in the twenty-first century, the design of a green building is possible only through the systematic integration of aspects such as architectural quality, transformability, resources, comfort, safety, constructability and cost from the beginning of the design process. Figure 2 illustrates the design of a multi-functional, transformable, energy efficient building whose final form is optimised primarily by its orientation, the path of the sun, climate conditions, transformation scenarios and maintenance strategy.

CONCLUSIONS

The different arrangement and hierarchy of building components respond to different use requirements. The main task of Design for Disassembly as a key to green engineering is to find a match between the desired performance of the building in use over time and its technical composition.

The end-of-life scenarios possible for a building and its materials are determined by its technical composition; whether it is possible to achieve environmentally preferable scenarios of re-use and reconfiguration compared with down-cycling and disposal of building materials. One can argue that the physical characteristics of a building are indicators of its sustainability. A major shift towards green design and engineering involves a shift from designing closed building systems and assemblies towards open and dynamic building assemblies made of independent and exchangeable building components and systems.

Different sub-assemblies are independent from each other and are connected via the base element of the assembly, similar to computer programs where independent modules can be independently upgraded, reconfigured and added to the existing architecture. Such a concept allows for future alterations to external screening and internal partitioning. It allows for services to be independent of the fabric, to provide for accessibility, servicing and alteration. It creates the provision for re-use and recycling and paves the way for designs of greater richness and diversity.

References:

Dias Natalis (2007). Speech by Prof. dr. ir. Jacob Fokkema, Rector of Delft University of Technology.

Greadel T E and B R Allenby (1996). *Design for Environment*. Prentice Hall, New Jersey.

CIB (October 2002). "Open Building, Proceedings Conference of CIBW104: Balancing Recourses and Quality in Housing". Mexico City.

CSB, 2007: Centre for Building Statistics in the Netherlands, Bouwvergunningen, huur-en koopwoningen, 2007

Durmisevic, 2006: E. Durmisevic, "Transformable Building Structures—Design for Disassembly as a way to introduce sustainable engineering to building design and construction", PhD thesis, University of Technology, Delft, February 2006.

Clift, 2003: M.Clift, "Life Cycle Costing in the Construction Sector", *Industry and Environment Review*, Vol. 26, No. 2–3 Sustainable Building and Construction 2003.

EDUCATION IN SUSTAINABLE ENVIRONMENTAL DESIGN

SIMOS YANNAS

INTRODUCTION

The Architectural Association (AA) School's involvement in the teaching and research of sustainable environmental design can be traced back to its Department of Tropical Studies (the AA Tropical School) which was set up in 1954 and operated successfully until 1971. The *Manual of Tropical Housing and Building Part 1—Climatic Design*, a classic textbook in this field, was one of the Tropical School's intellectual legacies. In 1974, in the aftermath of the first energy crisis, the AA launched the Environment and Energy Studies Programme (AA EE), one of the first postgraduate teaching and research programmes of its kind, within its newly formed Graduate School. AA EE has since become widely known internationally and has staff and graduates active in environmental teaching, research and practice in some 50 countries. The AA School currently offers a 12 month Master of Science (MSc) and 16 month Master of Architecture (MArch) in Sustainable Environmental Design.[1]

The main research object of these Masters options is the relationship between architectural form, materiality and environmental performance, and how this relation is to evolve in response to climate change and emerging technical capabilities. Sustainable environmental design is not a fixed ideal, but an evolving concept that should be redefined and reassessed with each new project. Observation, measurement and computer modelling and simulation are fundamental techniques that underpin the research undertaken within the programme. These are applied at various levels of detail and intensity, extending the understanding of theoretical principles and providing empirical and analytical inputs to the design process. With a current annual intake of 40 to 50 students from many different countries, climates and cultural backgrounds, the taught programme highlights the diversity of the environmental agenda, pinpointing similarities as well as differences between climatic regions, building types, environmental attributes and human behaviour.

KEY PROPOSITIONS

The objective of sustainable environmental design is to achieve thermal and visual comfort in and around buildings using nature's energy sources and sinks by means of architecture. In educating new generations of practitioners, it is desirable that claims to sustainable environmental design:

- Provide evidence on how a proposed scheme improves on built precedents
- Are open to scrutiny in both process and final product
- Treat the environment as a form generator and not as a wastebin
- View occupant comfort as architectural concerns not as engineering add-ons
- Conceive time as a design dimension
- Treat climate change as design parameter
- Learn from precedents and set realistic performance targets.

Research and practice over the last 35 years have shown that sustainable environmental design:

- Can deliver building performance without increasing cost
- Has creative and innovative potential that is largely unexplored
- Is not a self-taught skill and cannot be picked up from books or everyday practice
- Is based on simple principles that have complex and counter-intuitive outcomes
- Must be kept simple to succeed
- Can be informed by powerful simulation tools,
- Can help define an architecture of transitions that bridges past and future.

PEDAGOGIC OBJECTIVES AND OUTCOMES

Pedagogic objectives and outcomes of the AA School's MSc and MArch in Sustainable Environmental Design are:

- To provide a knowledge base from theory and built precedents
- To use environmental simulation tools to inform design
- To learn by doing with hands-on applications
- To combine environmental performance with architectural expression.

The taught programme is in two parts. The first part is common to both MSc and MArch candidates and is structured around a series of joint studio projects undertaken in teams combining the two groups.

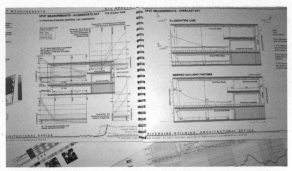

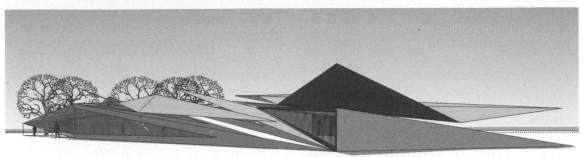

Projects are supported by weekly lectures, seminars and software workshops. These review theory and practice in sustainable design, case studies by leading researchers and designers, define performance criteria for different building types and climates and provide training in the use of environmental simulation tools and design analysis techniques. The second part of the course is organised around candidates' dissertation projects.

PROJECTS

What Can Buildings Tell Us, What Can We Tell Back

Study of built precedents provides an excellent vehicle for applying the principles and tools of environmental design.[2] The building studies undertaken as part of the MSc and MArch in Sustainable Environmental Design combine occupant and designer interviews with on-site observations and environmental measurements (Figure 1). Measurements help calibrate digital models which then provide initial conditions for simulations of environmental performance (Figure 2). Simulations of solar, thermal, daylight and airflow processes undertaken in the form of parametric studies provide the foundations of environmental design research aiming at insights into a building's performance if it were designed, occupied or operated differently.[3] Building studies are undertaken in teams. Buildings are selected for

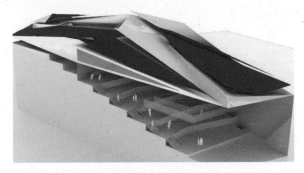

their architectural or environmental interest. London (Latitude 51° 32' N) offers a rich variety of buildings for study.[4]

Over the years a wide range of built environments have provided laboratories for these studies. These included dwellings, offices, schools, art galleries, railway stations, pavilions, streets, squares and other public spaces. The theoretical knowledge, survey methods, scientific instruments and software tools required for such studies are introduced by the taught programme in its weekly lectures and workshops over the three terms of the academic year. The findings from this first project provide starting points for design research agendas that are pursued in the following term of the academic year. The objective then is to explore environmentally performative designs, aiming at near-zero carbon buildings that make use of natural resources and can address climate change. While London continues to offer application

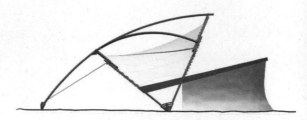

contexts, project teams can also choose sites in other cities and climatic regions *(Figure 3).*[5]

LEARNING BY DOING: HANDS-ON APPLICATIONS

Additionally, project work may include the design and making of small experimental structures. Two of these, built by students as part of short-term projects, are illustrated above.

Fixed Canopy for Archaeologists[6] A group of 20 Masters students collaborated on the design, fabrication, erection and testing of this small structure. It was conceived as a shelter for archaeologists carrying out work in sunny summer conditions on an Aegean island. Made of timber, hemp rope and cotton sailcloth, the structure was fabricated at the AA School's London and Hooke Park workshops. The form of the fabric cover was modelled on the sunpath aiming to shade the work area at all times during the summer months. The saddle shape of the tensile fabric works like an inverted wing; strong winds push the structure into the ground. The mesh skirt on the north side can provide protection against the disruptive northerly winds that affect the Aegean in mid-summer. The fabric can be soaked with water, providing evaporative cooling to the work area underneath. The structure was assembled and exhibited work on the island of Santorini (Latitude 36° 24' N) in the course of a study trip there in April 2004 *(Figure 4).*

Heliotropic Urban Bench[6] On a return study trip to Santorini, the Masters group got involved in the design and construction of another small structure. This was conceived as a piece of urban furniture providing users adaptive opportunities for controlling sun and wind by moving the structure's constituent

elements. The moving parts allow users to vary the proportion of the sky dome that is obstructed or exposed as well as expand or contract openings for air movement. The components were made from laminated timber at the AA School's Hooke Park and London workshops. The structure was assembled and exhibited at the Passive and Low Energy Cooling International Conference in Fira and on the main square of the town of Oia in May 2005 *(Figure 5).*

DESIGN RESEARCH

MSc and MArch dissertation projects provide opportunities for design research that reflect the programme's thematic areas as well as candidates' professional interests and backgrounds. The research component of the dissertation project combines literature review with field studies and analytical work. MSc dissertation projects aim to take the results of the research into the formulation of design guidelines for the chosen building type and climatic conditions. On the other hand, MArch dissertations conclude with a design project as an application of the research. The scale of the MArch design projects can vary considerably with context and design brief. Dissertation topics are decided midway in the course following a preparatory period and the submission of a research paper outlining the area of interest. Work on the dissertation research is supported by weekly

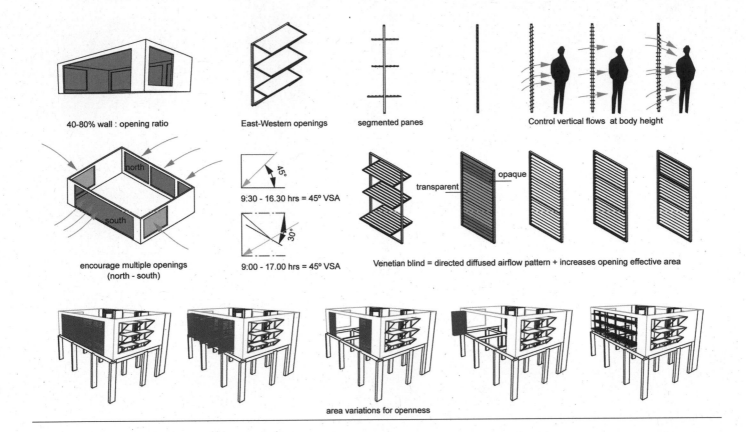

40-80% wall : opening ratio

East-Western openings

segmented panes

Control vertical flows at body height

encourage multiple openings
(north - south)

north

south

45°

9:30 - 16.30 hrs = 45° VSA

30°

9:00 - 17.00 hrs = 45° VSA

transparent

opaque

Venetian blind = directed diffused airflow pattern + increases opening effective area

area variations for openness

Figure 6: Openings, from Michael Smith-Masis' "Design Guidelines for Social Housing in the Warm-Humid Climates of Costa Rica".

seminars and tutorials. Some recent MSc and MArch dissertation projects are presented here to illustrate the range of topics studied.

Streets, squares, rooftops and the transitional spaces by which they are coupled to, or decoupled from, indoor spaces contribute to the unpredictable microclimatic diversity of cities. Field studies undertaken over the last 40 years in different climatic regions and building types show that inhabitants adopt behavioural patterns that help them adapt to prevailing outdoor conditions. In adaptive theory this is expressed as a numerical correlation between the outdoor temperature and the range of indoor temperatures at which occupants feel comfortable when able to make adjustments to their environment, clothing, activity or posture. On the other hand, the use of mechanical cooling appliances tends to weaken this relation, or even decouple indoor and outdoor temperatures altogether. The latter intensifies indoor-outdoor temperature differences, often creating conditions of acute discomfort at the thresholds.[7] When the outdoor temperature is too high and/or where mechanical cooling is to

be provided, convective coupling with the outside is better minimised, but stepped transitions are desirable as they can reduce cooling loads as well as prevent thermal shock. Each year several dissertation projects strive to come to grips with the issues of passive or mixed-mode design in tropical and composite climates. Effective solar protection through shaded openings, thresholds and transitional spaces combined with control over the air permeability of the building envelope provide architectural tools for passive design in those climates and these feature strongly in the projects illustrated below.

DESIGN GUIDELINES FOR SOCIAL HOUSING IN WARM-HUMID REGIONS OF COSTA RICA (LATITUDE 9° 55' N)

This study is notable for its successful translation of research into a visual language of environmental design that can be understood by all those involved in the process of housing provision. Focusing primarily on solar protection, natural ventilation and in improving the use of space in and around dwellings so as to limit or dissipate excess heat,

Top: Figure 7: From Nitin
Bansal's fieldwork and
simulation results for the High
Court site in Chandigarh.
Bottom: Figure 8: Site layout
arrangements, building
sections showing airflow and
temperature snapshots.

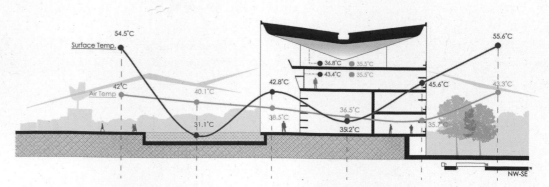

this MSc dissertation project concludes with a rich variety of constructional possibilities drawn from built precedents, the research literature and original analytical work *(Figure 6)*.[8]

LE CORBUSIER IN THE TROPICS

Vernacular and modernist buildings provide a rich source of built precedents for illustrating environmental design concepts and issues. They thus feature regularly as case studies in dissertation projects. A study of some of Le Corbusier's buildings in Chandigarh (Latitude 30° 44' N) observed that the architecture was rooted in the fundamentals of passive design:

"The brise soleil gave a protected permeability as it provided air and light along with protection from the sun. The parasol provides enough shading and

allows ventilation underneath... shaded arcades proved to be effective in reducing (the incidence of) solar radiation on the primary building surface and in providing transition from inside to outside and vice versa" *(Figure 7)*.[9]

On-site measurements and subsequent simulation studies also highlighted the climatic liability of over-reliance on concrete as the main material, a limitation that was especially apparent during the warm-humid period of the year.

LOW-INCOME HOUSING IN BANGKOK (LATITUDE 13° 45' N)

This project combines the study of vernacular precedents with a systematic review of literature and results of parametric studies, aiming to optimise passive design strategies providing adaptive

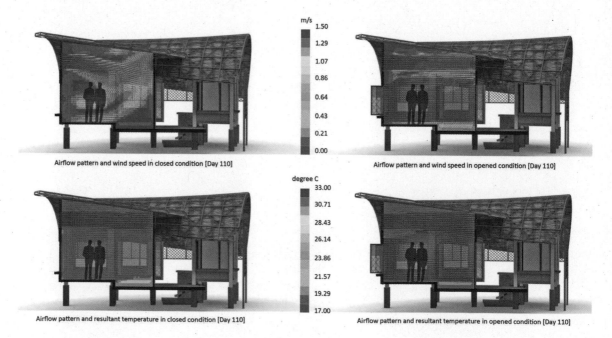

Airflow pattern and wind speed in closed condition [Day 110]

Airflow pattern and wind speed in opened condition [Day 110]

Airflow pattern and resultant temperature in closed condition [Day 110]

Airflow pattern and resultant temperature in opened condition [Day 110]

opportunities to make occupants comfortable. The architectural expression of the scheme is strongly influenced by the environmental strategies adopted (*Figure 8*).[10]

MASS HOUSING IN PUNE (LATITUDE 18° 31' N)

Plan depth is a critical issue for natural lighting as well as ventilation. In this project, plan depth is limited by design to ensure both these function naturally in the context—a dense, multi-residential mass housing scheme.[11] The residual spaces display similar environmental attributes and are landscaped for use as public spaces shared by the surrounding dwelling on each floor. The rigid floor plan of the apartment block is thus eroded, creating semi-outdoor gardens. The scheme underlines the functional and environmental role of transition spaces as an important architectural tool for cultures which have always used such spaces. Thermal simulation studies showed that living spaces in the dwellings could be maintained within comfort range by passive means for the whole year with the exception of the hottest days. Thermal performance of the units is critically dependent on adequate airflow, which is only possible if occupant control is available (*Figure 9*).

HIGH DENSITY LOW ENERGY HOUSING DESIGN AT HIGH LATITUDES

In cool climates at high latitudes, sunshine may be scarce but is almost always welcome. In addition to frequent overcast skies, there is unavoidable overshadowing caused by the urban surroundings as well as a scheme's own architecture. A design challenge resulting from the demand for higher built densities on urban sites is to provide solar access to residential developments where it is most appreciated. Knowledge of solar geometry can help map solar availability across the site as well as over daily and seasonal cycles. The dwelling types and occupancy characteristics required by the design brief can then inform the spatial distribution of living spaces, horizontally and vertically, so that solar access is achieved where and when most needed. Such design aims to combine amenity with whatever energy saving solar gains might provide while also leading

to architectural diversity. Following earlier research, the dissertation project illustrated here focuses on a large brownfield site in the Cork Street area of Dublin (Latitude 53° 20' N), a part of the city which has seen rapid densification of the urban fabric.[12] Starting with a series of solar access studies, run in parallel with calculations of space heating energy requirements to identify potential savings from passive solar gains, the study progressed towards its proposed site layout and built forms following evaluation of the multiple variables involved (*Figure 10*).[13]

URBAN ROOFTOPS

Around the Mediterranean, and at similar latitudes elsewhere, sunshine is abundant, but most urban centres are built to very high densities that limit winter solar access to the upper floors of the urban blocks. Exploiting the potential for passive

Left: Figure 11: Roofscape design proposal by Katerina Pantazi.
Right: Figure 12: Design proposal for urban square by Konstantina Saranti.

and active solar gain where this is available, and finding suitable alternatives where overshadowing prevails, provide the foundation for a range of research strands explored in recent research projects as well as MSc and MArch dissertations. Urban rooftops exhibit microclimatic conditions that are different from those at ground level. Their higher exposure to solar radiation and wind can be exploited as valuable resources. Roofs can be designed in protective ways, to reflect solar radiation and/or provide thermal insulation, but can also be made to act selectively, contributing to passive heating and cooling of buildings.[14] Moreover, study of the roofscape of residential urban blocks in central Athens (Latitude 37° 58' N) has highlighted considerable potential for creating new recreational uses from these currently unused waste spaces.[15] The geometry and microclimatic differentiations of the rooftop environment provided criteria for mapping spots for different activities and for

different users from among the inhabitants of the corresponding buildings (*Figure 11*).

DESIGN OF OUTDOOR SPACES AND URBAN MICROCLIMATES

At ground level, streets, squares and other open spaces are often overexposed to the sun, causing discomfort to pedestrians or those wishing to sit outside in the warm part of the year. Mapping of daily activity on Georgiou Square, a large public space in the centre of Patras, Greece, (Latitude 38° 14' N), provided starting points for a detailed study of possible microclimatic interventions.[16] These included the provision of extensive shaded areas, attention to the solar-optical properties of surrounding surfaces and study of the roles of vegetation and bodies of water (*Figure 12*).

References:

1 For course description see AA Prospectus and for detailed information Programme Guide MSc/MArch Sustainable Environmental Design, Architectural Association School of Architecture, London.

2 The environmental software used for analytical work on the projects illustrated here include Meteotest's Meteonorm v6.1 global meteorological database for weather data, Autodesk Ecotect for shading studies, Gregory Ward Larson's Radiance for daylighting simulations, EDSL Tas and Ambiens for thermal and airflow simulations and Michael Bruse's ENVI-met for urban microclimate modelling.

3 Budd, A, A Leedham, R Rodrigues, M Vitali (2009). *Keeling House*, Building Study. MSc/MArch Sustainable Environmental Design, Architectural Association School of Architecture, London.

4 For recent building studies in London see Yannas, S (2009). "What can buildings tell us, what can we tell back" in Proc. PLEA 2009 Conf. Quebec, pp. 472–477; and for study of outdoor spaces see also Yannas, S (2004). "Adaptive Skins and Microclimates" in Proc. PLEA 2004 Conf. Eindhoven, pp. 217–222.

5 Sabhaney, R (2009). "Knowledge Centre for New Delhi". Spring Term Design Project, MSc/MArch Sustainable Environmental Design, Architectural Association School of Architecture, London.

6 Yannas, S (2007). "Sustainable Design and Architectural Education". *AXIS*, pp. 108–129.

7 Yannas, S (2008). "Challenging the Supremacy of Air Conditioning". *2A Architecture and Art* Special Issue No.7 Gulf Research Project on Sustainable Design, pp. 20–43.

8 Smith-Masis, M (2008). "Design Guidelines for Social Housing in the Warm-Humid Climates of Costa Rica". MSc Dissertation, Sustainable Environmental Design, AA School of Architecture, London.

9 Bansal, N (2009). "'Corbu' in the Tropics: A Study of Environmental Strategies by Le Corbusier in Chandigarh". MSc Dissertation, Sustainable Environmental Design, AA School of Architecture, London.

10 Cholasuek, C (2010). "Sustainable Low Income Community in Bangkok". MArch Dissertation, Sustainable Environmental Design, AA School of Architecture, London.

11 Pandit, A (2010). "Contemporary Indian Housing, Pune, India—Making Use of Transition Spaces as Climatic and Social Mediator". MArch Dissertation, Sustainable Environmental Design, AA School of Architecture, London.

12 Yannas, S (1994). "Solar Energy and Housing Design". AA Publications, London.

13 Bruce, G (2007). "High Density Low Energy". MArch Dissertation, Sustainable Environmental Design, AA School of Architecture, London.

14 Yannas, S, E Erell, J L Molina (2006). *Roof Cooling Techniques—A Design Handbook*. Earthscan, London.

15 Pantazi, K (2010). "Urban Metaphors—Exploring the Urban Roofscape of Athens". MArch Dissertation, Sustainable Environmental Design, AA School of Architecture, London.

16 Saranti, K (2010). "Microclimatic Interventions on an Urban Square in Patras". MArch Dissertation, Sustainable Environmental Design, AA School of Architecture, London.

FROM THEORY TO PRACTICE: ON GREEN DESIGN

MICHAEL MCDONOUGH

INTRODUCTION

I will presage my remarks here by noting that Albert Einstein, a guy who surely knew a bit about theory, believed—and I am paraphrasing here—that if you can't explain your theory in plain language to an average person not involved in your profession, then your theory probably isn't very good. He was a theoretical physicist, of course, and I am an architect—but I agree.

And so I test my theories on taxi drivers. They tend to be savvy, and not too many of them are architects. Well, that often depends on the economy, but let's not belabour the point. Anyway, I call this test the "Taxi Driver Test". The Taxi Driver Test can be summarised as: "If I cannot explain my theory to a taxi driver, it is not worth a damn."

PART ONE: THEORY

So I say to a taxi driver: "Here's my theory: use less energy."

"Why?" says the taxi driver.

"You can save money", I say.

"Oh", he says, "I thought you were going to give me a big speech about saving the planet."

"I am", I said, "but I thought it would be better if I got you roped-in on the money thing."

"Well", he says, "I got kids and they are all about the planet being saved and the quality of their lives hanging in the balance, so I get that part. But I am a businessman, so I like numbers. You got some numbers?"

"Yes", I said. "Here are some numbers:"

"As you know, most of the energy we use is from fossil fuels, and that messes up our air, biodiversity, oceans, food, economies, geopolitics, and health…."

"But we need it to live", he says. "It is the foundation of our civilisation."

"Yes, we do, and it is, but we waste over 90 per cent of that fossil fuel energy", I say. "So we lose multiple times. We waste scarce resources and we damage the environment up to the point of no return, the industrialised nations have large armies wherever there are fuel reserves, food riots ensue and transportation workers go on strike when fuel prices spike, and all the rest: it is all linked."

"90 per cent?" he says. "How so?"

"Let me give you one simple example", I say. "Let's look at one light bulb in your house. First, you are only getting 40 per cent of the electrical energy you are paying for into your wall outlet. That is because 60 per cent is lost in transmission, noise and light energy travelling from the plant to you. After that the light bulb, if it is a conventional tungsten bulb, uses only five per cent of the energy it consumes to make light. So you are getting use of five per cent of 40 per cent of the power that is being put into the system so that you can, for example, read your electric bill, so that is…."

"Two per cent efficiency," he says "I am pretty good at running the numbers in my head with the fares and all. But what about my cab's fuel use? Am I the bad guy here because I have to drive you, Mr Architect, to the airport?"

"Transportation is about a quarter of the problem, but it is the sector everyone likes to focus on. You might be bad or not, but I and my fellow architects and engineers and others in the building sector are arguably worse."

"How come?" he says, looking at me in the rear view mirror.

"In actuality, it is buildings that are the real energy hogs, using about half of all energy consumed on the planet, and they waste up to 90 per cent of that. So it's not you as much as it is me, the architect, who should be worrying more about the problem."

"Proportionally, is it more your problem?" he asks.

"Right", I say, "and there is more that we architects can do that is fairly simple. Take lighting as an example. I can specify a dimmer where tungsten bulbs are used, specify super energy efficient LED bulbs and fixtures, emphasise daylighting, and have a control system that automatically turns the lights off when a room is empty. All that stuff works and, depending on your choices, you can gain back 90 per cent or more of your losses from the outlet to the bulb. The power plant part is more complex, but there are ways to get at that as well."

"Public policy?", he says.

"Right," I say, "and producing power on your roof top, and so forth. But that is not the Holy Grail here. It is not solar power, or wind power, or what have you, which are about producing energy. It is about reducing demand. That is where the 90 per cent saving is lurking—in the demand."

"So, use less energy is your thing?" he says. "But if it's not primarily in the light bulbs because we are messing with percentages of what is actually something like two per cent of the problem, and the power plants are hard to get at as an issue because they represent a significant extant infrastructure, where is it specifically?"

"You are pretty quick on the uptake", I said.

"I got some college", he said. "But, you know, the economic dislocations of late phase capitalism and all that…."

"Right, well, let's compare energy consumption related to heating and cooling in a typical modern glass high rise building to energy consumption in an ancient stone hut. How much better, more energy efficient, would you think the modern steel, glass, and computer modelled technological marvel is compared to the simple stone-on-stone hut?", I asked.

"I don't know", he said. "As a guess, I would say something like it's five times better. After all, it has got a lot of smart guys working on it. Plus there are laws and codes, and that green building thing, that LEED thing, I think it's called. You get tax breaks and stuff for it."

"They are exactly the same in terms of efficiency", I said.

"Or inefficiency", he said.

"Precisely", I said. "And because we are running out of easy-to-access petroleum, a prime source of fossil fuel energy, and because coal is a significant source of ground, air and water contamination, our global energy demand relating to buildings looks a bit like burning a nasty candle at both ends. When you add up the costs of fighting international resource wars, accelerating climate change, collapsing the ocean's bio-systems and species extinction at a rate of three species per hour,

it seems very inefficient indeed. And that inefficiency will very shortly irreversibly impact our ability to survive as an industrialised global culture."

"That guy, James Lovelock, the guy who invented the Gaia hypothesis, the idea that Earth is a self-regulating super-organism, he says that it's already over for civilisation as we know it", he said. "He thinks that when the Earth pushes back at us something like 80 per cent of humans will perish from starvation, disease and war by 2100 as the result of climate change."

"Yes, well, not everyone agrees, but I think we both get the drift here. It isn't good", I said.

"Hey, 90 per cent waste is bad business", he said. "So where do we go from here, theoretically, Mr Architect?"

"Theoretically, medium- to long-term, the sun", I said. "The sun provides us with thousands of times more clean and green energy than we need to run Earth. The numbers relating to available energy are 89,000 terawatts from the sun, 370 terawatts from wind, which is a by-product of hot and cold temperatures produced by the sun on Earth, versus 15 terawatts of demand. You also have bio-fuel and hydroelectric power and other alternative sources, but the big picture is that the non-fossil fuel energy is there if we can harness it. And we have many of the technologies we need to harvest that clean, green energy right now, today."

"You sound like a supply-sider", he said.

"Not really", I said. "After over 40 years of green building advocacy and practice, 'clean and green' energy is only about seven per cent of all energy produced, only five per cent of that seven per cent is related to solar and wind. The US has six per cent of the world's population and still uses 24 per cent of its energy; green buildings comprise only about five per cent of all new buildings and less than one per cent of all new and existing buildings in the US; and if you measure energy use in buildings using a real metric such as watts/square metre/year in the US it has actually gone up over the past few years. So LEED and the green building movement and solar and wind power have, to date, actually done nothing to reduce energy consumption in buildings."

"And that is half the battle", he said. "And you guys, all of us really, are losing it."

"Right", I said.

"So what are you saying? That we are we all doomed?" he said.

"No, I am saying that our emphasis needs correcting, that we architects really need to get the job done. Look, in the absence of truly energy-efficient buildings and viable, widely available alternative energy solutions that meet demand, we continue to turn to fossil fuels for energy, because

1. They are available and portable
2. They are cheap, at least relative to first costs
3. They work anywhere and all the time
4. They pack a lot of energy.

Specifically, on that last 'pack a lot of energy' point, a single barrel of oil provides energy equal to 25,000 man hours of labour for what is, after all is said and done, a relatively small amount of money. And because alternative energy has availability, intermittency, cost, durability and efficiency issues, using fossil fuels like oil remains a very seductive proposition. Unfortunately, that oil won't last much longer as an available and cheap fuel source, and the longer term consequences are disastrous.

Meanwhile the green design advocates like to tell everyone that we have all this free sun and wind energy, and it is easy to just switch over. But that isn't right either. There really are technological issues. Both sides of the equation are attractive in their way and both sides have issues—neither can meet demand. Fact is, no matter what fuel type you choose, you cannot produce your way out of a problem where waste is 90 per cent of the problem.

So we should stop wasting 90 per cent of what we have left or can produce. We should use less energy...."

"OK, I get it", he said.

"… and that is my theory", I said.

He drove quietly for a while, and then turned around and asked me "How did you figure out that theory?"

I smiled.

"Practice", I said.

PART TWO: PRACTICE

"You see," I went on, "it didn't come to me all at once. I had been thinking about the problem for about 30 years, starting way back when I was in architecture school. I studied a lot of other stuff along the way: art, poetry, materials, industrial design, language, culture, science, technology. And around ten years ago I had an idea for a house that could mash-up all that knowledge, turning it into something useful. It would show people how to make small changes in their lives to effect big changes in the world around them. That was the idea, and it started as a sketch on paper.

I called it e-House.

Its organising principle was rooted in ideas revolving around science and nature. It fascinates me that both ancient Eastern mysticism and modern Western physics have both tended to the idea that reality is ultimately unknowable and that our basic physiology as human beings colours how we see, experience, and ultimately define that unknowable", I said.

"It's that 'the observer alters the observed' idea, right?" he said.

"Sort of", I said. "For me it seems that the idea of 'science' is one way to observe the world, and that the idea of 'nature' is another way to observe the world. They meet up in technology, which draws on both worlds; it is part science and part nature. After all, both science and nature claim to describe the universe, so they have to overlap somewhere", I said.

"And for you it was in this e-House?" he asked.

"Yes. The house relates strongly to the always-changing but ever-constant patterns of sunrise and sunset. You can see the light of dawn and dusk from every major room, but the sun's movement and the moon's cycle make the house seem different every day and night. That way you experience the benefits of what is called circadian rhythm, the patterns of light from dawn to darkness to dawn again each day, the light that we evolved with as a species. One big section of the house hangs off the southeast corner of the centre mass of the building to catch the first light and passive solar heat of dawn—the 'Light Catcher'. Another hangs off the northwest, to catch a wonderful view of a verdant

green meadow, the 'View Catcher. That is the technology of nature.

The e-House also has the technology of science: basically a lot of machines that help the house make productive use of the energy that is all around it to create an ideal indoor environment on a minimal energy budget. The centre of the house is a sort of block with a big stair cut into it. It completes a journey from the ground, through the house, and ultimately to the ambiguous sky. The house elevates you, physically and spiritually. You feel that connection to the sky, the dome of heaven.

At first, the idea was to simply find everything I needed to build e-House online: The House that Google Built. I loved the idea that you could construct a very forward-looking building using what was readily available. I liked the idea that you could drop-ship the future. I also wanted to explore the idea that we had, as a technological society, developed solutions for most of our energy problems, but that the experience required to gather them into one project was lacking. That was my mission: to get the best of the best from an environmental and energy perspective into one house.

Initially, in 1999, I spent a year researching, contacting and visiting over 100 of the most advanced green building product manufacturers, fellow professionals, environmentalists and scientists in the world, and then created a website and used it as a forum for the participation of that community in conceptualising the house. It was a prototypical blog in a way; a blog before there were blogs; an open source project cloud", I said.

"I follow you", he said. "Social networking with a productive end in mind."

"I started to build e-House in upstate New York in summer of 2000, reporting the results of that process though a series of articles, email exchanges, site tours, online videos, slide shows, interviews, documentary films and international exhibitions, lectures, and seminars over a period of five years. The project got its share of recognition. I completed the building to the point that it could be lived-in and monitored, and we tested a lot of technologies that are now becoming more and more common: near laminar flow balanced displacement ventilation, high thermal mass in-floor hydronic radiant heat, superefficient

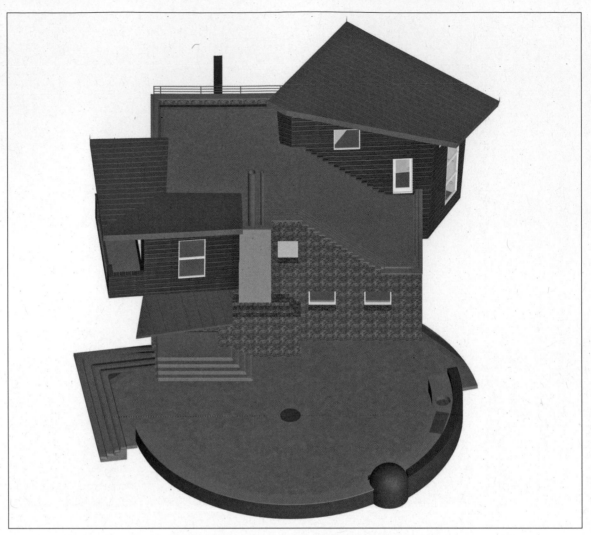

e-House isometric rendering showing western aspect, outdoor kitchen and terrace, and recreational roof details.

bio-mass supplemental heat, daylighting, passive solar heating and advanced lighting controls."

"It sounds like you became a sort of green geek", he said.

"We were testing all this stuff in a climate that can be as cold as Moscow, as warm as Cairo, as humid as Hong Kong, as dry as the Negev, as windy as Boston and has tornadoes, hurricanes and more snow than Alaska. We demonstrated that a well-designed and well-constructed house in a wide range of climates could reduce energy consumption by 50 per cent just by carefully selecting materials, systems, and controls and assembling them carefully, and that felt pretty good. It turned out that you could get the most benefit from paying attention to the way the walls, windows and doors were put together. It was that simple. God was in the detailing, to paraphrase Mies van der Rohe", I said.

"I don't know who that is", said the taxi driver. "But I get the gist of it. It is about the barrier the house forms between inside and outside. Like a car. So then what happened?"

"As I was building e-House, I learned more and more about the possibilities of going beyond energy conservation to what is called 'net-zero energy', the idea that the building uses no more energy than it can produce on site averaged over a year. So I stopped in year five of construction and began to experiment with net zero energy and zero carbon footprint systems, and to invent new technologies to make them feasible.

So I looked anew at all the different climate and energy aspects of the spot where e-House is located, all the problems and opportunities, and tried to match them up in a matrix—to study the genius loci, the 'genius of the place'."

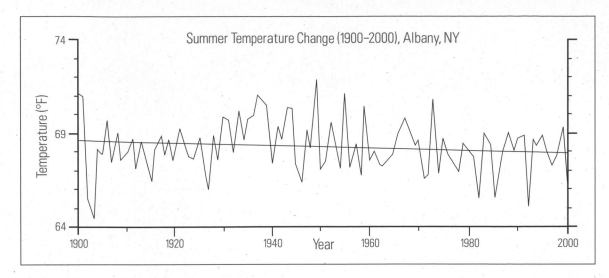

"New York State has that extreme climate you mentioned: record low of -46°C (-52°F); record high of 42°C (102°F). Some genius of a place", he said.

"It depends on how you look at it", I said. "It is all just energy and all energy is from the sun. There is sun energy in the atmosphere, in the ground, in the earth's rotation, in the water cycle of evaporation, condensation and phase change and in the plants and animals and how they work as bio- and eco-systems.

If you think of energy as just watts per square metre per year, it gets boring fast. Like if the only thing you knew about a car was its miles per gallon rating. But if you think, well, how would an artist or poet look at energy, you could see it in a new way."

"Like what way?" he asks.

"Well, in unexpected ways. I looked at the climate and ordinary objects around me in unexpected ways. New York is very humid—up to 100 per cent relative humidity in the summer—and the average annual temperature is 10°C (50°F), which is also the temperature of the ground water. This is also the temperature you need to dehumidify and air condition your house, about 10°C (50°F). Essentially, I figured out, the climate that makes your glass of iced tea sweat in New York in August is a possible way to air condition your house. So when I asked 'How is an iced tea like a house?' the unexpected answer was that they both relate to air conditioning.

The thing is, you normally expend a lot of energy to get that 10°C or 50°F by using an air conditioner—and air conditioners are energy hogs, using four times more energy to cool than to heat the same space. They also don't dehumidify very well, so you can get mould and mildew and feel cold and clammy. So you spend all your money on air conditioning and get a mouldy basement and a summer cold."

"That I know", he said. "My brother-in-law in Florida has to run his heater and air conditioner at the same time for part of the year just to keep the house from mildewing."

"At e-House we looked at the problem in that unexpected way", I said. "I looked at the energy in the sweating iced tea glass carefully. I found out that most of the energy in air conditioning—70 per cent of it—is used to overcome the heat stuck in the high humidity air. This is the same high humidity air that forms as water, or condenses, on the outside of your iced tea glass. And the iced tea glass actually does a better job, a more energy efficient job, of dehumidifying than a conventional air conditioner.

So, with the support of New York State, we built what was conceptually a long, twisting tube of iced tea, a coil, which is sort of like the radiator in your car. We stuck it in the house's ventilation duct and connected it to a well and pumped well water through the coil. We eventually found that the house could be made comfortable using less than half the energy of a conventional air conditioning system. My team calculated that if the system were commercialised and broadly adopted, it would eliminate most of energy used by air conditioning for two thirds of the population of Earth", I said.

"So, what else?" he asked.

"We also developed a three-part design approach to net-zero energy/zero-carbon buildings based on e-House. It says that if you have well-insulated high thermal mass walls and roof and balanced ventilation with energy recovery, you can use on-site alternative energy cost-effectively and achieve net-zero energy/zero-carbon buildings now. Without getting too technical, you can buy all this stuff now and build market rate projects that tend toward net zero-energy/zero-carbon buildings. New Jersey, which has weather that is almost as extreme as New York's, adopted this three-part approach into its State Energy Policy in 1999. Now we are designing pilot and proof of concept projects there.

One of the tricks learned from e-House involves using a product called autoclaved aerated concrete (AAC), which is basically concrete posing as limestone, for the building's walls. It is just like the limestone you have had here in Jerusalem for 3000 years. AAC makes heat energy do a U-turn before it can get into the building, and saves 50 per cent or more of the energy you would normally use. Essentially the walls become a functioning part of the heating and air conditioning system.

We are also developing net-zero energy/zero-carbon agriculture at e-House. We are working with people from the United Nations Food and Agriculture Organisation, a series of manufacturers, farmers, a university and, again, New York State. Through this project we will develop self-watering, passively cooled, peak energy reducing growing environments that eliminate all weather-related losses.

The system is planned to provide fresh local produce at e-House while eliminating 60–80 per cent of all irrigation demand, and providing four double-crop seasons per year. The crops are organic, and require no tillage or nitrogen-based fertilizers. Yields are projected to produce ten times the equivalent of conventionally grown crops on any given parcel of land, thereby freeing 90 per cent of the land for other sustainable uses. I see sustainable agriculture as an integral part of future housing design.

This system is fully portable and can be deployed on any number of locations: an urban roof top, a brownfield, exhausted agricultural land, a suburban plot, a shopping mall parking lot and any number of other sites. Modules can be as small as eight metres square or as big as eight metres by 60 metres or more. High efficiency LED grow lights that run on power from solar electric photovoltaic systems make sunlight optional, and allow for the extended growing seasons", I said.

"I get it", said the taxi driver. "Your 'Use Less Energy' theory was tested in practice at this little house and now its starting to have some impact. Pretty nice. You got anything else?"

"Well, I am working on a poem for my friends and colleagues at the symposium I am travelling to now", I said.

"Take a shot", he said.

BUILD AND BE

The same thought and syllable
Uttered by that upright apish man
Or man-ish ape so many years ago
Expressing thought beyond its brutish needs
By lips and tongue
Beyond the mere grunt—
Here was intent, you see:
I am and think and build,
And then: homo sapiens,
The Knowing Ape
As we call
Both you and me.

So it began.
Stone on stone,
And self-awareness,
Farming, trade,
And linear time itself.
And right and wrong
(As if we've got that straight).

Ba, the linguists claim,
Was that very sound
In Proto-Indo-European utterance.
Remembered now, perhaps,
In the German Bau and
English Build and Be
(As I have noted at the top).

For as we build
And what we build
We are.

ORGAN TRANSPLANTS IN ELECTRONICS

DOMINIC MUREN

HOW LESSONS FROM FOODIES AND KIDNEYS WILL HELP USERS TAKE BACK CONTROL OF TECHNOLOGY

Consumer electronics is one of the most valuable market sectors worldwide. In 2008, the US cellphone market was $2.4 billion, according to a study published by market research group NPD. This puts the cellphone market in the US ahead of the GDP of 30 countries. Though popular and useful, these products pack incredible negative environmental impact. Despite the best efforts of talented designers, changing the size, cost, material or durability of these devices has done little to mitigate their impact. Electronics remains among the most tenacious contributors to toxic waste. For example, in the United States in 2006 consumer electronics accounted for 70 per cent of heavy metals in landfills, but only two per cent of total landfill waste, and are among the most energy intensive objects we know how to make— one kilogram of laptop requires almost 100 times as much energy to make as one kilogram of wood, and ten times as much as one kilogram of aluminium. They remain among the shortest lived products—the average American cellphone lifespan is 18 months, less than that of most T-shirts. As product designers fail to address these problems with superficial solutions like bamboo laptop sleeves and corn plastic housings, the answer to the world's e-waste problem may be found in the work of an Italian foodie.

THE SLOW FOOD EFFECT

In 1986, an event took place which would shake the world. A small group of Italians gathered near the Piazza di Spagna in Rome, waving bowls of penne pasta in protest. They were united in opposition to a McDonald's restaurant planned to be built nearby. From this first protest grew Slow Food, an international movement focused on counteracting "fast food and fast life, the disappearance of local food traditions and people's dwindling interest in the food they eat, where it comes from, how it tastes and how our food choices affect the rest of the world". Slow food operates on the principle that informed consumption of locally produced foods has significant positive consequences for the health of farmers, eaters, communities, eco-systems and economies. And it is working. Slow food has been a major force

behind the growth in availability of organic fruits and vegetables, non-intensively grazed livestock and whole foods. More importantly, it has re-opened the conversation between farmers and chefs, butchers, bakers, greengrocers and homemakers about what types of foods are good, and what costs— environmental, nutritional, social and economical—are affordable. Because of slow food, and organisations like it, customers have a voice in what the marketplace should provide for them, not only in terms of products, but consequences.

Humans are the tool maker, and while other animals might make and use tools, no other creature so completely alters their local environment—even their local culture—through the tools they make. And no other animal's tools have such far-reaching side effects resulting from their production. Considered in this way Slow Food advocates not only local food, but local consciousness and intention in all products which affect our lives. Put another way, Slow Food advocates local production in general, and the positive consequences of enabling conversations between makers and users of things.

THE LIE OF ELECTRONICS RECYCLING

Almost no product is further from local production than the average computer. Take a laptop sold in Seattle, in the United States. Shipped over on a boat, it was most likely assembled in Southern Asia. At this factory, electronic components were gathered from around Asia, Eastern Europe, North America and Russia. These components—chips, capacitors, resistors, wires—almost definitely contained minerals from Australia, Africa, Russia, South America and Asia. That computer represents the end of one of the longest, most complex supply chains on Earth. Part of the massive energy embodied in a laptop comes from this collection process—just getting all these components together from all over the world requires a mammoth effort. However, these are also complicated components themselves. The balance of embodied energy comes from organising the incredibly complicated structures within these components. Even the simplest parts like a resistor or capacitor might consist of ten to 20 different materials, all arranged precisely to provide the right function. More complex parts like batteries or hard drives might have hundreds of components, often layered in microscopically thin stacks or arrays. And the most complicated parts—processors, RAM or image sensors—might have billions or even trillions of individual transistors, minutely carved into silicon or metal films by light and acid. Each of these objects stands in direct violation of the second law of thermodynamics—that the disorder of a system must generally increase. Of course, those familiar with entropy know that it can be reversed by applying energy, and this is exactly why creating these highly ordered objects requires so much energy. The energy required to make a laptop, or any piece of consumer electronics, goes primarily to informing rough matter with the order which makes it an electronic component.

Once this fact is understood, current electronics recycling programmes seem much less effective. Electronics recycling is already maligned as a result of dishonest and dangerous practices. For example, despite international laws banning the practice, large amounts of electronic waste are shipped to China, India and Africa, where lax regulations allow dangerous reclamation practices.

But even if this grind-and-reclaim recycling is executed safely, there is still a significant loss. If a computer is ground and pulverized as generally happens during recycling, and all elemental components are safely recovered, the order within the components is lost. This is a little like thinking that a pig could be made into sausages and then somehow made back into a pig again. This is obviously ridiculous—the order that let the pig walk and squeal is simply gone. Every time a computer is ground up, melted down and re-processed into new computers, the energy needed to re-order these components on a microscopic level must be spent again. Over time, this energy usage adds up to a real expense. This is felt by the computer customer, who pays the same for a computer which uses recycled parts as for a 'virgin' one. Perhaps more importantly, it is felt by the environment, for whom energy spending nearly always means greenhouse gas emissions and accelerated climate change.

So electronics recycling doesn't work, because it destroys the order invested into existing electronics at a high energy cost. Localised manufacturing isn't possible, because the manufacturing infrastructure needed to impart that order to matter is too large, expensive, dangerous and unsightly to locate within communities. Futurists envision a world where technologies like molecular printers using carbon (which is almost infinitely available everywhere on Earth) will make recycling and printing of everything, including electronics, almost breathlessly simple. But that future is far off. What can be done today? A solution to both problems can be found by re-examining the previously stated problem of making sausages into pigs.

As pointed out before, sausages have lost some fundamental essence of pig which cannot be regained. But why should it be lost? In fact, humans re-arrange organisms all the time—many readers may have organs within their bodies which are not theirs. Hearts, livers, kidneys, even bone marrow, can all be transplanted thanks to nature's modularity. Rather than being one unified mass of intermingled cells, animals' guts are separated into functional units.

Nature understands that it is the complex structure of a heart or lung which is difficult to replicate, and so it keeps these designs intact, even across species. In order for consumer electronics to retain the order they contain, modularity of a similar kind must be introduced. This would, in turn, provide multiple advantages for local manufacture, repair and customisation. A modular framework for building electronics should be informed by nature's methods for arranging modules to form an organism.

SKIN/SKELETON/GUTS

One such modular framework is the Skin Skeleton Guts (SSG) system for building electronic devices. By adapting the best parts of nature's structural organisation, electronics built in this way can gain serious modularity and flexibility, while staying achievable. All animals derive their functionality from a collection of guts. The specifics of these guts determine what an animal may eat, how it thinks, how fast and far it can run, how it sleeps and reproduces. Each of the gut components is specialised and grouped together to fit within the overall shape of the animal. Connections between organs are flexible in the extreme—often the organs themselves are also flexible. This is by design, since the organism must move, and during movement the organs themselves slide, bump and shift against one another. A solid, brittle animal wouldn't last long.

Electronics could likewise be arranged into functional modules, connected by a shared bus, in the same way that USB peripherals can be added to a computer or video cards added to the motherboard of a computer. A device like a cellular phone might include a module for processing data, a module for charging a battery with a battery on board, a module for controlling the device (for example, a touchpad), a module with a cellular modem and a module with screen and control software. These modules would need to be flexible in their functionality to enable maximum compatibility with other modules. In order to achieve this, each module would be re-programmable with new firmware to allow differential functionality and communication with other modules. Like real organs, these blade-like modules would be constructed using flexible circuit boards so that they could be re-arranged to fit a variety of potential device configurations.

Guts, whether in animals or electronics, are fragile and need protection. Guts need form; giraffes and horses might have similar guts, but their skeletons give them vastly different functional form. However, this form must not be rigid. As with guts, non-moving animals don't get very far.

SSG electronics have skeletons of solid material which are located together by sets of protrusions and depressions, rather than by screws or glue. As with natural bones, this allows the skeleton to jostle in a fall, and avoid fracture, while protecting the guts components from damage. Likewise, solid bones help protect the guts from sharp objects like pens, and coins in pockets. The simple shape of individual bones within a skeleton lends itself to a variety of means of fabrication from 3-D models. Bones might be printed on a 3-D printer from plastic, or, if local labour was cheap enough, carved from wood. In the phone concept shown, the skeleton is printed from a translucent photo-cured resin on a 3-D printer. Different skeletons might give similar collections of guts vastly different functionality.

Skeletons derive their flexibility by being held together by a skin of stretchable, flexible material—

ligaments, tendons and an outer protective skin. This skin gives aesthetic beauty to the collection of an organism. Again, horses and giraffes may have different skeletal forms, but it is their skin coloration which is most visible and memorable. The skin also gives functional qualities. Basic smoothing of the skeleton allows a human to carry a backpack on what would normally be a very sharp, awkward skeleton. Abrasion resistance, stickiness and optical properties like reflection or transparency might all be provided by a skin.

The Skins in SSG products act in place of the glue or screws, holding the skeleton together firmly but flexibly, so that broken skeletal parts are much less likely—small plastic parts generally break at the screw, hinge or snaps. In addition, the skin gives the final aesthetic finish, colour and smoothes the underlying skeletal form—and any imperfections of the bone fabrication process. Since they are sewn from low cost sheet materials like leather, fabric and synthetic non-woven films, skins can be replaced cheaply and easily, either to give a worn product a new finish or to achieve a new styling without discarding all the value embodied in the guts and skeleton.

Products made in this way achieve radical modularity with current technology. This modularity allows for remixing of modules into entirely new functional configurations. Such remixing is theoretically possible using existing manufacturing, but few people can participate since the infrastructure required to make an electronic device with a monolithic circuit board and injection moulded plastic case is large, inflexible and very expensive. The SSG framework is optimised for maximum participation via small-scale local fabricators at every level.

DESIGNED TO BE REMIXED

This optimisation for participation can be seen well in the Makerwatch SSG prototype. Each of the SSG levels—skin, skeleton and guts—is editable using widely available or easily accessed tools.

The skin becomes obsolete most rapidly, either through wear or through the march of fashion. Accordingly, it is made from low cost fabric or other sheet material and sewn on a standard sewing machine—one of the most widely available fabrication machines on Earth. All communities have either tailors or hobbyists capable of producing a skin. The files describing a skin are also the easiest to create, share and output, since they are simple 2-D patterns which can be edited with ubiquitous image editors or on paper in the absence of computers. Patterns can be output physically by laser cutting fabric, printing a paper pattern for cutting or tracing a paper pattern for cutting. In this way, maximum participation in generating new skin shapes or patterns can be carried out locally.

The skeleton is designed to resist breaking and will not need to be replaced as often as the skin. This allows it to be slightly more complex to edit or reproduce, which would require 3-D model editing skills and access to a computer. These skills are widely distributed among young people in the developed world, who use them to edit characters of video games—and this literacy is growing. Sharing of skeleton parts is facilitated by sites like Thingiverse.com, Google Warehouse and other file repositories. Output of these files is easily possible if access to a 3-D printer is available. If such devices are rare, then service bureaux like Shapeways.com and Ponoko.com will print or cut skeletal parts from uploaded files.

The guts are the most complicated component to design and fabricate. In fact, they are the only component which would still benefit from mass production, at least until printable electronics assemblies become more feasible. Thus, if various modules were mass produced, but could be re-programmed individually and re-combined in different configurations for different overall functionality, the process of re-mixing guts would still be accessible to anyone with a computer and collection of modules. Even re-mixers who weren't adept at programming might download firmware from internet repositories to upload to their modules. Even with mass production, sharing the designs of individual modules as open source specifications online would allow small-scale producers to produce runs of modules using pick-and-place machines or online services at close to competitive prices.

At this point it is worth noting that open specifications —for software, hardware, 3-D and 2-D models—are crucial to the success of a model like this. Products which do not have openly published descriptions of their manufacture and operation benefit from this secrecy by creating an artificial monopoly on production. While the sales of these products may be lucrative in the short term, proprietary products are by their nature incompatible with competitors' products, so re-mixable modules would be impossible.

If, on the other hand, these same products were fully open in their description and methods of construction, they become more valuable if more of their competitors share the same standards—the more available modules, the more opportunities there are for realising any conceivable design. Furthermore, by building a rich eco-system of potential modules, manufacturers might sacrifice some profits in the near term in exchange for a more loyal customer base in the long-term.

AN ECO-SYSTEM OF PARTS

Perhaps the most compelling attribute of an SSG-based product system is this increased possibility for re-using components rather than recycling them. Modern electronics recycling wastes the complex order embodied in electronic assemblies, and the energy it took to inform matter with that order. In contrast, SSG-based product assemblies can be dissolved into their component modules and reconstituted into entirely new products without significant energy inputs.

For example, as previously suggested, a point-and-shoot camera might be changed into a more feature-rich camera by simply housing the same guts collection in a larger, more holdable and stable skeleton and skin. The file of this skeleton might be flexibly defined such that it would be printed with a variety of bayonet mounts to accept different professional lenses.

In another example, the cellular phone described above might be converted into a wirelessly connected e-reader. With the addition of new battery and screen modules and a new skeleton and skin, a device which was no longer needed could contribute the bulk of its components (and embodied energy) to a newly useful device. Additionally, if the unused modules from the old phone were still functional, they would likely find buyers in a used-module marketplace —perhaps e-Bay.

Such production models are already being explored, if only in the most cursory way. Desktop computers have long separated their functional components—motherboard, graphics card, sound card, hard drives—in order to allow for specialisation and the functional improvement that comes with it.

Some companies are even going so far as to create collections of interchangeable electronic modules which are very much like the guts described in SSG. Liquidware offers an extensive line of 'shields' which are compatible with the Arduino micro-controller board and another group of boards which interface with the Beagleboard microcomputer. All these devices are open-source and specifications are freely available for them, giving their community of users much more flexibility in their implementation. Open hardware modules like these have given rise to a vibrant community of hardware hackers and makers, creating novel devices which are too specific to be economically viable for mass production, but nevertheless meet real user needs.

THE FUTURE IN AN SSG WORLD

A global economy based a modular, re-mixable, openly described manufacturing method like SSG would be fundamentally different from the one we live in today. The central feature of such a world would be a global cloud of open source product module descriptions. In much the same way that cloud computing is poised to change the way that people interface with information, this new world would allow cloud manufacturing. Products could be crystallised as needed from this cloud of potential modules, either by printing them from raw materials or assembling them from collections of existing reprogrammable modules.

In this world, the very concept of a product would change. Even today, technology is a result of a conversation (however one-sided) between inventors who dictate what is possible and users who dictate what is desirable. Products today are static, dead objects, set in their ways, out of touch with the conversation and waiting to become obsolete. SSG products crystallised from the global cloud would be frozen moments from this on-going conversation, as up-to-date as their user desired. As this local

conversation shifted and the product became inadequate, it could be dissolved and re-crystallised into a new form, relevant and functional within a new conversational context. In this new economy, 'consumers' would no longer exist—rather, users would be important participants in defining the directions that the development of the global object cloud would take.

The global nature of this information cloud is worth emphasising. Traditional notions of 'developed' and 'developing' world would be invalid. Rather, since all manufacturers would share access to the same set of potential module descriptions, the technological development of a local region would depend more on what objects were appropriate based on local culture, materials, manufacturing methods and functional needs. In addition to stemming the loss of cultural diversity that comes with global product homogenisation and marketing, this localised manufacturing model would improve regional resilience in the face of natural and political disasters like hurricane or war.

Most importantly, the SSG model works within existing free-market economies. Open design of objects doesn't mean that objects are free—matter still matters. In fact, the differences in the experience of buying a phone or camera in this new economy might be unnoticeable. But rather than creating a selection of different cameras by over-producing cameras, SSG allows retailers to produce cameras on demand, to fit the exact specifications of the user. Likewise, camera users need not invest in the functionality of a new camera only to throw it away when they upgrade.

Perhaps the most tantalising image that might become commonplace in an SSG-based economy would be of the high school graduate preparing to head off to university. Gathering toys and games accumulated over years of childhood, she sets out, not to the thrift store to donate them, but to her local SSG tailor who will work with her to re-crystallise these old parts and some new ones into a computer suitable for her new life of study. In this future, she is not a consumer of technology, but a master of it. She—and everyone else in this future—can finally reclaim their birthright as humans: to be the toolmakers.

BIOGRAPHIES

KEN YEANG

Dr Ken Yeang is an architect-planner, ecologist and author best known for his signature and innovative green buildings and masterplans. He is regarded as one of the foremost designers and a noted authority on ecologically-responsive architecture and planning. He has authored several books on ecological design and tall building design, the latest being *Ecodesign: Manual for Ecological Design*.

He has pioneered the passive low-energy design of tall buildings, which he calls the 'bioclimatic skyscraper' and has received numerous awards for his work including the Aga Khan Award for Architecture, RAIA International Award, Prinz Claus Award and UIA Auguste Perret Award. His built works include the Menara Mesiniaga Tower (Malaysia), the National Library (Singapore) and the Great Ormond Street Hospital Extension (UK).

He is an Honorary Fellow of the American Institute of Architects, past Chairman of ARCASIA and has served on the Royal Institute of Architects Council. He is the distinguished Plym Professor at the University of Illinois and Adjunct Professor at the University of Hawaii and University of Malaya. He is a principal of the UK architecture and planning firm, Llewelyn Davies Yeang and its sister company, Hamzah & Yeang (Malaysia).

ARTHUR SPECTOR

Arthur Spector completed his preliminary education in architecture at Rensselaer Polytechnic Institute in Troy, New York. He travelled to Israel for a one year work fellowship and decided to remain there. He formed his primary partnership of Arthur Spector, Michael Amisar, Architects in 1972.

In 1992 he initiated, together with the Rothschild Foundation, The Jerusalem Seminar in Architecture. In 1996, Rizzoli published an anthology of the first three seminars called "Technology, Place & Architecture" which he edited together with Professor Ken Frampton.

Spector Amisar has focused primarily on the planning and implementation of public buildings. More recently, he formed together with Arie Shauer, Spector Amisar Shauer (SAS Architects) for the planning of hospitals and healthcare-related buildings.

The firm masterplanned the Government Precinct in Jerusalem, the Israel Convention Centre and the Israel Museum with Professor Julian Beinart of MIT.

Arthur Spector has won numerous awards including the Rechter Prize for Architecture for both Shaltiel Community Centre in 1987 and Beit Gavriel in 1995. More recently, he has received an AIA Citation for the Davison Medical Tower at Hadassah. He has taught at Bezalel Aademy in Jerusalem and was a Hallmark Fellow at the International Design Conference in Aspen.

MIKE WELLS

Dr Mike Wells is a consultant ecologist and urbanist with almost 30 years' experience of ecological science and 20 years' in environmental private practice. Mike co-founded Biodiversity by Design in 2006 to help promote truly exemplary development projects that enrich local biodiversity, nurture social equity and provide sustainable economic returns. Mike focuses on exploring the 'creative gaps' between disciplines including Architecture, Landscape Architecture, Ecology, Engineering and Art.

Mike is co-author of the UK's guidance on ecological impact assessment, and of many papers and articles on biodiversity, ecologically informed sustainable urban design and ecological masterplanning. He is a long-term external lecturer and Visiting Research Fellow at Bath School of Architecture and Civil Engineering.

Mike is a board member of the UK Landscape Foundation, the Bristol Urban Design Forum and the Technical Implementation Board of the UK's Sustainable Environment Foundation. He is also Chair of the Bath branch of the Wildlife Trusts. He is a regular collaborator with Ken Yeang on development proposals and projects around the world.

FLEUR TIMMER

Beginning a career as a restaurateur in her early twenties, Fleur soon decided to return to her dream of being a designer. Retraining in furniture design, then landscape architecture and urban design, she now works in ecological practice. The fact that she has studied various design disciplines to a high level and chosen to apply these skills to multi-functional eco-urbanism is testament to her keen interest in facilitating much needed collaboration between disciplines to realise truly sustainable development.

The quest for the comprehensive understanding of the bigger picture for the survival of man and nature continues to fascinate Fleur to the extent of further study in the subject of ECO-City planning as the reality of newly created cities upon our world is escalating at great speed. Her special interests lie in vegetated architecture for both roof and facade, the design of hi-tech biodiverse food production areas and water-intelligent landscapes.

ALISTAIR CARR

Alistair Carr is a professional ecologist who has been in environmental practice for nearly twenty years. He joined Biodiversity by Design in 2006, soon after it was established. Before that, he worked in the UK's water industry for over fifteen years where he was involved in pioneering work in the establishment of water quality monitoring systems. He then employed data acquired from such systems to model the effects of proposed urban developments on the aquatic environment.

Alistair now specialises in sustainable urban habitat design and management. He focuses on the use of native and local plants, whether the design relates to a green roof in London or the provision of street shade and dust attenuation in the United Arab Emirates. His work often has a strong additional focus on he selection of non-native planting that is of particular value to native fauna and also provides other urban eco-system goods and services.

MICHAEL PAWLYN

Michael Pawlyn founded Exploration in 2007 to focus on biomimicry—an emerging discipline offering innovative architectural solutions inspired by nature. From 1997–2007 he worked with Grimshaw Architects and was instrumental in the design development of the Eden Project. He was responsible for leading the design of the Biomes and proposals for a third major climatic enclosure. He developed the Grimshaw environmental management system, the company becoming the first architects to achieve certification to ISO14001 in December 2000.

He has lectured widely on sustainable design in the UK and abroad and in May 2005 delivered a talk at the Royal Society of Arts with Ray Anderson, CEO of Interface. In May 2009, he opposed the renowned environmental sceptic, Bjorn Lomborg, at the BCO Conference in Edinburgh.

In 2006, he was appointed to represent Grimshaw as a Founder Member of the UK Green Building Council and in 2007 was elected a committee member of 'The Edge', a think-tank dedicated to addressing important political, social and professional issues.

BERT GREGORY

As CEO of Mithun, Bert Gregory, FAIA has led the firm to national recognition for concept-based, environmentally intelligent design. He is an expert in the development of resource-efficient structures and communities, and serves as a national leader, speaker and advocate for sustainable building and urbanism. His perspective reaches beyond traditional architecture to merge science and design—an interdisciplinary approach that creates lasting places for people. Bert strives to expand the reach of the firm to inspire a sustainable world

through integrated design. Awards include four AIA COTE Top Ten Green Projects, two ASLA national honour awards and the AIA national honour award for regional and urban design. Bert currently serves as Vice-Chair of the USGBC LEED® Neighbourhood Development core committee and the Washington Clean

Technology Alliance steering committee. Mithun is laying the groundwork for a new paradigm of economic development and urban living, ranging from an individual site to a neighbourhood to an entire region.

STEFAN BEHNISCH

Stefan Behnisch studied philosophy and economics in Munich and architecture in Karlsruhe, Germany. He worked as an architect in Behnisch & Partner, the practice founded by his father, before establishing his own practice in 1989.

Stefan Behnisch has been an advocate of sustainable design since he started working as an architect. Many of his buildings received prestigious awards, and the Genzyme Center in Cambridge, MA was rated LEED Platinum.

Marco Polo Tower in Hamburg's Hafen City. Among current projects are the John & Frances Angelos Law Centre for the University of Baltimore and a new building for Amherst College in the USA.

In 2007, Stefan Behnisch received a Global Award for Sustainable Architecture (one of five) and in 2009 a Good Design Award in the category "People" presented by the Chicago Athenaeum and the European Centre for Architecture, Art, Design and Urban Studies. In 2008, he was named Honorary Fellow of the American Institute of Architects. Stefan Behnisch has been the Eero Saarinen Chair Visiting Professor at Yale School of Architecture in 2005, 2006, 2008 and 2009, is Miller Visiting Professor at the University of Pennsylvania, Philadelphia and Harry W Porter Jr. Visiting Professor at the University of Virginia School of Architecture.

DAVID LLOYD JONES

David Lloyd Jones is a founding director of Studio E Architects. Prior to setting up Studio E he was a director of RMJM where his work ranged from research into housing and university standards to commercial centre city development. In the early 1980s he was responsible for the design of the seminal, highly acclaimed, low energy NFU Mutual & Avon Insurance Group's Head Office at Stratford upon Avon. He is an acknowledged expert and innovator in energy conscious and sustainable architecture.

At Studio E, David has led a succession of sustainable projects including the Solar Office Doxford International incorporating, at the time, the largest photovoltaic array anywhere, numerous government sponsored R&D projects, and more recently Beaufort Court, the first commercial zero-emissions building in the world.

Current projects include the Pakistan Islamic Arts Institute in Lahore, a sports centre in Southwark Park, the master planning of the City of London Freemen's School, extensions to Bacon's City Technology College and a pan-European high-insulating window R&D project. He has presented papers at conferences around the world and has contributed to many publications. His book, *Architecture and the Environment*, was published by Lawrence King Publishing and is available in six languages.

He is a member of CABE's School Review Panel, the RIBA Sustainable Futures Forum and a Fellow of the Royal Society of Arts and Science. He guided Studio E to the 2010 Queens Award for Enterprise: Sustainability, only the second architectural practice to win this prestigious accolade.

THOMAS HERZOG

Studied architecture at TUM Technische Universität München, where he received his Diploma in 1965. Herzog was Professor of Architecture at the University of Kassel from 1973, and later in TH Darmstadt, and TUM Technische Universität München. He was Dean of the Faculty of Architecture and 2007 Emeritus of Excellence at TUM and Guest Professor in Lausanne (EPFL), Beijing (TSINGHUA), Philadelphia (PENN) and Copenhagen.

Prof. Herzog founded his own practice in 1971. Since then he has worked jointly with different partners (housing, administration, industrial and exhibition buildings, etc.), since 1994 in partnership with Hanns Jörg Schrade.

Thomas Herzog has won numerous awards for his research work and projects, among which are the Mies van der Rohe Prize, the Gold Medal of the Bund Deutscher Architekten, the Auguste Perret Prize from the International Union of Architects, Den grønne Nål from the Federation of Danish Architects, Grand Médaille d'Or, Académie d'Architecture, Paris, Fritz Schumacher Prize for Architecture and the Leo von Klenze Medal.

JOSEPH CORY

Specialising in innovative design and committed to sustainability, Joseph Cory founded the GEOTECTURA office, which provides creative and practical architectural solutions to social and environmental challenges using multidisciplinary research methods and open source design.

Cory received his diploma from Israel Institute of Technology (Technion) and is currently a senior lecturer and faculty member in the Department of Interior Building and Environment at Shenkar College of Engineering and Design. Dr Cory teaches sustainable architecture at the Technion and lectures worldwide on his visionary design.

KHEE POH LAM

Khee Poh Lam teaches architectural design (focusing on systems integration), building performance modelling, building controls and diagnostics as well as acoustics and lighting. His fields of research are total building performance and diagnostics and the development of computational design support systems.

Professor Lam is a member of the US Energy Foundation Board of Directors. He is also working specifically with their China Sustainable Energy Program on a range of activities including green building codes and standards, education and training as well as green design of various demonstration projects in China.

Professor Lam was Director of the Graduate Program in the School of Architecture at Carnegie Mellon. He is currently Visiting Professor at the School of Architecture, Chinese University of Hong Kong and Xian Jiaotong University as well as the School of Environmental Science and Technology, Tianjin University, China.

NADAV MALIN

Nadav Malin is the building industry's acknowledged go-to resource for thoughtful perspective on the materials and design solutions that define sustainable building practice. As president of BuildingGreen, he oversees the company's industry-leading information and community-building resources, including *Environmental Building News*, its sister publication *GreenSpec* and the project certification help tool *LEEDuser*. He also lends his technical expertise and vision to McGraw-Hill Construction, serving as executive editor of the award-winning *GreenSource* magazine.

Nadav led the team that created the US Department of Energy's High Performance Buildings Database and continues to oversee BuildingGreen's responsibility for ensuring the quality of case studies and the collection of meaningful data on actual building performance.

STEVEN J STRONG

Steven Strong is President of Solar Design Associates, Inc. (founded 1974), a group of architects and engineers dedicated to the design of environmentally responsive buildings and the engineering and integration of renewable energy systems which incorporate the latest in innovative technology.

Over the last 25 years, he has designed dozens of homes and buildings powered by solar electricity. In 1984, working with New England Electric, he completed the world's first photovoltaic-powered neighbourhood in central Massachusetts. He recently completed the design and installation of a new 'solar skin' for the US Mission to the United Nations in Geneva, Switzerland and is currently working on powering the US Embassy in Athens with solar electricity and upgrading the UN Headquarters in New York City with building-integrated PV.

Steven Strong has received numerous awards for his pioneering work and represented the US on the International Energy Agency's expert working group on Solar Electricity in the Built Environment for eight years. He is the author of *The Solar Electric House and Solar Electric Buildings, an Overview of Today's Applications.*

SIMON WOODS

Simon Woods is currently an Associate and Chartered Engineer with design consultants Ramboll and has over 25 years experience of the design and installation of engineering infrastructure systems both within buildings and in the wider masterplanning context. Originally trained in environmental engineering, Wood has also incorporated research experience at Manchester University in the urban regeneration and development sector to enable masterplanning schemes to be developed on a sustainable basis combining the various disciplines. Recent projects have concerned developments in Eastern Europe including major town expansion schemes in Kazakhstan and airport redevelopment in St Petersburg.

ELMA DURMISEVIC

Dr Elma Durmisevic is head of the 4D architects office in Amsterdam, associate professor at the University of Twente and project leader of the first green design related master track at the University of Twente.

Durmisevic completed a PhD at Delft University of Technology in 2006 on the subject of Transformable Building Structures, and since then has initiated research, education and innovation projects at the research centre for Green Transformable Buildings at the University of Twente and the multidisciplinary Green Design Festival in Sarajevo, design studios for the development of flexible and sustainable buildings and the experimental green building lab at the University of Twente in partnership with the construction industry.

SIMOS YANNAS

Professor Simos Yannas is Director of the Environment and Energy Studies Programme at the Architectural Association School of Architecture in London, where he is responsible for the MSc and MArch in Sustainable Environmental Design and Director of the AA School's PhD Programme. He is a Sir Isaac Newton Design Fellow in Architecture at the University of Cambridge and Visiting Professor at Queensland University of Technology.

He has been involved in environmental design research, teaching and consultancy since the mid-1970s and has lectured in schools of architecture and professional institutes in some thirty countries. Design research undertaken within the MSc and MArch courses has been exhibited and published internationally at scientific conferences and in architectural journals in many countries.

His latest book, a collection of papers titled *Lessons from Traditional Architecture* is due to be published by Earthscan in 2010. He was awarded the Passive and Low Energy Architecture International Achievement Award in 2001 and 2008.

MICHAEL MCDONOUGH

Michael McDonough is an award-winning architect, industrial designer and author who designs and consults on environmentally appropriate systems and advanced building technologies. He specialises in zero-energy/zero-carbon footprint buildings and related systems and has designed a wide range of projects including offices, airports, galleries, multi-media environments, resort buildings, multi-family residences, shops, custom residences and urban planning as well as furniture, exhibits and jewellery.

He has published over 80 articles and two books on architecture and design. Long an active artistic collaborator, he has also exhibited in museums and galleries worldwide and worked with painters, sculptors, writers, designers, filmmakers and scientists, notably award-winning author Tom Wolfe, industrial designer Hartmut Esslinger, lighting designer Howard Brandston, fashion designer Steven Sprouse and environmentalist Linda Garland.

He also designed and built e-House, a net-zero energy/zero-carbon design and building science laboratory, which the international press has termed "the most sustainable building in the world" having "the coolest rooms on the planet".

DOMINIC MUREN

Dominic Muren writes and lectures on industrial and interaction design at the University of Washington. He founded the popular industrial design blog IDFuel.com and served as a contributing writer for Treehugger.com—dubbed "The Green CNN"—for over five years. His writing explores the interconnections between designed objects, the environment and society—the complicated factors that make products "work" within different systems. His book *Green's Not Black & White: The Balanced Guide to Making Eco-Decisions* has been reprinted in six languages.

He was awarded a 2010 TED Global Fellowship for his work on Humblefacture.com, an evolving manifesto which argues that by bringing factories down to a local, accessible scale, manufacturing can be made more environmentally, socially and functionally positive. In addition to his writing and teaching, Dominic is an award winning industrial designer and principal of The Humblefactory, a design laboratory in Seattle, Washington with a works-in-progress blog at Humblefactory.com.

BIBLIOGRAPHIES

CHAPTER 4

1 United Nations (2010). *World Urbanization Prospects, The 2009 Revision. Highlights*. UN, New York.

2 United Nations (2010). *World Urbanization Prospects. The 2009 Revision. Highlights*. UN, New York.

3 Giradet, H (1999). *Creating Sustainable Cities (Schumacher Briefing)*. Green Books, London.

4 Rogers, R (2005). *Cities for a Small Planet*. Faber and Faber, London.

5 Goode, D (2000). "Cities as Key to Sustainability". In D Poore (Ed.) *Where Next? Reflections on the Human Future*. The Board of Trustees, Royal Botanic Gardens, Kew.

6 Register, R (2006). *Ecocities: Rebuilding Cities in Balance with Nature*. New Society Publishers,Canada.

7 Glaeser, E L (2009). "Green Cities, Brown Suburbs". *City Journal*, 19(1): 1–5.

8 Hall, P (1999). *"Sustainable Cities or Town Cramming?"*Town and Country Planning Association, London.

9 Farr, D (2007). *Sustainable Urbanism: Urban Design with Nature*. John Wiley & Sons, London, p.103.

10 Goodacre, R (2006). "RECEP Urban Environments Desk Study: The Benefits of Urban Living. Report to the Royal Commission on Environmental Pollution". HMSO London.

11 Nicholson-Lord, D (2003). *Green Cities: and Why We Need Them*. New Economics Foundation, London.

12 Frith, M and Harrison, M. "Decent Homes, Decent Spaces. (Undated). Report as Part of the Neighbourhoods Green. Improving Green Spaces for Social Housing Project". Peabody Trust, London.

13 Montgomery, D R (2001). "Soil Erosion and Agricultural Sustainability". *Proc. Nat. Acad. Sci.* 104(33): 13268–13272.

14 Best Foot Forward Ltd (2002). "City Limits. A Resource Flow and Ecological Footprint Analysis of Greater London". City Limits Project Partnership, London.

15 Porritt, J (2010). "Do the Maths". In E Yarrow (Ed.) *The Global Environment*, Edition 2. Circle Publishing, Richmond.

16 Hofman, N (2001). "Urban Consumption of Agricultural Land". *Rural and Small Town Canada Analysis Bulletin*, 3(2): 1–13.

17 Giradet, H (1999). *Creating Sustainable Cities (Schumacher Briefing)*. Green Books, London.

18 Newman, P and I Jennings (2008). *Cities as Sustainable Ecosystems*. Island Press, Washington.

19 Viljoen, A (2007). *Continuous Productive Urban Landscapes: Designing Urban Agriculture for Sustainable Cities*. Architectural Press, London.

20 Knowd, I, D Mason and A Docking (2006). "Urban Agriculture: The New Frontier". *Changing City Structures*, 23: 1–23.

21 Despommier, D (2009). "The Rise of Vertical Farms". *Scientific American*, 301, pp. 80–87.

22 Nelkin, J and T Caplow (2008). "Sustainable Controlled Environment Agriculture for Urban Areas". *Acta Hort.* ISHS, 801: 449–456.

23 Hassel, M V (2005). "Community Gardens in New York City: Place, Community and Individuality". In P F Barlett (Ed.). *Urban Place: Reconnecting with the Natural World*. MIT Press, London, pp 91–116.

24 Stuart, S M (2005). "Lifting Spirits. Creating Gardens in California Domestic Violence Shelters". In P F Barlett (Ed.). *Urban Place: Reconnecting with the Natural World*. MIT Press, London, pp. 61–88.

25 Jenkins, M (2003). "Prospects for Biodiversity". *Science*, 302: 1175–1177.

26 De Leo, G A and S Levin (1997). "The Multifaceted Aspects of Ecosystem Integrity". *Conservation Ecology*, 1(1): 1–23.

27 Goulson, D, G C Lye and B Darvill (2008). "Decline and Conservation of Bumble Bees". *Annu. Rev. Entomol*, 53: 191–208.

28 De la Rua, P, R Jaffe , R Dall'Olio, I Munoz and J Serrano (2009). "Biodiversity, Conservation and Current Threats to European Honeybee". *Apidologie*, 40 (3): 263–284.

29 Southwick, E E and L Southwick Jr (1992). "Estimating the Economic Value of Honey Bees (Hymenoptera: Apidae) as Agricultural Pollinators in the United States". *Journal of Economic Entomology*, 85 (3): 621–633.

30 Kevan, P G and T P Phillips (2001). "The Economic Impacts of Pollinator Declines: an Approach to Assessing the Consequences". *Conservation Ecology* 5(1): 8. http://www.consecol.org/vol5/iss1/art8/

31 Pretty, J N, C Brett, D Gee, R E Hine, C F Mason, J I L Morison, H Raven, M D Rayment and G van der Bijl (2000). "An Assessment of the Total External Costs of UK Agriculture". *Agricultural Systems*, 65 (2):113–136.

32 Pimentel D, C Wilson, C McCullum, R Huang, P Dwen, J Flack, Q Tran, T Saltman and B Cliff (1997). "Economic and Environmental Benefits of Biodiversity". *BioScience*, (47) 11: 747–757.

33 Balmford, A, A Brunder, P Cooper, R Costanza, S Farber, R E Green, M Jenkins, P Jefferis, V Jessamy, J Madden, K Munro, N Myers, S Naeem, J Paavola, M Rayment, S Rosnedo, J Roughgarden, K Trumper and R K Turner (2002). "Economic Reasons for Conserving Wild Nature". *Science*, 297: 950–953.

34 Goode, D (2000).

35 Mayor of London. (2006). "London's Urban Heat Island: A Summary for Decision Makers". Greater London Authority.

36 Gill, S E, J F Handley, A R Ennos and F Pauleit (2007). "Adapting Cities for Climate Change: The Role of the Green Infrastructure". *Built Environment*, 33(1): 115–133.

37 Yukihiro, M (2009). "Biodiversity and Ecosystem Services in Urban Areas for Smart Adaptation to Climate Change". *Proceedings of the Second International Conference on Urban Biodiversity and Design*. URBIO(2010). J Imanishi and J Hon (Eds.) Nagoya, Japan, 18–22 May 2010. URBIO2010 Organising Committee. http://www.jilac.jp/URBIO2010/doku.php

38 Ruano, M (1999). *Ecourbanism: Sustainable Human Settlements. 60 Case Studies*. Gustavo Gilli,Barcelona.

39 Ipsen, D (1998). "Ecology as Urban Culture". In J Breuste, H Fledmann and O Uhlmann (Eds.). *Urban Ecology*. Springer, Berlin.

40 Sukopp, H (1998). "Urban Ecology—Scientific and Practical Aspects". In J Breuste, H Fledmann and O Uhlmann (Eds.). *Urban Ecology*. Springer, Berlin.

41 Thompson, I (2006). *Ecology, Community and Delight. An Inquiry into Values in Landscape Architecture*. Routledge, London.

42 American Society of Landscape Architects (2009). "The Case for Sustainable Landscapes". ASLA, Washington DC.

43 Millennium Ecosystem Assessment (2005). "Ecosystems and Human Well-Being: Synthesis 1". http://www.millenniumassessment.org/documents/ document.

44 Costanza, R, R d'Arge, R de Groot, S Farber, M Grasso, B Hannon, K Limburg, S Naeem, R V O'Neill, J Paruelo, R G Raskin, P Sutton and M van den Belt (1997). "The Value of the World's Ecosystem Services and Natural Capital". *Nature*, 387: 253–260.

45 Goode, D (2006). "RECEP Urban Environments Desk Study: Green Infrastructure". Royal Commission on Environmental Pollution, London.

46 The Royal Commission on EnvironmentalPollution. (2007). "26th Report. The Urban Environment: Chtr 4: The Natural Urban Environment". HMSO, Norwich.

47 Town and Country Planning Association (2008). "The Essential Role of Green Infrastructure: Ecotowns Green Infrastructure Worksheet. Advice to Promoters and Planners". TCPA, London.

48 Yeang, K (2009). *Ecomasterplanning*. John Wiley and Sons, London.

49 Town and Country Planning Association. (2008).

50 CABE Space (2003). "Does Money Grow on Trees?" CABE, London.

51 Lancaster University and Centre for Ecology and Hydrology (2004). "Trees and Sustainable Air Quality". Lancaster University, UK.

52 Oberndorfer, E, J Lundholm, B Bass, R R Coffman, H Doshi, N Dunnett, S Gaffin, M Køhler, K K Y Liu and B Roe (2007). "Green Roofs as Urban Ecosystems: Ecological Structures, Functions and Services". *Bioscience*, 57(10): 823–833.

53 Mentens, J H, D Raes and M Hermy (2006). "Green Roofs as a Tool for Solving the Rainwater Runoff Problem in the Urbanized twenty-first century?" *Landscape and Urban Planning*, 77: 217–226.

54 Rhode, C L E and A D Kendle (1994). *Human Well-Being, Natural Landscapes and Wildlife in Urban Areas—A Review*. English Nature, Peterborough.

55 Ulrich R S, R Simons, B d Losito, E Fiorito, M Miles and M Zelson (1991). "Stress Recovery During Exposure to Natural and Urban Environments". *J. Exp. Psychology*: 11, 201–230.

56 Ulrich, R S (1999). "Effects of Gardens on Health Outcomes: Theory and Research". In C C Marcus and M Barnes (Ed.) (1999). *Healing Gardens*. Wiley, New York, pp. 27–86.

57 Royal Commission on Environmental Pollution. (2004). "Desk Study: Urban Nature". RCEP, London; Nicholson-Lord, D (2003). *Green Cities: and Why We Need Them*. New Economics Foundation, London.

58 Nicholson-Lord, D (2003). *Green Cities: and Why We Need Them*. New Economics Foundation, London; Burls, A and W Caan (2005). "Human Health and Nature Conservation". *BMJ*, 331: 1221–1222.

59 Burls, A and W Caan (2005). "Human Health and Nature Conservation". *BMJ*, 331: 1221–1222.

60 Sullivan, W C (2005). "Forest, Savanna, City: Evolutionary Landscapes and Human Functioning". In P F Barlett (Ed.). *Urban Place. Reconnecting with the Natural World*. MIT Press, London, pp. 237–252.

61 Douglas, I (2005). "Urban Greenspace and Mental Health. Discussion Paper for the UK Man and the Biosphere Urban Forum". UKMAB, London.

62 Kaplan, R and S Kaplan (2005). "Preference, Restoration, and Meaningful Action in the Context of Nearby Nature". In P F Barlett (Ed.). *Urban Place: Reconnecting with the Natural World*. MIT Press, London, pp. 273–298.

63 Stone, D (2006). "Health and Nature: Critical Elements for Sustainable Developments". In E Williams (Ed.) *Proceedings of the 22nd Conference of the Institute of Ecology and Environmental Management 2005. Sustainable New Housing and Major Developments—Rising to the Ecological Challenges*. IEEM, Winchester, pp.61–66.

64 Fuller, R A, K N Irvine, P Devine-Wright, P HWarren and K J Gaston (2007). "Psychological Benefits of Greenspace Increase with Biodiversity". *Biological Letters*, 5: 352–355.

65 URBED (2004). "Biodiversity by Design. A Guide for Sustainable Communities". Town and Country Planning Association, London.

66 Harrison, C and G Davies (2002). "Conserving Biodiversity that Matters: Practitioner's Perspectives on Brownfield Development and Urban Nature Conservation in London". *Journal of Environmental Management*, 65: 95–108.

67 Mitsch, W J, N Wang, L Zhang, R Deal, X Wu and A Zuwerink (2005). "Using Ecological Indicators in a Whole-Ecosystem Wetland Experiment". In S E Jørgensen, R Costanza and X Fu-Liu (Eds). *Handbook of Ecological Indicators of Ecosystem Health*. Taylor and Francis, London.

68 Millet, M (1997). "Demonstration Reedbed Filtration Systems". WWT, Slimbridge

69 Biologic Design. http://www.biologicdesign.co.uk/page.php

70 Nicholls, C (2004). *Biodiversity and Pest Management in Agroecosystems*. CRC Press, Oxford.

71 Loreau, M. (2000). "Biodiversity and Ecosystem Functioning. Recent Theoretical Advantages". *Oikos*, 91: 3–17.

72 Rural Economy and Landuse Programme (2008). "Eating Biodiversity: an Investigation of the Links Between Quality Food Production and Biodiversity Protection". Relu, Newcastle-upon-Tyne.

73 Kendle, T and S Forbes (1997). *Urban Nature Conservation*. E & FN Spon, London.

74 Plant, C W and P Harvey (1997). "Biodiversity Action Plan. Invertebrates of the South Essex Thames Terrace Gravels—Phase 1: Characterisation of the Existing Resource" (three volumes). Unpublished report number BS/055/96. English Nature, Colchester.

75 Harvey, P (2000). "The East Thames Corridor: a nationally important invertebrate fauna under threat". *British Wildlife*, 12 (2): 91–98.

76 Kadas, G (2004). "Rare Invertebrates Colonizing Green Roofs in London". *Urban Habitats*, 4(1): 66–86.

77 Wells, M J (2001). "Rarity on the Roof? Finding Partial Solutions to Challenges of Brownfield Redevelopment". *Ecology and Environmental Management In Practice*, 33: 14–15.

78 Ecoschemes Ltd and Studio Engleback (200 3). "Green Roofs: Their Existing Status and Potential for Conserving Biodiversity in Urban Areas. English Nature Research Reports", No. 498. English Nature, Peterborough.

79 Burga, C A, F Klötzli and M Gloor (2001). "Orchiden-Wiesen in Wollishofen (Zürich)—ein Erstaunliches Relikt aus dem Anfangdes 20. Jahrhundrets". *Vierteljahrsschrift der Natureforschenden Fesellschaft in Zürich*, 146(2–3): 39–52.

80 Gedge, D and G Kadas (2005). "Green Roofs and Biodiversity". *Biologist*, 52(3):161–169.

81 Hochschule Wädenswil and Living Roofs (2005). *Green Roofs and Urban Biodiversity. Science and Technology Transfer*. Hochschule Wädenswil, Wädenswil.

82 Wells, M J and G Grant (2006). "Biodiverse Vegetated Architecture Worldwide: Status, Research and Advances". In E Williams (Ed.) *Proceedings of the 22nd Conference of the Institute of Ecology and Environmental Management 2005. Sustainable New Housing* and Major Developments—Rising to the Ecological Challenges. IEEM, Winchester, pp. 61–66.

83 Town and Country Planning Association (2009). "Biodiversity Positive: Ecotowns Biodiversity Worksheet". TCPA, London.

84 Staddon, J E R (1975). "A Note on the Evolutionary Significance of Supernormal Stimuli". *The American Naturalist*, 109 (969): 541–545.

85 Jorgensen, A (Ed.) (2007). *Urban Wildscapes*. Sheffield University, UK.

86 Barker, G (Ed.) (2000). "Ecological Recombination in Urban Areas: Implications for Nature Conservation". English Nature, Peterborough.

87 Lynch, B D and R Brusi (2005). "Nature, Memory and Nation: New York's Latino Gardens and Casitas". In P F Barlett (Ed.). *Urban Place: Reconnecting with the Natural World.* MIT Press, London, pp. 191–211.

88 Newman, P and I Jennings (2008).

89 Pretty, J. and P F Barlett (2005). "Concluding Remarks: Nature and Health in the Urban Environment". In P F Barlett (Ed.). *Urban Place. Reconnecting with the Natural World.* MIT Press, London pp. 273–298.

90 Sukopp, H (1998).

91 Morris, R K A, I Alonso, R G Jefferson and K J Kirby (2006). "The Creation of Compensatory Habitat— can it Secure Sustainable Development?" *Journal for Nature Conservation,* 14 (2): 106–116.

92 Treweek, J (1999). *Ecological Impact Assessment.* Blackwell Science, Oxford.

93 Goode, D (1998). "Integration of Nature in Urban Development". In J Breuste, H Feldmann and O Uhlmann (Eds.). *Urban Ecology.* Springer Verlag, Berlin.

94 Morris, R K A, I Alonso, R G Jefferson and K J Kirby (2006). "The Creation of Compensatory Habitat—can it Secure Sustainable Development?". *Journal for Nature Conservation,* 14 (2): 106–116.

95 Bradshaw, A D, D A Goode and E H P Thorp (Eds.) (1983). *Ecology and Design in Landscape.* Blackwell Scientific Publications, Oxford.

96 Kusler, J A and M E Kentula (1990). Executive Summary. In J A Kentula and M E Kentula (Eds.) *Wetland Creation and Restoration: The State of the Science.* Island Press, Washington.

97 Emery, M (1986). *Promoting Nature in Cities and Towns.* Croom Helm, London.

98 Baines, C and J Smart (1991). *A Guide to Habitat Creation.* London Ecology Unit, London.

99 Merritt, A (1994). *Wetlands, Industry and Wildlife. A Manual of Principles and Practices.* Wildfowl and Wetlands Trust, Slimbridge.

100 Rodwell, J and G Patterson (1994). "Creating New Native Woodlands. Forestry Commission Bulletin 112". HMSO, London.

101 Parker, D M (1995). "Habitat Creation—a Critical Guide. English Nature Science Series No. 21". English Nature, Peterborough.

102 Dryden, R (1997). "Habitat Restoration Project: Fact Sheets and Bibliographies. English Nature Research Report 260". English Nature, Peterborough.

103 Helliwell, D R (1998). *Case Studies in Vegetation Change, Habitat Transference and Habitat Creation.* Reading Agricultural Consulant, Didcot.

104 Kendle, T and S Forbes (1997).

105 Gilbert O L and P Anderson (1998). *Habitat Creation and Repair.* Oxford University Press, Oxford.

106 Wells, M J, M Luszczak and B Dunlop (1998)."Sustainable Habitat Creation on a Former Industrial Site". In H R Fox, H M Moore and A M McIntosh (Eds.). *Land Reclamation: Achieving Sustainable Benefits.* A A Balkema, Rotterdam.

107 Mitsch, W J and J G Gosselink (2000). *Wetlands (3rd Edition).* John Wiley and Sons, New York.

108 Penny Anderson Associates (2002). "Highways Agency Task C002. Chalk Grassland Habitat Creation. A Literature and Project Review". PAA, Buxton.

109 White, G and J Gilbert (2003). *Habitat Creation Handbook for the Minerals Industry (RSPB Management Guides).* RSPB, Sandy.

110 Betts, C J (2003). *British Wild Plants in Natural Associations: A Database for Landscaping, Habitat Creation and Local Planning.* Christopher Betts, Worcester.

111 Dunnett, N and J Hitchmough (2004). *The Dynamic Landscape.* Spon Press, London.

112 Luscombe, G and R Scott (2004). *Wildflowers Work. A Guide to Creating and Managing New Wildflower Landscapes.* Landlife, Liverpool.

113 Hitchmough, J and K Fieldhouse (2004). *Plant User Handbook A Guide to Effective Specifying.* Blackwell Science, Oxford.

114 Nottage, A and P Robertson (2005). *The Saltmarsh Creation Handbook: A Project Manager's Guide to the Creation of Saltmarsh and Intertidal Mudflat.* RSPB, Sandy and CIWEM, London.

115 Earth Pledge (2005). *Green Roofs. Ecological Design and Construction.* Schiffer Books, Atglen.

116 Newton, J, D Gedge, P Early, and S Wilson (2007). *Building Greener: Guidance in the use of green Roofs, Green Walls and Complementary Features on Buildings.* CIRIA, London.

117 Environment Agency (2009). "Estuary Edges. Ecological Design Guidance". EA, London.

118 Urbanska, K M, N Webb and P Edwards (1997). *Restoration Ecology and Sustainable Development.* Cambridge University Press.

119 Fox, H R, H M Moore and A M McIntosh (Eds.) (1998). *Land Reclamation. Achieving Sustainable Benefits.* A A Balkema, Rotterdam.

120 The River Restoration Centre (2002). *River Restoration Manual of Techniques.* RRC, Silsoe.

121 Eades, P, L Bardsley, N Giles and A Crofts (2003). *The Wetland Restoration Manual.* The Wildlife Trusts, Newark.

122 Rooney, P, P Nolan and D Hill (2005). "Restoration, Re-Introduction and Translocation. Proceeding of the 20th Conference of the Institute of Ecology and Environmental Management". IEEM, Winchester.

123 Rodwell, J (1991–2000). *British Plant Communities,* five volumes. Cambridge University Press.

124 Goode, D (2005). "Connecting with Nature in a Capital City: The London Biodiversity Strategy". In T Tryzna (Ed.) *The Urban Imperative: Urban Outreach for Protected Area Agencies.* California Institute of Public Affairs, Sacramento.

125 Harrison, C, J Burgess, A Millward and G Dawe (1995). *Accessible Natural Greenspace in Towns and Cities: A Review of Appropriate Size and Distance Criteria.* English Nature, Peterborough.

126 Town and Country Planning Association (2008).

127 Institute of Ecology and Environmental Management (1996). *Guidelines for Ecological Impact Assessment.* IEEM, Winchester.

128 Kusler, J A and M E Kentula (1990).

129 Box, J (1998). "Setting Objectives and Monitoring for Ecological Restoration and Habitat Creation". In H R Fox, H M Moore and A M McIntosh (Eds.) *Land Reclamation. Achieving Sustainable Benefits.* AA Balkema, Rotterdam, pp. 7–11.

130 Global Invasive Species Database. http://www.issg.org/database/welcome/

131 Robertson, B A and R L Hutto (2006). "A Framework for Understanding Ecological Traps and an Evaluation of Existing Evidence". *Ecology,* 87(5): 1075–1085.**132** Klem, D (2006). "Glass: Deadly Conservation Issue for Birds". *Bird Observer,* 34(2): 73–81

133 Longcore, T and C Rich (2004). "Ecological Light Pollution". *Front Ecol Environ,* 2(4): 191–198.

134 Sherwood, B, D Cutler and J Burton (2002). *Wildlife and Roads: The Ecological Impact.* Imperial College Press, London.

135 English Nature (1994). *Planning for Wildlife in Towns and Cities.* English Nature, Peterborough.

136 UK Biodiversity Action Plan. "UKBAP Priority Species and Habitats". Accessed 2010 at http://www.ukbap.org.uk/newprioritylist.aspx

137 Hill, D. (Ed.) (2007). "Making the Connections: A Role for Ecological Networks in Nature Conservation". *Proceedings of the 26th Conference of the Institute of Ecology and Environmental Management.* IEEM, Winchester.

138 Town and Country Planning Association (2009).

139 Semlitsch, R D and R J Bodie (2003). "Biological Criteria for Buffer Zones around Wetlands and Riparian Habitats for Amphibians and Reptiles". *Conservation Biology,* 17(5): 1219–1228.

140 Melles, S J (2005). "Urban Bird Diversity as an Economic Indicator of Human Social Diversity and Economic Inequality in Vancouver, British Columbia". *Urban Habitats,* 3(1): 1541–7115.

141 Kuo, F E and W C Sullivan (2001). "Environment and Crime in the Inner City: Does Vegetation Reduce Crime?". *Environment and Behavior,* 33(3): 343–367.

142 Lancaster University and the Centre for Ecology and Hydrology (2004). *Trees and Sustainable Urban Air Quality: Using Trees to Improve Air Quality in Cities.* University of Lancaster, Lancaster.

143 Mayor of London (2002). "Connecting with London's Nature: The Mayor's Biodiversity Strategy". Greater London Authority, London.

144 Singapore National Parks Board and Convention on Biological Diversity (2009). "User's Manual for the Singapore Index on Cities' Biodiversity". CBD, Montreal.

145 Wells, M J and L Engleback (1997). "Ecological Sustainability in Urban Design: Aspirations and Achievements". *Environmental Policies in Europe: Towards Sustainability. Proceedings of the 1997 European Environment Conference.* ERP Environment, Shipley.

146 Wells, M J (2006). "Ecologically-led Landscape Design in Brownfield Regeneration Projects". In E Williams (Ed.). *Designing Nature into Urban Development and Regeneration. Proceedings of the 16th National Conference of the Institute of Ecology and Environmental Management 2002.* IEEM, Winchester, pp. 156–171.

147 Douglass, I and J Box (2000). "The Changing Relationship between Cities and Biosphere Reserves". Report prepared by the Urban Forum and the UK Man and Biosphere Committee. http://ukmaburbanforum.org.uk/Publications/Cites

148 Goode, D (2006).

149 de Leo, G A and S Levin (1997). "The Multifaceted Aspects of Ecosystem Integrity". *Conservation Ecology* (online), 1(1): 3.

150 Jørgensen, S E, R Costanza and X Fu-Liu (Eds) (2005). *Handbook of Ecological Indicators of Ecosystem Health.* Taylor and Francis, London.

151 Imanishi, J and J Hon (Eds) (2010). "Proceedings of the Second International Conference on Urban Biodiversity and Design. URBIO(2010)". URBIO2010 Organising Committee. http://www.jilac.jp/URBIO2010/doku.php

152 Reynolds, P (1998). "Wildlife Corridors and the Mitigation of Habitat Fragmentation. European and North American Perspectives". Capreolus Wildlife Consultancy, Garvald, Scotland.

153 Andrews, J (1993). "The Reality and Management of Wildlife Corridors". British Wildlife, 5(1): 1–8.

154 Kirby, K (1995). Rebuilding the English Countryside:Habitat Fragmentation and Wildlife Corridors as Issues in Practical Conservation (English Nature Science Series, 10). English Nature, Peterborough.

155 Dawson, D (1994). "Are Habitat Corridors Conduits For Animals and Plants in a Fragmented Landscape?" (English Nature Research Report, 94). English Nature, Peterborough.

156 Farr, D (2007).

157 Newman, P and I Jennings (2008). Cities as Sustainable Ecosystems: Principles and Practice. Island Press, Washington.

158 Dunnett, N and J Hitchmough (2004).

CLIXTown and Country Planning Association (2009). "Biodiversity Positive: Ecotowns Biodiversity Worksheet". TCPA, London.

CHAPTER 11

1 "Energy Efficiency in Buildings: Facts and Trends, World Business Council for Sustainable Development", 2007. http://www.wbcsd.org/DocRoot/H94WhkJolYq5uDtsLfxR/WBCSD_EEB_final.pdf

2 http://www.nytimes.com/2007/10/26/business/worldbusiness/26cement.html

3 http://en.wikipedia.org/wiki/Theory

4 http://www.epa.gov/greenbuilding/pubs/about.htm#1

5 Ruck, N C (Ed.) (1989). *Building Design and Human Performance.* Van Nostrand Reinhold, New York.

6 Thomas, R (Ed.) (2002). *Environmental Design: An Introduction for Architects and Engineers, 2nd Edition.* Spon Press, London.

7 Yudelson, J, (2009). *Green Building Through Integrated Design.* McGraw-Hill, Maidenhead.

8 Loftness, V, V Hartkopf, P Mill. "A Critical Framework for Building Evaluation: Total Building Performance, Systems Integration and Levels of Measurement and Assessment". In Wolfgang F E Preiser (Ed.) (1989). *Building Evaluation.* Plenum Publishing Corporation, New York.

9 Lam, K P and V Srivastava, "Living in the Intelligent Workplace—Structuring and Managing Building Operation Information". In M Chui (Ed.) (2005) / *CAAD Talks 05: Insights of Smart Environments.* Garden City Publishing Ltd. Taipei, Taiwan, pp. 297–314.

10 Lahlou, S. "The EDF R&D Laboratory of Design for Cognition (LDC)". http://www.rufae.net/tiki-download_file.php?fileId=7.

11 Su, V. "The URA Centre". *Skyline,* Nov./Dec. 1999. Urban Redevelopment Authority, Singapore, pp. 8–12.

12 "Redefining the Library: The National Library of Singapore". National Library Board, Singapore, 2008.

13 Gallaher, M P, A C O'Connor, J L Dettbarn Jr, andL T Gilday (August 2004). "Cost Analysis of Inadequate Interoperability in the U.S. Capital Facilities Industry". Research report sponsored by National Institute of Standards and Technology, Advanced Technology Program.

14 Mattar S G (November 1983). "Buildability and Building Envelope Design. Proceedings of the Second Canadian Conference on Building Science and Technology", Waterloo.

15 Loftness, V, K P Lam and V Hartkopf, "Education and environmental performance-based design: a Carnegie Mellon perspective". *Building Research & Information,* Vol. 33, No. 2/March–April 2005, Routledge, United Kingdom, pp. 196–203.

16 Mahdavi, A and K P Lam, "A dialectic of process and tool: knowledge transfer and decision-making strategies in the building delivery process". In K Mathur, M Betts, T Kwok Wai (Eds) (1993). *Management of information technology for construction,* World Scientific and Global Publication Services, Singapore, pp. 345–356.

17 "National Building Information Model, Version 1, Part 1: Overview, Principles and Methodologies". US National Institute of Building Sciences, 2007. http://www.buildingsmartalliance.org/nbims/

18 Wilson, A (April 2005). "Making the case for Green Building". *Environmental Building News,* No. 4. http://www.buildinggreen.com/auth/article.cfm/2005/4/1/Making-the-Case-for-Green-Building/

© 2011 Black Dog Publishing Limited, London, UK,
the authors and architects. All rights reserved.

Edited and designed by Wordsearch
www.wordsearch.co.uk

Black Dog Publishing Limited
10A Acton Street
London WC1X 9NG
info@blackdogonline.com

British Library Cataloguing-in-Publication Data. A CIP
record for this book is available from the British Library.

ISBN 978 1 907317 12 5

Black Dog Publishing Limited, London, UK, is an environmentally
responsible company. *Green Design: From Theory to Practice* is printed
on FSC certified paper.

IMAGE CREDITS

page 40 Vladimir Wrangel—Fotolia.com
page 43 Image courtesy of Mithun
page 45 Image courtesy of Mithun
page 46 Image courtesy of Mithun
page 47 Image courtesy of Mithun
page 52 Behnisch Architekten
Page 53 Roland Halbe
Page 54 Behnisch Architekten
Page 55 Jürgen Landes
Page 56 Roland Halbe
Page 60 Killian O'Sullivan
Page 61 Marie-Louise Halpenny
Page 62 Killian O'Sullivan
Page 63 Tim Soar
Page 67 Top: Verena Herzog-Loibl
Page 67 Below: Heike Seewald

Page 68 Top: Horst Goebel
Page 68 Below: Klaus Kinold
Page 92 Nadav Malin
Page 96 Photo courtesy of Solar Design
        Associates, Inc.
Page 97 Photo courtesy of Solar Design
        Associates, Inc.
Page 98 Photo courtesy of Solar Design
        Associates, Inc.
Page 127 Michael McDonough Architect PC
Page 128 Michael McDonough Architect PC
Page 129 Michael McDonough Architect PC
Page 138 *Michael Pawlyn*, Kelly Hill
Page 139 *Stefan Behnisch*, Christoph Soeder
Page 139 *Joseph Cory*, Kfir Malka

architecture art design
fashion history photography
theory and things

black dog publishing

www.blackdogonline.com

london uk